About the author

The author is a self-described ordinary, middle-aged bloke with a healthy dislike of routine. He was born sometime in the later fifties in Wales and spent his formative years in Cardiff and the Midlands, where the swinging sixties largely passed him by.

Taking early retirement from a career in engineering, confined to a desk and meeting rooms, he gave away his textbooks but was not yet ready to till an allotment like his father. On seeking his wife and dogs' wise counsel, he began long-distance walking, losing weight and developing a 'six-pack' just about visible in the right light.

After chafing his thighs on Offa's Dyke Path and reading all the Brontë books on the Pennine Way (well, almost all), his sights turned to Europe. This book is the result.

SIX PAIRS OF BOOTS
SPAIN TO CYPRUS ON THE E4 TRAIL

JOHN PUCKNELL

SIX PAIRS OF BOOTS
SPAIN TO CYPRUS ON THE E4 TRAIL

Vanguard Press

VANGUARD PAPERBACK

© Copyright 2021
John Pucknell

A CIP catalogue record for this title is
available from the British Library.

ISBN 978 1 80016 140 5

Vanguard Press is an imprint of
Pegasus Elliot Mackenzie Publishers Ltd.
www.pegasuspublishers.com

First Published in 2021

Vanguard Press
Sheraton House Castle Park
Cambridge England

Printed & Bound in Great Britain

Dedication

Dedicated to Cathy, my lovely wife, who has encouraged me to
follow my dreams.

Contents

Chapter 1: Introduction — why and how

Imagine waking on a mountain campsite, the grey pink stain of dawn over the distant grey mountains, pinpricks of orange lights from some distant village twinkling in the valley far, far below. Then walking an hour or two, listening to birds singing, before stopping at a bar for your first, small, strong coffee of the day and maybe a slice of toast and marmalade. Imagine completing a long day's walk in the sweaty heat, the water in your bottle now unpalatably warm, then rewarding yourself with a cold beer, intense pleasure rippling out as you swallow the first mouthful. Imagine stumbling on some surprise event, a wedding where you are offered a plastic cup of cider and a slice of cake outside a church or a village festival celebrating some historical event. Imagine seeing a wild boar snuffling among the pine needles, its tail wagging vigorously, or finding a clear crystal of selenite on a mountain track. Imagine the glow of satisfaction, the pride on reaching some lonely destination, maybe a mountain ridge, looking down on the clouds, powered by your legs alone, all you need carried on your back, achieved by yourself alone. But there is no need to imagine; all this you can experience for yourself with time and persistence by walking a European Long-Distance Walk, and the further you walk, through different countries and landscapes, the more pleasure you will receive.

My home country of Britain has several long-distance paths: the Pennine Way, Offa's Dyke, the Thames Path, to name a few. They are 250 to 400 kilometres long (150 to 250 miles). For those wanting to walk further to gain simple pleasures such as those described above, there are several ultra-long-distance walks in the world that extend over 1,600 kilometres (1,000 miles), taking several months or more to walk. The Appalachian Trail and the Pacific Crest Trail in the USA are among the most famous, familiar to readers of Bill Bryson and viewers of the film *Wild*. Very considerably less well known, even to some of the local tourist organisations, are the twelve European Long-Distance Walks that crisscross Europe, ranging in length from 1,800 to 12,000 kilometres.

So why pick one of these little known, somewhat obscure European trails, and why specifically the E4 Long Distance European Trail? For myself, it is the enormous variety the E4 has to offer: from 1,000-metre climbs up to the mountain passes of the Pyrénées and the narrow ridges in Bulgaria, to the Great Plain of Hungary, where the only climb will be up the stairs of your hotel; from walks along the great River Danube to little streams in northern Greece; from lush green pastures in Switzerland to parched desert landscapes in southern Spain. Yet, the variety is not confined to scenery; the E4 crosses many different countries and cultures. I met many interesting people on the route, although, as some eight languages were involved, none of which I can speak, lengthy conversation was not normally possible. But the range of food speaks for itself, from *'Lomo de Cerdo'* in Spain to *'Sauerbraten'* in Bavaria; from *'Shopska'* Salad in Serbia to fondue in Switzerland; from freshwater carp in Austria to cod in cream in France, from quiche in the Cevanne to *'Langos'* in Hungary and I could never resist a *'Kaffee und Kuchen'* in Bavaria. This list does not begin to scratch the surface. Plus, there is a wealth of history: Stone Age sites on the banks of the Danube, castles from the Reconquista in Spain, religious wars between Catholics and Huguenots (and Cathars) in France, and more recent monuments from World War Two. With luck, you will hit a festival, such as a "Moors and Christian" re-enactment in Spain or Bastille Day in a small village in France with a handshake from the mayor as the band prepares to play.

This book is a description of my walk along the E4. At 6,600 miles, or 10,600 kilometres, which sounds better, it is not something you can fit into a two-week holiday. It requires a little time and hence is an ideal project to undertake in one's retirement, not being too strenuous for this sixty-year-old, who spent most of his working life sitting behind a desk. While a little camping is necessary to cover the complete route, the E4 does not involve weeks of trekking in the wilderness with the fitness of a marine. A good cup of coffee, or a cold beer, is not usually far away.

In retirement, my father, in the time-honoured fashion of many a male (and female) of a certain age, acquired an allotment. It started as an abandoned plot, but he dug it up and planted it with potatoes, lettuce and runner beans, some apples and gooseberry bushes, supplementing tomatoes he grew at home in his greenhouse. Such produce helped to feed my wife and me when we visited from distant parts, washed down with his home-made wine, which had a most individual flavour. He had a little shed on his allotment plot with his bits and pieces in, its roof feeding a water butt and a barrel that you put weeds and cuttings in and then rotated to encourage the formation of compost. Soon he joined the committee. On certain Saturdays, he manned the allotment shop selling fertiliser and seeds. An important event in the calendar was the Annual General Meeting of the Allotment Association, which I once attended with him, my wife and my mother. It was held in the Conservative Club, of which Dad was a member, despite being a lifelong Labour supporter (although this did not progress to joining the line-dancing class). Years passed, and it became my turn to retire. I felt my Dad, and Sainsbury's did a better job of growing vegetables than I could ever aspire to and instead decided to walk across Europe.

The reason I felt that trans-European peregrinations were more exciting than the size of my tomato crop probably has something to do with my reading earlier in life. Laurie Lee's *Cider with Rosie* was required reading at school. At the time, I was not sure exactly what happened at the end of the book, but I was sufficiently interested to read the sequel, *As I Walked Out One Midsummer Morning*. In this book, Lee walks across Spain with little money and a violin. It seemed enormously exciting, very romantic and very brave. Far braver than I was. At the age when Laurie Lee was crossing Spain, I was completing "A" levels at school and going to university. I did not have the courage to take a gap year and travel or anything like that, but I hope my parents were proud of my achievements. When I later progressed to a company car, I arranged a black Rover, the kind of car I thought Dad would approve of.

Nowadays, I no longer have a father to impress, but I do have a little more courage to do something different, plus a wife, better than I deserve, willing to support my wayward ways. My sister gave me a book on Patrick Leigh-Fermor, who walked across Europe in the 1930s, which reminded me what an adventure such a trip could be (I would later meet someone who knew him in the Mani, Greece). I do not have his way with people (and most certainly not with women), but this did not stop me wishing I could follow in his footsteps (at least as far as the walking).

Well, not quite in his footsteps. As a result of a trip with my sister and mother to Spain and specifically to Andalucía, I discovered the E4 Long Distance European Walk. While Mother and sister visited some villages in the Alpujarra, I walked a section of footpath shown on a map from the local Tourist Information office. This was part of the GR7 path, which crosses Spain and also Andorra and France. Although GR stands for *'Sendero de Gran Recorrido'* in Spain and *'Grande Randonnée'* in France, I could not say what it stands for in Andorra or even which the official language is. It skirted the south side of the Sierra Nevada Mountains as a dusty track. I walked down through a whitewashed village, crossed a narrow valley and past abandoned farm buildings, through occasional trees, by stone walls with occasional views across the lower-lying land to the south covered with olive trees and small farms. Somewhere I must have crossed a bridge by the farm owned by Chris Stewart, who wrote about it in *Driving over Lemons*. I found this a very enjoyable book, and clearly, I was not the only one, as when I later returned along this path a few years later, farm buildings I remember as abandoned and crumbling seemed to have been turned into attractive dwellings. It was a beguiling walk and one marked with signs indicating that it was not only the GR7 national footpath but also the E4 international footpath.

Never having heard of the E4, I looked it up on the internet on my return home. I discovered it was one of the twelve trails across Europe promoted by the European Ramblers Association, an association of rambling associations from across Europe. These European long-distance walks were, in general, created by joining together existing long-distance footpaths running through each country, footpaths such as the GR7 in Spain and the Pennine Way in Britain. I also found a blog by John Hayes, describing his epic six-month walk along the E4 from Spain's southernmost point to Budapest. While still working, I spent many pleasant evenings following his daily updates as he journeyed across Europe. As he was a similar age to me, it made the trip seem eminently doable, and so the idea formed in my mind that on finishing work, I would make a similar trip.

Well, similar-ish... although John Hayes completed his trip across Europe in one go, I felt that breaking the E4 into five-week sections was more manageable. It meant that I would not be away from my wife (and Mother while she was alive) for too long a stretch and that I could fit other activities into my life... walking our dogs, completing a "round the world" trip (using aeroplanes) with my wife, some consultancy work. Shorter trips would mean that there would be more expense and time spent getting to and from each section of the walk, but it also meant I could research each section in more depth before each trip, and the planning and associated anticipation is very much part of the fun, and generally means a more successful and interesting trek. First, though, I had to get a few long-distance walks in the UK under my belt to make sure I was both up to it and would actually enjoy it.

In consequence, having left my job of thirty-odd years on a Friday, I set off to walk the length of the Offa's Dyke National Trail on the Sunday, starting at Prestatyn on the north coast of Wales and heading south along the 285 kilometres (177 miles) path that follows the route of the dyke along the border between England and Wales. This earth embankment was thought to have been built by King Offa in the 8th century, maybe to keep the Welsh out of his kingdom of Mercia. The first day's walk was glorious, climbing out of Prestatyn, looking back at the sea as it progressively moved further away. I arrived at the campsite where I stayed the first night well ahead of schedule at two p.m. Unfortunately, the following day was not so successful. The long day spent climbing up and down the peaks of the Clwyd Mountains was a shock to the system. On the last long descent, my knees were so weak and wobbly I was seriously thinking of giving up, and it was only my second day. A year earlier, I had undergone an arthroscopy and knee surgery, which was something to do with cutting a loose, flappy bit off the thing that is in the middle of my knee joint. When I asked the surgeon about future walking expeditions, he said it was fine but that I should avoid playing squash and not walk if my knee (any knee) became inflamed. That night in the toilet, I examined my knees closely under the cold fluorescent light, and they maybe were inflamed... or maybe they always looked like that. My wife, ever the source of useful advice, said to make the following day a short one and see how things went. I did, and my knees were fine—but then it was the turn of my thighs. After a few days, chafing was seriously affecting the inside of my thighs, so that I was starting to walk like John Wayne (did he suffer the same problem with all that horseback riding?). At Knighton, a town roughly half way along the Offa's Dyke Path, I consulted the local chemist and ended up with a heap of supplies: glucosamine, ibuprofen, a knee-support bandage and most usefully (and possibly the only useful thing) a yellow tube of anti-chafing cream—the ingredients suggested it was actually a silicone grease. Whatever it was, it seemed to work, and I successfully rendezvoused with my wife at the service station café on the old Severn Bridge, a bit beyond the end of the Offa's Dyke trail. I was very proud of my achievement and, despite the medical issues, rather enjoyed it.

I later walked the Pennine Way and a few other long-distance paths, which I found a lot easier than my first walk along Offa's Dyke. In addition, I enjoyed the solitude of walking alone, the changing landscape, the food choices and the little unexpected events that happen on a walk, as well as the challenge of completing a walk, despite rain and mist and hail and unplanned detours of various sorts. In consequence, after doing a few other things, I was ready to start planning for the E4 trail.

The next step was gaining my wife's agreement. Fortunately, she was very supportive and wanted me to follow my dream… but she had a couple of concerns. First that I might find some other woman, globetrotting, attractive, free-spirited and available, on the trail. This was not even a remote possibility as no one could be better than my wife, and besides, most of the people I had met on my walks so far seemed to be middle-aged men like myself (apart from the beards). Secondly, she worried about me getting run over while I daydreamed my time away walking down or across a busy road. More likely maybe, as road accidents are the major cause of accidental death in the UK at least, but hopefully a risk I could manage by careful attention on roads. My mother was more concerned that I would be beaten up and robbed. Foreign office advice suggested this was unlikely provided I avoided wandering around big towns late at night and did not accept offers from beautiful girls. As the E4 avoids built-up areas and I am more of an early bird, enjoying a good dawn, I felt fairly confident of my safety from this perspective.

Despite her fears of crime in Europe, my mother also wanted me to travel, something she valued highly.

Having gained the necessary permissions, I turned my attention to what gear to take. Discussions of gear fill many pages of magazines and hours of conversation between hikers.

My research suggested that accommodation was often, but not always available, on the E4. To avoid having to make complex arrangements in a foreign language with taxis or big detours, I decided to take camping equipment so I could 'wild camp' in remoter places where a hotel or hostel was not available. By wild or 'free' camping, I mean pitching my tent in some trees or a field rather than an official campsite. For reasons to be explained later, I was not always happy about wild camping and would certainly prefer a comfortable, if modest, hotel, but it made arrangements a lot simpler on certain sections. Besides, waking up on the side of a mountain, miles from anywhere, looking down on the clouds below, or listening to the dawn birdsong in some woods, has the capacity to fill me with happiness and contentment; it has a certain romance. Camping at official campsites where they existed on the E4 also appealed as a means of keeping down costs (something my father would have approved of). On my preliminary walks in the UK, I used an inexpensive backpacker's tent that served me well, but for a backpacker, weight is everything. The lighter the load on your back, the more pleasant things are. So for my first trip on the E4, I bought a lightweight tent that at 0.85 kg was half the weight of my previous tent and, in consequence, cost seven times more and did not last as long. I had bought my sleeping bag fifteen years before, and my rucksack was a veteran of twenty-five years' service. Both had served me well, and I saw no point in changing them as modern alternatives had similar weights. I debated taking a sleeping mat but decided against it on my first trip due to its weight and bulk.

In keeping with an old-fashioned approach, I took two aluminium water bottles rather than one of those off-putting plastic bladders with pipes you suck through. However, they were nice, modern aluminium bottles with brightly coloured enamel on the outside. I took a one-litre bottle and a one-and-a-half litre one. For times when I had to use stream water, I took chlorine dioxide tablets to sterilise the water, which Chris Townsend's book *The Backpacker's Handbook* recommended.

Boots are key to a comfortable walk. I wore some leather 'Brasher' boots that I had used on a trip on the GR20 in Corsica a few months before without any blisters. Leather, as they are easy to clean and make presentable for visits to restaurants, and because I found bits tended to come unstitched on fabric boots, I had owned earlier before the soles wore out. The leather boots I chose were made of a small number of leather pieces. When I later tried a more expensive pair made out of a jigsaw of sections, they again failed due to bits coming undone. I also took some very cheap slip-on canvas shoes for use in the evenings; I could feel every bit of gravel through the thin soles, but they were very light in weight and took little room in my rucksack.

Outdoor shops are fun places to visit for my wife and me, and we rarely leave empty-handed. I found some underpants and tee shirts (sorry, base layers) made of Cocona, a thin mixture of merino wool with other stuff to stop them from smelling if you did not wash them. These seemed ideal, especially as they were lightweight and dried very quickly so they could be washed in a hotel sink and dried overnight, something I did whenever possible to make sure I did not become too malodorous. My wife feels I have too many socks, but new, woollen, bouncy walking socks always feel luxurious, and I might have sneaked some in.

Over my state-of-the-art underpants, I wore some hiking trousers in lightweight fabric with lots of pockets in which to forget where things are. I also had a crease-resistant button-up shirt to maintain sartorial standards when visiting hotels and restaurants, and a fleece or two for cold nights. I took a Gore-Tex jacket, and waterproof trousers to handle rain, gaiters to avoid the bottom of my trousers getting muddy, and sunhat and sunglasses to handle the sun. Almost all my clothing was some shade of blue, which my wife thought a bit boring.

My toilet bag had soap in a plastic container (donated by my wife), toothpaste, toothbrush, dental floss, a comb and a couple of disposable razor blades, but no shaving foam. I used the soap for shaving and shampooing based on the recommendation of some guide or other. A separate bag had various tablets and medicines, plasters, lip balm (to avoid the cracked lips I gained on previous trips), insect repellent, sunscreen and toilet paper and a handful of dog poo bags.

Based on my research (Chris Townsend again), poo disappears pretty fast and, provided you do it somewhere well out of the way and cover it with stones or leaves, it should not cause anyone any distress. Toilet paper is another matter and takes a long time to decompose. It is easy to spot well-used toilet spots on the trail from the discarded toilet paper, fortunately, bleached by the sun and rain. So I put my used toilet paper in a dog poo bag until I could dispose of it in a dustbin somewhere.

As I planned to eat at cafés and restaurants wherever possible to enjoy the local cuisine, I did not take any cooking equipment, which would just add weight. For occasions where I had to fend for myself, such as lunches on the trail, I took a pen knife and a plastic 'spork' (a cross between a spoon and a fork—a waste of space as it soon snapped in half). I packed some (dried) fruit and nuts, flapjacks and oatcakes in my rucksack in the UK in case I could not find suitable food to eat on the trail in Spain. I thought of these as emergency rations (but more pleasant). My wife recommended flapjacks as they are made of oats, which give a slow release of energy, and sugar or similar for an immediate energy boost. I particularly liked the Cherry Bakewell flavour. Fruit and nuts also have a surprisingly high energy value, and oatcakes are useful for eating with cheese or tinned tuna.

For navigation, I bought a guidebook for the first part of my walk along the GR7 in Andalucía, a compass (which I did not use and left behind on subsequent trips) and a Garmin e30 GPS. GPS stands for Global Positioning System; the device shows your location based on signals from satellites. Mine was a small, handheld, reasonably robust, and waterproof device with a small screen on which I could see my position on a map of Spain. The map was loaded on an SD card. Old school types are not keen on the use of a GPS, preferring a map and compass. To use a map and compass in featureless terrain, you start from a known location and then count steps, or time yourself, as you walk along a particular compass direction. From the number of steps or time you have walked, you can work out the distance you have travelled from your starting point, and from that, you can find where you should be on the map.

Alternatively, you look out for features you can see on the map; these need to be distinctive, as one stream or mountain can look much like another. The traditional approach relies on good, detailed maps, which are not available in many countries, and even if they are, carrying enough large-scale maps for a long-distance walk like the E4 would mean that there would be little room in your rucksack for anything else. If you prepare well, a GPS is far better, as it can tell you where you are in longitude and latitude or in alternative coordinate systems like the National Grid or the WGS (World Geodetic System). Having spent time in the mist on featureless moors in the Pennines, I soon discovered that in such conditions, a compass and map are not very useful for telling you where you are. Others possibly have a greater aptitude than me for counting steps and following compass directions. Still, all too often, especially when surrounded by a white fog, I daydream while following some transient path or other until I start wondering, where am I? Having not estimated my distance or direction from some known starting point, a map and compass in a white-out may look professional but does not actually tell you where you are, unlike my trusty GPS. However, the position given by a GPS is not enough on its own, as by itself, it does not tell you where to go. Your GPS needs to be loaded with a suitable map, purchased on the internet. Although a map is necessary, as the screen on a typical GPS is only an inch or two across, it is difficult to work out how to get to some point well off the edge of the screen, avoiding obstacles in your way. To resolve this, you should load a 'track' of your planned route onto your GPS before leaving home. Either this can be obtained from some internet site as what is known as a 'GPX' file, or else you can create it on your laptop before your trip using the map purchased for your GPS. Such preparation is essential. Once you have created a suitable 'track', navigation becomes a simple matter of following it on the GPS (after making it a suitable colour like bright pink so that it stands out from the colours on the map). Where possible, I loaded a couple of GPX tracks from different sources on the internet as they did not always agree. Some long-distance walkers I have met use their smartphones for navigation, these have a GPS function built-in, and you can download one of several apps with maps and tracks people have uploaded to guide you where you wish to go. For myself, I preferred to save the battery power on my phone for emergencies and use a dedicated GPS that is not also trying to find a mobile signal. I also find the buttons on my GPS easier to use in rain or with gloves than a touch screen, although I have known hikers use their nose to operate their smart phone when encumbered with gloves. This takes a bit of skill. Despite my comments above, I sometimes take a large-scale map, so I can get a bigger picture of where I am and can make sense of signposts to nearby towns.

Other 'gear' included a head torch for camping with spare batteries, my smart phone with charger and continental plug adapter (later replaced by a continental charger avoiding the weight of an adapter), a Kindle with a selection of books and the Kindle charger (until I realised, I could use my phone charger), a Spanish phrase book and a small digital camera. I could have used my phone as a camera, but it had no telephoto option, and, as mentioned, I wanted to save its power for emergencies, so I walked with it switched off. This also avoided nuisance phone calls. Switching it on just to take a photo was not practical when trying to catch a shot of a squirrel. In fact, nothing is very practical when trying to catch a shot of a squirrel scampering away. I had a wad of small denomination euros (always wise, as I discovered shop keepers do not appreciate you buying an ice cream with a fifty-euro note), a credit and debit card. Finally, and most importantly, my passport, printouts of bus and flight tickets and what I called my itinerary. My itinerary was the result of extensive research. It included when my bus and flights left, the towns and villages I would pass through, the accommodation options in those towns and the distances between them. With this information, I could work out where best to stop for the following nights, given how tired or not I felt. Such research, anticipating my trip and the places I would visit, was very much part of my enjoyment of the E4.

I loaded everything into dry bags in case it rained. As the name suggests, these lightweight nylon bags keep your clothes, Kindle and passport dry while water is dripping down your neck or penetrating the gap between your waterproof jacket and waterproof trousers, making it look like you have wet yourself. The alternative to dry bags is to use a rucksack cover, but the only one I had said 'Trespass' on the back, which

I did not think a very good advert for hikers; it also tended to accumulate water in its base and blow away in windy weather. My rucksack weighed in at about 13 kg, which would increase to over 15 kg when the water bottles were full. Then I was ready—or so I thought.

Chapter 2: Tarifa to Ronda — sun and sickness

A pleasant start

The E4 starts in Tarifa in the south of Spain and follows the GR7 footpath through Andalusia. Some sites claim the E4 starts in Ceuta, a Spanish outpost on the coast of Morocco. I could find no references to anyone ever starting there, and, as Ceuta is rather a small place, not even in Europe, I did not feel it worth the ferry trip to go there. Instead, I started at Gibraltar, a British outpost on the coast of Spain. This was the nearest airport to Tarifa I could conveniently fly to. (Later, I walked from Cabo de São Vicente in the south-west corner of Portugal to Tarifa, which is a possible extension to the E4 and described in Appendix 2.)

Gibraltar was a spectacular place to start from. My flight landed in the midday heat on the last day of August 2014, beneath the giant rock of Gibraltar. The runway is squashed between the rock and the border fence with Spain and beyond the runway's end is the sea on the other side of the peninsula. It did not seem to leave much room for pilot error. Leaving the airport building, I walked into town. This involves crossing the runway, possibly the only one in the world crossed by a main road. After checking into my hotel, I headed for the Mediterranean Steps, TripAdvisor's top recommendation. These wind around the rock, eventually taking you to the top past some dramatic views and through a few tunnels excavated into the steep sides of the mountain. I visited more tunnels later, dug out of the rock as part of the island's defence against attacks from Spain in the 18th century and against Germany in the last war. The red telephone boxes, fish and chips, pubs and the full English breakfast next morning highlighted how British Gibraltar wanted to be, although the monkeys on the rock, trying to investigate the plastic bag I was carrying, seemed to indicate a more exotic connection.

The next day I crossed the border into Spain and the town of La Linea. The helpful lady in the empty and cavernous concrete tourist office pointed the way to the bus station (all the tourist offices I visited in Spain were very helpful). As I had spare time, I wandered around the dusty town, picking up some pears at the market before catching my bus for Tarifa. I had visited Tarifa some thirty years earlier, when my wife and I found a quiet, dusty outpost, with the distinction of being the southernmost point of mainland Europe. Things had changed. It was now the hip, kitesurfing or kiteboarding capital of the world, or at least in the top ten. As I walked along the beach, the many colourful fabric wings billowed out, pulling surfers on boards at speed through the waves, as they showed off with jumps and twists. At the edge of Tarifa's old town, close to where I dined on tuna and Coke, there was a board marking the start of the *'Sendero Europeo E-4 Tarifa-Atenas'*, or 'European Footpath E4 — Tarifa to Athens'. The E4 does not go to Athens and now extends to Cyprus, but who wants to be picky?! The E4 has been extended at various times, and different signs in different countries give different start and end points. Unfortunately, this particular sign was defaced by anarchist graffiti for no obvious reason.

In most of Spain, the E4 follows the GR7. GR stands for *'Gran Recorrido'* in Spain, or 'Long Journey'. Waymarking of trails is by red-and-white marks or signposts. Sometimes the waymarking is enthusiastic, but at other times there is none, and I soon lost the path before I was even through the outskirts of Tarifa. Not that it mattered. I followed the sea, then a boardwalk through a nature reserve behind the beach, crossing onto the beach for a while and stopping for a cold Coke in the heat before ending up at the campsite at Torre de Pena. My pitch was nicely shaded by eucalyptus trees close to the tower that gave the campsite its name. Perfect, I thought, until I tried to get the tent pegs into the hard-baked ground. I managed to get the four pegs of my tent into the ground, gently hammering them in with the aid of some rocks, handily piled nearby. Fortunately, and impressively, unlike the tent pegs I remembered in my youth, the yellow 'DAC' aluminium tent pegs did not bend, and the tent stayed up despite the fabric flapping in the wind blowing in from the sea and the meagre number of pegs.

I enjoy walking on my own. There is no one to be responsible for or worry about, and no one I have to struggle to keep up with. If I take the wrong path, there is only myself to feel frustrated, and if I wish to make an unplanned diversion, stop early or carry on late, I need not consult anyone. I do not need to entertain people with conversation or motivate others to carry on; I can just think my own thoughts. This is fine except in the evenings. The campsite had a lovely restaurant overlooking the sea, and, as I sipped a glass of cold white wine, watching the sunset shed its pink colours over nearby couples as I enjoyed grilled fish, I thought it would have been lovely to have my wife with me...

Road to Los Barrios — a hot, hot day

Suitably excited to be on my way, I started off early the next day, as it would be around 37 km to Los Barrios, the first place where there were a hotel and restaurants. Thirty-seven kilometres is a long day, and now I would not plan on a day longer than 32 kilometres or 20 miles. The sun was still behind the mountains as I walked along the road up the first valley heading north. Gradually the pink sun cleared the far ridge, giving grazing cows sharp shadows. I had a slight problem when the road split into two directions, but which arm to take? I switched on my GPS to check which way to go, but the 'track' I was planning to follow had disappeared! A passing (non-English speaking) jogger looked over my shoulder while I retrieved the 'track' and then followed it in the wrong direction. Just because you download a track from the internet does not mean it goes the right way! However, whoever recorded the 'track' eventually got back on the right route, and I followed them.

The only problem now was that I had picked up two very friendly dogs. Bored by their farm guarding duties, they obviously thought they could start a new life walking with me as I hiked through the Mediterranean scrub. I tried "shoo" and "go away", English phrases with which they were clearly unfamiliar. Eventually, I had to resort to throwing a few sticks in their general direction, trying to convey hostile intent while carefully missing them. Then I rushed off down what I thought was the right footpath, hoping they would not follow. It was close to the right path, but maybe not actually on it, as I pushed my way through some prickly bushes before eventually reaching a group of houses and a section of road.

My next encounter with dogs was not so good. I misread a GR7 sign which appeared to be pointing past some houses. As I crossed in front of a cottage, another dog, clearly a matriarch with puppies close by, circled around me and bit my calf from behind. Some dogs can be very sneaky when they attack you. Trying to get behind you seems a common tactic with a smaller kind of dog. I rushed off again in the wrong direction and dropped down through bushes to the gravel road I should have been walking along. Finding a quiet spot, I examined the bite. It was arguable whether the dog's teeth had broken the skin, a fleck of red but no bleeding. I cleaned it up with a sterile wipe from my first aid pack (which I had inconveniently packed deep within my clothes) and wondered about rabies.

The day moved into the afternoon. I wandered along the road as the heat increased. No one else was in sight, maybe because of the area's remoteness, or maybe they were sensible and stayed indoors during the heat of the day. I had been warned by a guy in an outdoor shop that August would be too hot for walking in Andalucía, and maybe the 2nd of September was too close to August. There was one diversion through a wooded area by a stream, possibly a good place for a campsite had I known better, but I headed on. The sun reflected off the white dust of the track, and shade was in short supply as I reached a sign saying 'Los Barrios 14 kilometres', still a long way to go. I tend to breathe through my mouth when walking, and in the heat, it rapidly dried out along with the back of my throat. I took frequent gulps of water, now lukewarm in the sun and not refreshing. It crossed my mind that I had not passed water since first thing that morning, making me wonder about dehydration. I was certainly releasing a lot of sweat which dripped into my eyes, making them sting. At one point, the GR7 took a footpath off the road I was following, but the Cicerone guidebook warned of a possible obstruction. I preferred the certainty of an alternative road route to the risk that I would have to retrace my steps, which would be very depressing.

Finally, tired and thirsty, with only a small amount left of the 2 ½ litres of water I started with, I reached the junction with the main road where there was a petrol station, offering a selection of cold drinks. Sitting on some propane tanks outside, I downed a can of cold Coke, the most amazing, refreshing experience, quickly followed by some mineral water, but there were still three kilometres to go. They went very slowly, but the heat gradually reduced as the sun moved lower in the sky. It was getting on for seven p.m. when I arrived in Los Barrios where I then faced my second problem. I knew there were a couple of hotels in town, but where were they? I could see no sign of them in the town centre. I walked back in case I had missed them. I asked as best I could in phrasebook Spanish, but no one seemed to recognise the name of the road where the nearest hotel was located. A lady even found a map for me to look at. Eventually, I found it a short distance beyond the town centre. It was on a small road running parallel to the main road, which had a different name. Fortunately, a room was available, and I quickly showered and phoned my wife, telling her of my mishap with the dog.

I returned to the town centre thinking of whether I might get rabies and where I could get food. There were plenty of people about, chatting to each other and eating ice creams. The Spanish eat late and enjoy socialising in the evenings, sometimes over ice cream; given the heat of the afternoon, I could understand why. Nearby was a medical facility, and I considered going in and asking about my bite, but seeing the waiting room with some obviously ill people, my scratch seemed too small to bother them with. I had read somewhere that pharmacies offered advice, so I looked up the word for dogs ('*perros*') and entered a *Farmacia* clearly marked by a green cross sign. I made the actions of a dog biting my calf and said the word '*perros*'. The lady behind the counter offered me a choice of three creams. I picked one and headed off, only to discover later that it was for insect bites. At this point, a fortuitous phone call from my wife, who, in the meantime, had been doing some research online, confirmed that Spain was currently rabies-free. At last, as nine p.m. arrived, I found a place on the square serving hamburger and chips, for which the translation was not too difficult (*"hamburguesa y patatas fritas"*), and there was a menu so I could point.

Finally relaxing over a drink, I reflected on some of the lessons of the day: firstly it is hot in September in Andalusía, so lots of water is a good idea, or better still, walk at some other time, and secondly, waymark the hotels on your GPS so you can find them.

The long road to Castillo de Castellar

The next day was another long one, 33 kilometres. In future, I would try to avoid consecutive long days, but this trip was very much an education for me. I again started early to maximise the cooler hours and the pleasant light. Refreshed, I soon reached the petrol station that had been so welcome yesterday and then headed into the hills. The guide said to go through a gate to some military barracks. I came to a gate after passing a few army type buildings, but some men waiting by their cars prevented me from going through. This was the first time I was stopped that day. I pointed to a GR7 sign trying to explain I was following the footpath. Unfortunately, the sign pointed back to Los Barrios, and they thought I wanted to go there; at least their gesticulations suggested that was the case. So I gesticulated that I had just come from there. Unfortunately, I was never any good at playing Charades, but eventually, mutual understanding prevailed, and they pointed to a path at right angles to the road. It turned out that the gate referred to in the guide no longer existed, and the gate that I had been so eager to enter led to the firing range. Probably fortunate that I was redirected.

After wandering through some hills with red earth, shrubs and low trees, I reached a rubbish dump where the guide said turn left. In this, it was supported by an old wooden sign. I was soon stopped for the second time that day. This time the men had a few English words, along the lines of "industrial site, no entry". Fiddling around on my GPS, I found an alternative road route. Like those at the firing range, the men were very friendly and offered me a lift. Since I was aiming to walk across Europe, this was not possible, but I appreciated the sentiment. It was by no means the only time I would have to decline an offer of a ride. The first part of the road was not pleasant as large trucks passed me on their way to the landfill site on a road not really wide enough; however, adventurous journeys are all about surviving hazards and handling the unexpected.

After lunch at a roadside restaurant, reluctantly served to me at midday, far too early, it appears, for Spanish waiters, I started a two-hour walk along a busy road, which was the official route for this part of the GR7. The 'track' I had downloaded onto my GPS took a different route, but I did not risk it in case I was stopped for a third time on the same day.

Fortunately, the road had a cycle path to walk on and lacking any cyclists, it was safe if a little boring. After a few more roads, I reached the base of the mountain on which the town of Castillo de Castellar is located. There was meant to be a campsite here, but seeing no sign of one, I started the climb up into town.

Old Spanish towns like Castillo are beautiful, with stone buildings lining narrow alleyways, evocative of ancient times, but they tend to be on hills. No doubt there were sound defensive reasons for this with the wars between the Christians and Moors. However, the problem for long-distance walkers is that it means a long climb at the end of the day when you are hot and tired and fixated on a cool beer. My reward for the climb was a gorgeous room in an only moderately expensive hotel. It was in what may have been the castle. The interior walls of my room were white, I had a modern bathroom to shower in, a choice of beds and the small windows through the thick walls gave views all the way back to the Rock of Gibraltar, which looked ever more beautiful as the sun set and day turned to night. The friendly receptionist spoke English and flattered me when I revealed a few words of Spanish, but best of all was a cold (if expensive) beer before a meal that seemed to be a mixture of fried bread and sausage at a nearby restaurant (although a little lonely as I was the only one eating).

Two days of heat

The following day I only had to walk 20.5 kilometres, so I was hoping for some respite, but it was not to be, and I arrived at Jimena de la Frontera hot, sweaty and tired. This was despite a long section on flat ground surrounded by cotton fields and farms. As it was another old town built on a hill, the last uphill stretch has really hard work. Heading for the first bar, I downed two Cokes before enquiring where the town's campsite was. There were guesthouse options, but I thought to save money, I should camp. The barman was most helpful in giving me a map of the town. At the campsite, the ground had been baked solid in the burning sun, from which straggly trees gave little respite, and the water supply was warm and tasted of the plastic pipe. The campsite manager suggested I pitch my tent before paying. Possibly he thought I might give up and want to stay at some cool, shady room in a *'hostal'*, but I was made of tougher stuff (or so I told myself). The campsite swimming pool looked cool, blue and inviting and full of people enjoying themselves but I had saved weight by not bringing swimming trunks, which had seemed a good idea at the time. Instead, I went into town and bought several litres of cold mineral water, then visited the castle, an Arabic fortress with an impressive entrance gate. A dog was roaming around, and given my experience a few days before, I explored no further. It was not such a bad campsite, it had a restaurant, at which I was the only diner, despite waiting until a Spanish nine p.m. The young waitress was being trained by an older lady, who gave instructions from a nearby door. Thankfully she successfully delivered an enormous salad followed by an enormous main course, *'Lomo de Credo'* (fried pork loin) and chips, which was to be a bit of a staple across Spain.

The next morning, suitably refreshed, I left my sleeping bag at dawn for yet another long day, 35 kilometres to Ubrique. The morning was beautiful. As I climbed the hills behind Jimena de la Frontera, the view became larger and larger. I could see not only the Rock of Gibraltar but across the water of the Gibraltar Straits to the mountains of Morocco beyond. The paths and tracks I followed led through low trees with dusty leaves in the dry landscape with rocks and dry-stone walls and stunted bushes. Even the flowers looked like they would suit a dried flower arrangement, yellows among the sun-browned leaves. By eleven a.m. I was getting tired. I started stopping for fifteen minutes every hour for a rest, and after those fifteen minutes I did not want to start again. Some men in a white pick-up who had been collecting something in the woods stopped and offered a lift. Being a long-distance walker, I refused, of course, but there was some doubt in my mind. The last eight kilometres to Ubrique were not enjoyable. Hot, sweaty, tired, the rucksack digging into my shoulders, I was losing interest in my surroundings; all I cared about was finding my way into town.

Finally reaching the town of Ubrique, I again knew the town had hotels but had not recorded where they were. Thankfully the first person I asked checked his smart phone (why had I not thought of that?) and pointed out the way to a comfortable hotel. As I showered, the first water that fell across my lips tasted salty as it washed my sweat away.

Unpacking my rucksack, the sight of my warm, Gore-Tex jacket made me break out into a sweat again.

I rang my wife each night, both because I love her and so that she knew where I was in case something happened to me. I told her that I would take a rest day in Ubrique tomorrow, being so knackered. Then I had a variety of tapas in the bar attached to the hotel, leaving most of the choices to the young waitress.

Returning home

The next day started well. After some fumbling with words and pointing to what a nearby customer had, I managed to order coffee, orange juice and toast with butter and marmalade, a fairly typical breakfast for me in Spain. *"Café, zumo de naranja, tostada, mantequilla y mermelada"* was a phrase I became familiar with, adding a belated *"por favor"* (which means 'please') as I remembered to be polite.

Next, a visit to the tourist information to learn what the sights were in the town. The young lady was delighted to tell me there was an art event today and, indeed, artists were dotted around the town, painting street scenes in their own styles. The museum I visited was dusty, empty of people and not very interesting.

By noon my digestive system was starting to complain and seemed ungrateful for the glass of lemonade I offered it. Returning to the hotel, I lay down and felt worse. Then I got up and spent a long time in the en-suite toilet. I distracted myself reading about diarrhoea, heat exhaustion and heat stroke on my phone, which was a bit alarming, heat stroke being a fairly rapid cause of death. By the evening, I was no better. Not feeling like much to eat, I bought what I thought was yoghurt that would be good for my stomach. I may have got the names confused, and it was actually for babies. I made a decision. Head back home until it was cooler and my bowels were back in order, but first, I would walk to Ronda.

So the next day, I was on my way at dawn, climbing out of town on an old cobbled Roman road. I crossed yellow, dry grass fields, passed a herd of black pigs, walked through low holm oaks, passed tumbledown dry-stone walls and hiked along gravel roads through stony hills. I reached a cool bed and breakfast place on a street in the village of

Montejaque without too much pain, and even enjoyed a beer in the evening, but did not manage to finish my pizza, my bowels still complaining.

Then it was a shortish walk to the historic town of Ronda through dry meadows with yellow fennel flowers and occasional sheep. I had visited Ronda before, but today I was feeling too poorly to enjoy its sights, instead I was focussed on catching an aeroplane home. I had purchased a ticket from Alicante for a few weeks in the future when I had thought to finish my walk. A mistake as now I had to change the departure date. It was surprisingly easy to do via the airline's phone app, albeit at a cost. In future, I would only book my return flight home when I was within a few days of finishing my walk, which gave needed flexibility on departure date and airport. I could even use my phone as a boarding card. Amazing!

Getting to Alicante was not so easy. On entering Ronda, I first stocked up on Imodium to plug my bowels and avoid any accidents, then it was a train to Granada. I was too late arriving for the onward bus, so I stopped at a busy campsite near the bus station and had a burger at a crowded Burger King restaurant because it was less likely to add to my stomach woes than anything more Spanish. In the morning, a bus to Alicante, another one to the airport, then a flight arriving at Bristol airport in the early hours of next morning. I then had a few hours to wait for the bus back home. I lay on the floor of the coffee shop and felt ill. By lunchtime, I was in bed at home, my wife ministering to my needs and asking if I had given up on my dream…

Chapter 3: Ronda to Cieza — discovering success

My Return to Spain

My dream was still alive, and after two weeks, I was fully recovered from my stomach problems and ready to go again. On adding up daily distances, I was pleased to discover that on my first trip, I had walked 170 kilometres (over 100 miles) over seven days! This convinced me there was a good chance that I would be able to cross the remaining 565 kilometres of Andalusía. I had made some changes to my packing, such as dumping my heavy Gore-Tex jacket for a lightweight waterproof jacket which we used to call a cagoule. The cagoule proved useful. As I finished my first day's walk from Ronda to Arriate, I was caught in a heavy rain storm; the hot, dry weather of my previous trip was changing for the better (i.e., cooler). The next day, the dust on the track had turned to mud, very sticky mud, which added an inch or so to the soles of my boots, as if I was wearing platform shoes. The rain was, however, an exception; the late September and October weather was now perfect for walking.

I was enjoying my food again. At lunchtime in a bar in Arriate, an enthusiastic owner fed me tapas which included a slice of beef tomato, dressed lightly with olive oil, grown by himself he proudly told me, to go with a Coke. Simple but surprisingly full of flavour. I had booked an apartment online for the night on the outskirts of town. I walked to the GPS coordinates indicated by Booking.com and knocked on the door of the house. No one was around, just some dogs who sniffed at me as I wandered through their garden calling out. On ringing the telephone number given for the reservation, and a difficult conversation between people lacking a common language, the owner drove up. It was then I realised I was at the house next door! I was glad the dogs were not fiercer and more protective of their garden. Wonderful though a GPS is, they are only accurate to ten metres or so, so that you are liable to find yourself not on the welcoming patio of the local hostelry but conducting a meet and greet with next door's guard dogs.

Much of the next three days was spent on gravel roads among hills with olive groves, some wooded areas and much sparse vegetation. I covered good distances without too much effort, which helped to rebuild my confidence. There were a few sights of note: a Roman bridge before the old town of Ardales; the ruins of the Bobastro Moorish village, cut into the rock, and a reservoir above the village of El Chorro (maybe a pumped storage scheme?). El Chorro is famous for the *'El Camino del Rey'*, a vertiginous walkway along the side of a gorge. A cause of some deaths it was being rebuilt when I passed; now finished, I must visit the area again and try it. As it was, I walked down an attractive path on the side of a cliff, into the village, where an older lady at the railway station café provided me with a cheese and ham sandwich. El Chorro is in a valley which meant the next section was a climb out over the hills to the village of Valle de Abdalajis. I am not entirely sure I followed the right route, but I arrived without too much trouble. Then I spent some time looking for the *hostal* I planned to stay in, which was marked in the wrong location on Google, something which was to happen again in the future. It was a welcoming, whitewashed building, which I eventually found. A *'hostal'* in Spain is not the same as a 'hostel' in Britain; it does not mean dormitory sleeping and instead usually refers to inexpensive rooms associated with a bar, often above it. Handy, as it means someone is generally around when you arrive, avoiding a fraught telephone call to an owner, complicated by language difficulties.

After crossing more hills through farmland and olive groves, I arrived at the larger town of Antequera. There were some lengthy suburbs to walk through, but the centre was historic with streets of whitewashed buildings, a cathedral and a Moorish fort. The history of the area is dominated by the Moors. These Muslim believers of Arab and Berger origins invaded Spain from North Africa in 711, conquering much of the country. Christian kings took until the end of the 15th century to drive the Moors out, a process called the *'Reconquista'*. The remaining Muslims and Jews had to convert to Christianity. The Moorish influence remains significant; even the name Andalusía is from the Arabic *'al-Andalus'*. Although the E4 does not visit Seville and Granada with their famous Moorish buildings, the Alcazar and Alhambra, it visits smaller sites such as at Antequera, and there are details such as irrigation systems left by the Moors. The location of villages at defensible, strategic locations on ridges and hillsides, with a castle at the highest point, is also a sign of these unsettled times.

After a tapas of beans and ham, I visited the major sights, somewhat encumbered by my rucksack, its weight on my shoulders detracting from my admiration of Moorish gardens and Mudejar ceilings. Sometimes I leave it at a ticket office or similar location after removing any valuables, but I am never sure how secure that is. Losing it would bring an abrupt end to my expedition. The helpful Antequera tourist information office confirmed that a campsite to the south of town was open, so I headed out of town past some old mills by the river. The lady at the office had warned me of some bad weather that night. Her forecast was correct. Given the difficulty I again experienced, hammering my pegs into the hard-baked and stony ground, it was perhaps surprising that only one peg was later pulled out by the wind, necessitating a struggle in the middle of a dark, wet and windy night to secure the pegs further by piling rocks on top of them.

Through the Alpujarra — no lemons were damaged in transit

After Antequera, the GR7 splits into two alternatives, a northerly and a southerly route passing each side of the Sierra Nevada mountain range. There was a consensus among the sources I consulted that the southerly trail was better, so I chose that one. It goes through the popular Alpujarra area with many tourist facilities. I subsequently walked the northerly route (see Appendix 3), and certainly, the southerly route is a more varied experience. However, the first section is not too inspiring, much of it walking on a tarmac road. The day's walk ended at the village of Riogordo. Accommodation at a Hospederia before the town was referenced in the guidebook, but this looked pretty closed when I reached it. The ubiquitous dog was amiably patrolling and a radio was playing inside, but nobody answered my call, and the place had an abandoned look. I was disappointed as I had found no other accommodation nearby in my research. It was a farming area with orchards and not ideal for wild camping. I walked into Riogordo to get some supplies and was gratified to see some signs to the Molino de Las Tablas Bed & Breakfast. There I was welcomed by the owner's mother, and despite language difficulties, I soon settled down with a cold beer. At first, I thought the other guests were speaking German, but it was actually Flemish, a mistake I made more than once on my trip.

As I walked into the mountains the following day, a restaurant with a terrace and view attracted my attention for lunch. While admiring the view, I tried some traditional Andalucian food, *ajoblanco*, a white garlic soup, which I was surprised to find was served cold, and *migas*, fried breadcrumbs with additional unidentifiable ingredients. The later part of the day took me on the route of an old railway line along the steep side of the rocky mountain range. A short tunnel took me into the mountain. Daylight on the other side revealed a different vista, the town of Ventas de Zafarraya at the edge of a plateau, farmed for vegetables. Before dinner, I wandered around the town. I noticed several half-built buildings, maybe abandoned due to the recent recession. Several Africans were employed on the farmland, where I later saw them harvesting a huge field of lettuces. I tried an old bar, recommended somewhere. Like most such places, it was full of men, the television on the wall tuned to the hunting and fishing channel. The programme seemed to be about well-built men shooting wild boar, the dead animals lined up in a row. Not being to my taste, I returned to my *hostal*. The helpful man behind the bar seemed to work there all day and all night; I never saw the bar without him. I ordered some ham and cheese for tea and watched a quiz show on the TV, called '¡Boom!' Despite it being in Spanish, I could work out some of the answers to the questions, which were typed on the bottom of the screen. For some reason, the contestants had to cut the lines into a 'bomb', and if they cut the wrong one, the 'bomb' exploded, covering them in coloured paint, which was curiously amusing. A lot more interesting than watching hunters and dead animals and a favourite for watching over dinner on my trip through Spain, along with a programme called 'Tony's Gym' of which I understood nothing, but it looked vaguely fun.

The next day took me to Alhama de Granada. Before the town, there is an impressive gorge. Swallows flew above the attractive old buildings, and the tourist office helpfully booked my next night's accommodation at a place I had not been aware of. This was at a restaurant by a lake, slightly off the GR7, where I spoke to my first English people on my trip. They had rented a cottage nearby. Having now mastered the Google Translate app, I was able to help them by telling them the Spanish for cinnamon (*'canela'*), which they wanted for their melon. The following day started with a dog which loped along beside me; maybe he thought we were going hunting together; he looked the type. Thankfully, after some considerable difficulty, I managed to shake him off and soon after met a man and his daughter who stopped their pick-up by me. From their expressions, I presumed they wanted to know what I was doing on their land. It is useful on these occasions to know where you are going, and I told them the name of the next town, Jayena, evidently pronouncing it correctly—j's being h's in Spanish, as they confidently pointed in the direction I had just walked from. I dug out the Cicerone guidebook and showed it to them. Noting their blank looks, I pointed out the route, which was via a place called *'La Resinera'* (where they used to process pine resin). This they recognised and pointed up the farm track in the direction I was walking. I thanked them and headed off, having formed the impression that they thought me a very silly person to take such a roundabout route. The Spanish are not great long-distance walkers and, like many people in Europe, no doubt think it is a lot easier to drive. I walked through Jayena, picking up some bread and cheese before camping at a forest campsite. There were locked toilets, and no doubt you could get a key from the local town hall (or *'ayuntamiento'*), but this would involve walking back to Jayena in the morning to return the key and much effort explaining what I wanted, given my extremely limited Spanish. Now well into October, some of the trees were now an attractive shade of yellow, contrasting with those still green.

The following day was a longish walk, through scrubby vegetation over hills, with some good views. Out of curiosity, I timed my progress which averaged 3.8 kilometres per hour, including breaks, which was to be fairly typical of my walk across Europe. Most of the day was on gravel tracks, but at one point, the route went down a small valley beside a dry stream bed. Somewhere or other, I missed the path up the side of the valley onto a track above. Progress became challenging, involving climbing over large boulders and, realising my error, instead of retracing my steps, I climbed up the steep side of the valley. A silly, beginner's mistake; it was covered in prickly bushes I had to push my way through. Inevitably I stumbled, put out my hand to avert a fall and was rewarded with a palm-full of thorns. Reaching the track above, I pulled most of them out, but a few were embedded. I was not brave enough to dig them out with a needle like my wife does, so they took several days to grow out. After a long day, I was relieved to reach Albunuelas, a village where I booked a Bed & Breakfast. I had a little trouble finding it, asking for Calle Horno, but somehow, I cannot grasp the silent H in Spanish words. In the end, I showed the address written down to a man standing outside the town hall, and, after giving me a leaflet on language lessons, he pointed out it was just around the corner.

It was in the Bed & Breakfast, over a dinner of curried chicken, that I met two Englishmen in their seventies who were about to start walking a section of the GR7. At one time, I thought being over seventy meant you were confined to an armchair by the fire, but it turned out that the English couple running the Bed & Breakfast was also over seventy. As I was approaching sixty, this gave me a warm feeling inside and the hope that I would still be enjoying striding out for many years to come. Over the next three days, I crossed paths with these two gentlemen several times. They walked slower than I did but started earlier in the day. Although they were hoping to wild camp, the area was not that suitable, with orchards and olive groves or bare hills, so we all stayed in hotels at Niguelas and Lanjaron. I was a little upset at the latter hotel. The motherly lady on reception carefully pointed out to me the washing facilities on the roof, consisting of concrete basins, with integral ribbed sections for scrubbing your clothes and washing lines for drying them, facilities I did make use of. When I later passed her, she made scrubbing actions to make sure I had been conscientious in my washing. Yet it appeared she made no mention of these laundry facilities to my fellow walkers, who had arrived a little later after an early beer. Was I especially smelly, I wondered? Whenever I have a room of my own at a hotel or Bed & Breakfast, I wash some items of clothes in the bathroom basin, especially tee shirts and underpants that can emit some odours. Woollen socks are more problematic as they take longer to dry and fleeces take forever, so they rarely get a wash on my travels.

After Lanjarron, the GR7 takes you across the Alpujarra, an area popular with tourists due to its villages of whitewashed houses with flat grey roofs, narrow streets and cosy bars, set off by the sunny weather. This also meant more facilities for accommodation and eating. I stayed at campsites at Pitres, Trevelez and Laroles, and *hostals* in Cadiar and Yegen. The latter was run by a friendly Irish lady who served me pigs' cheeks for dinner with vegetables in a light batter. Pigs' cheeks are much nicer than they sound; a local dish, it seems. I also had excellent food at a restaurant in Pitres, overlooking a valley. I was much impressed by the salad; in addition to the expected lettuce and tomatoes, it had apricots and nuts. The meal on the terrace ended with a complimentary spirit of some kind, and the general view of the diners was very complimentary (although a Dutch lady was a little irritated when I thought she was German). Elsewhere I tried the *'conejo'* (rabbit), which often reached the menus, popular in Britain when my mother was young, but not often eaten now; maybe people think of them as too cuddly and cute. There were also cafés and bars en route advertising tapas with their drinks in English for the benefit of passing tourists; it's surprising how a slice of cooked potato with a bit of pepper and olive oil can make a tasty snack.

The Alpujarra is the area on the south side of the Sierra Nevada, which Chris Stewart helped to make famous in his book *Driving over Lemons*. Much of the trail is along the side of the mountains among scrubby vegetation, up and down valleys, visiting the little whitewashed villages and passing olive groves and tumbledown stone buildings, now often being restored for visitors. Villages often had a little 'fountain', where water trickled out of a pipe set in a wall, into a stone trough. The climate is dry and these water supplies were clearly important. In places, the path follows little aqueducts (*'acequia'* in Spanish) that channel water for irrigation. Some date back to the times when the Moors occupied the area, bringing farming technology from the Middle East. There are some interesting landscapes. A small path went down a gorge somewhere between Trevelez and Cadiar; at its start, there was a 'No Waiting' sign and a prohibition for vehicles over four tonnes; however, as the path was only a few feet wide, it looked like official overkill. Between Cadiar and Yegen, there was a section of 'badlands', where the loose soil was deeply eroded into multiple valleys and ravines. In one place after Yegen I passed a ferruginous spring, depositing material red with its iron content.

Leaving the campsite at Laroles early in the morning, I headed north to cross the Sierra Nevada range. Stopping for a breakfast of *tostada* and coffee at a café at Bayarcal, I noticed how many of the men were drinking an early morning spirit, something that seems common in rural Spain. The TV is invariably on in these cafés and, although in Spanish, one could more or less decipher the weather forecast from the chart and some news from the pictures. After Bayarcal, the path climbed upwards, more or less following the road. Looking down, I saw a shepherd and his dogs lead his flock of sheep up a path along the stony sides of the valley. The highest point on my crossing was the Puerta de la Ragua at some 2,040 metres. The *alberge* there was closed, so I ate the food I had brought at a nearby picnic table by the trees.

The path down the other side of the Sierra Nevada was not at all clear. I followed the track on my GPS, through trees, across a firebreak and through the undergrowth. It was not too difficult, but near the bottom, I found myself on the wrong side of a wall to where I think the path was. A GPS is only accurate to several metres, and maps and tracks downloaded from the internet are no more accurate, so even if your GPS tells you that you are on the path, the actual trail may over a nearby fence or among some nearby vegetation. Nevertheless, I reached the village of La Calahorra and booked into a nearby hotel. A prominent castle sits on a hill beside the town. Unfortunately, as so often happened in this case, I had arrived too late and would be leaving too early to visit it.

Having conquered the Sierra Nevada, the next day involved crossing a wide flat valley before climbing the less-visited mountains of the Sierra de Baza. Crossing the flat agricultural valley, I passed a sizeable solar power station. It was a type that used lines of curved mirrors to focus the sun's heat on liquid pumped through a tube at the mirror's focal point. The liquid was heated to such a temperature that on releasing the pressure, it vaporised and drove a steam turbine which turned an electricity generator (at least that was what I assumed happened). As the sky was overcast, it was unlikely they would produce much power today. I impressed myself by ordering a ham and cheese sandwich for lunch (in Spanish) at a bar in Charches, a village I had been looking at from several kilometres away since I left La Calahorra.

After lunch, I headed into the tree-covered mountains on a gravel road. I was somewhat nervous as the lack of accommodation meant I would need to wild camp in a Sierra de Baza National Park where signs stated that camping was prohibited. But what can you do? There were some refuges, buildings that were locked and no doubt involved some impractical arrangement for the lone walker to obtain keys. From my research, I knew where a previous couple had camped, and indeed it looked an excellent spot, on a little promontory, flat ground, unimpeded by undergrowth, hidden by trees from the road with a view back to the Sierra Nevada. I pitched my tent and ate some food I had brought, listening carefully for the noise of anyone approaching who might tell me off. I was nervous, as I had only ever wild camped alone once before. I only heard the sound of one car, which quickly passed. In my imagination, as I prepared for this trip, I would sit and look at the stars and the lights of villages in the valley below, but it was surprisingly cool and, having abandoned warm clothing after my earlier trip, I soon found myself tucked up in my sleeping bag for warmth, reading my Kindle until I felt ready for sleep. In complete contrast, the following night, I was in a spacious wood cabin at a mountain resort at Narvaez after a late and surprisingly good lunch.

The scenery changed as I walked into the town of Baza. I admired a park with neatly trimmed hedges and statues, stocked up on some *'fruto seco'* (nuts) and sat down in a café for coffee and a 'madelaine' (a small cake) while I made a call about some consultancy work, I would complete on my return to Britain. It was a sign that already my trip was nearing an end. The next few days were across drier landscape. In places it was a white, dusty desert with sparse vegetation and low hills, banded with cream and red ochres. Between dry hills there was a lake and cultivated area with fields of lettuces being harvested, large lorries taking the freshly picked produce away as quickly as possible. Another time I walked across a large, dry plateau on a gravel track among acres of stubble or dry grass. In some of the small towns, dwellings were built into caves dug into the soft rock behind dazzling, white frontages, whitewashed chimneys poking out of the hillside behind; on another occasion, dwellings were built into the rock of a cliff. A little colour was provided by religious images of 'Our Lady' and similar, painted on tiles attached to the walls of buildings.

At the ancient-looking village of Orce, the place where I planned to stay was locked with a number to ring by the door, but my phone failed me saying 'network busy' and the tourist office was closed. I wandered around trying to find another guesthouse but it was not at the address I had. So I walked on to the next town as the day headed for evening, briefly following a flock of sheep being taken home for the night by their shepherd. At Galera I asked where the hotel was, again struggling with the pronunciation of the almost silent 'h', but one local fellow finally understood me and pointed the way. It, too, was closed but this time my phone worked and soon I had a room for the night. At a nearby bar, I bought a beer and something to eat. Some loud Englishmen nearby were drinking pints (beer was usually served in smaller glasses in Spain) their wives trying to chivvy them into leaving for some evening engagement, but the men bought another round and so the womenfolk left without them.

Two days later I was walking out of Huescar, a town with a number of older baroque-style buildings and a bandstand in the square. The first ten kilometres was up a straight road, tarmac lined along its length with thin cypress trees in a row, past olive groves and an old factory, leading into pine-clad mountains. Where a stream ran down a valley, the pines were replaced by a ribbon of deciduous trees, their leaves now an autumnal yellow, an increasingly picturesque scene as I looked down on it from my vantage point high up on the mountainside. On the other side of the mountain was Puebla de Don Fadrique, the last town on the GR7 in the province of Andalucía. Over a pizza at a busy hotel beside the main road, I contemplated the route into the next province of Murcia the following day. I was a bit apprehensive as John Hayes — whose blog I had been following — had been confronted by two-metre-high deer fences and had problems finding the path. However, the GPS 'track' I had downloaded together with a handful of GR7 signs led me without difficulty along farm tracks to the Andalucía—Murcia border, marked by a stone post. Then it was across some farmland to the village of Canada de la Cruz and a climb up into the pine-covered Sierra de Moratella Mountains, where I camped near the road's summit on a ploughed field hidden by some trees. I passed a number of tumbledown buildings, including some with curious metal chimneys shaped like a cone, with the wide end pointing to the sky. For the next two days I followed a valley down to the town of Moratella, through some impressive gorges and across a few plateaux. Yellow-leaved poplars and orchards of yellow and russet colours contrasted with the green pines in an autumnal haze. However, the weather was still warm as I enjoyed a Coke and bar of chocolate from a small shop in the remote village of El Sabinar. October seemed a pleasant time to walk across southern Spain.

At my wild campsite there was no mobile signal, so I was unable to make my daily call to my wife. In addition to keeping in touch with each other, this call ensures that if anything should happen to me, my wife knows more or less where I am, and if I do not call for a day or so, will know to raise the alarm. I leave details of my itinerary with her. The next day, again failing to get through to her, I managed to get my mother on the phone, but this proved a mistake as the poor signal cut out again almost immediately. Always concerned for my safety, she feared I was in trouble and phoned my wife in some distress. For the next few hours several anxious calls passed between wife and mother, until I was able to make contact again and reassure them all was well. That evening I stayed at an isolated boutique hotel—its only resident, something that was becoming common as I left the more touristic areas and with the summer season ending. As the lady running it spoke no English, she phoned someone else through which I arranged a solitary dinner and breakfast.

The town of Mortella marked the end of the mountain range. I stayed at a pension on the upper floor of a building above a bar. To gain entry, the barman shouted up for the lady in the floor above to open the door, which she did, accompanied by her Chihuahua. Even the cheapest places I stayed at in Spain were always clean and tidy, but this pension did not quite make the standard. The landlady gave me a long explanation in Spanish pointing to her knee which had a row of large, black stiches evidently from some recent operation. At the local tourist information office, I surprised a girl behind the desk asking her what I should see in the town. She gave me a map and I wandered up to the castle.

I crossed a broad valley to the town of Calasparra passing ploughed fields, a path through wilder vegetation and along a *'via verdes'*, or green road. A farmer stopped his pick-up by me and tried to direct me, pointing to the path I had just come from (at least I think that was what he was saying). Sometimes it is difficult to explain which direction you are going! After Calasparra, it was over a final mountain range before a view of the white buildings of the historic town of Cieza opened up beneath me in a broad valley. I visited the museum and tried to find out how to reach Alicante airport; the man at the tourist information office professed that he did not know, but after a little time on the computer, he worked out it would be a bus to the town of Murcia, then another bus which went direct to the airport. Then I ate the final evening meal of my trip which turned out to be a very large steak, medium rare, studded with grains of salt, and little else.

Chapter 4: Cieza to Solsona — a Walk in Winter

Into Valencia

Having successfully reached Cieza on the E4 in October 2014, walking 880 kilometres (which sounds better than the equivalent 550 miles) I was feeling confident, pleased with myself and keen to hike the next section as soon as possible. This was up the eastern side of Spain through the provinces of Valencia and Catalonia, in the ranges of mountains that lie around fifty kilometres inland from the coast. Consulting average temperatures for eastern Spain, I decided that the 1st of February was the earliest I could start without risking sub-zero temperatures, so the 2nd of February found me in Cieza ready to continue my trek.

Anticipating cooler weather, I took my warmer Gore-Tex jacket, long-sleeved base layers and a warm hat to wear. I packed an old 'Thermarest' self-inflating mat to sleep on when camping out, as on previous trips in Britain in colder weather the ground below had sucked the heat out of me, making it harder to sleep. Just having a thin, air-filled mat seems to provide a lot of insulation. I had also used foam sleeping mats in the past, but these are very bulky and make it look as if you are on an Everest expedition.

A few weeks beforehand I had walked along the Wales Coast path for a few days to get into condition after maybe overeating a little at Christmas and to break in my new walking boots. The walk along the little visited Carmarthenshire coast was memorable for views of large sand banks in the estuaries, visiting the location of the Rebecca riots (where men dressed as ladies in protest at toll charges) and stopping at Larne, home of the poet Dylan Thomas, where I listened to the folk music at the Brown Hotel. Unfortunately, my new boots produced a huge blister on my ankle, which did not subside in the remaining two weeks before I left for Spain. Fortunately, I am blessed with a practical wife, who dressed my ankle with material from her first aid bag for our dogs, packed me a supply of suitable dressings, and sent me on my way.

Although I have enjoyed all my trips on the E4, I remember this one as special, in part for my experience of solitude high in the mountains. Whereas the GR7 across Andalucía was covered by a guide, had many tourist facilities and at least some sections were frequently walked, this next section was more of an unknown with fewer tourist facilities. Furthermore, I was walking it out of season when many of those limited facilities were closed. I felt like a true explorer, and it annoyed me a little when people referred to my trip as merely a 'holiday'!

Having stayed the night in the friendly Hotel San Sebastian among the narrow streets of the ancient centre of Cieza, for much of the first few days I walked across farmland, past orchards covered in netting to keep the birds out, the branches naked of leaves at this time of year and fields of vines, just stumps, having been pruned back to the brown soil. Rare farm workers in fields or on a tractor looked at me quizzically as I passed them on farm tracks. I camped the first night of the walk among some small pine trees, hidden from a farm track by some uneven ground (although not so hidden to a dog (?) which came snuffling around in the night; I kept very still and it went away). The next day along the track I noticed the remains of some old system of underground tunnels, beneath what looked like wells, presumably some ancient system for distributing water from higher ground. They reminded me of some similar tunnels I had seen in Uzbekistan. The red-and-white painted waymarks and signs were reasonably good and I was pleased when I reached the stone pillar marking the boundary between the provinces of Murcia and Valencia. I sat down, resting with my back on it for a little while, and a man in a white pick-up stopped to check I was OK. Throughout this trip orchards of almond trees were in blossom, brightening a drab landscape with drifts of pale pink, a welcome precursor of spring. Dogs were, as ever, a nuisance, barking noisily as I passed, but, fortunately in Spain, they were usually secure behind a fence. After the big town of Elda, the route passes under a main road and into the 'Natural Park El Arenal', with its curious 'sand dunes' and a climb over some rocky, pine-covered hills to Castella. Castella is an old town full of historic buildings and narrow streets, with a castle on a hill within it. The helpful man at the tourist information office was pleased to see me—tourists in February seemingly pretty rare, and asked me to sign the visitors' book. He said the castle was closed on the day I was there. Many of the houses had plastic bottles of water on their doorsteps. I wondered if it was a local religious custom or ancient superstition, but instead I was told it was to stop dogs peeing on your doorstep.

After Castella the route led into mountains. A little powdery snow, like a dusting of icing sugar, coated the ground in places and thin ice covered some puddles. Over breakfast in a bar, I noticed the local paper reporting Siberian weather and illustrating it with a pond lightly covered in ice. Not too much to worry about! Elsewhere in Spain the evening news was showing snow ploughs pushing through great thicknesses of snow, rescuing villagers. For most of my walk I saw few people outside the towns, but the two days after I left Castella were a weekend, and while cool, they were sunny enough to bring out day walkers, friends and families in brightly coloured coats. On Saturday night I stayed at a hotel in Alcoy, leaving early in the morning before the sun had risen above the mountains. So early that couples seemed to be just returning from a very, very late night out. As I started the climb up a rock-lined gorge back into the mountains, I was surprised by red moving lights coming towards me. A group of runners was getting some early morning exercise led by a dog with a collar studded with flashing red LEDs. As I climbed up the gorge one side was tinted pink by the rising sun, the shaded side a whitish grey. Later on, walking across the mountainside, the near ground was variously greyish green, grey and white while the distant hills graded into blue above haze-filled valleys, below a pale blue, translucent, cloudless sky.

At the town of Bocairent, I stumbled across a 'Moors and Christians' festival, a multi-day event where the local inhabitants dressed up in colourful costumes as either ancient Moors or Christians to celebrate the 'Reconquistor', when the Moors were driven out of Spain. A brass band played, large multicoloured candles were sold, crowds spilled out of bars and a small castle had been built in the main square. I wandered around the cobbled streets and plazas of the old town, admiring the costumes. As I left town the following day, there was the sound of cannon fire, as the festival entered its final day, when the 'Moors' were expelled from the makeshift castle. One of the pleasures of a walk like mine is the events that you unexpectedly arrive in.

47

In Vallada, a town two mountain ranges away, I only knew of one place to stay, Giner's apartments. On this trip many of the rooms I stayed at were above bars, or the hotels had a staffed reception, so it was not necessary to book ahead as there would be someone around to ask for a room, and, if open, they were unlikely to be full at this time of year. Apartment-type accommodation however, had to be called beforehand if it could not be booked online, otherwise there would be no one around. The kind hotel owner at Bocairent rang to make a reservation, but only after I struggled to name the place. 'G' in Spanish can take on a range of sounds very different from the English pronunciation. As my Spanish comes out of a phrasebook, and unlike the hotel keeper at Hotel Estacio, most people in Spain do not speak English, I had a number of struggles with language. I could generally make myself understood asking a question from my phrasebook or pointing to an item on a menu, but the answer often confounded me. The most helpful people kept their answers simple and brief, so I could pick up the odd word like *'si'* or *'no'*, or else they conducted the conversation in mime. Unfortunately, on realising I was not understanding, some people would enter into a long explanation in Spanish; unfortunately, adding more words did not make them any more understandable. A more helpful approach was taken by one hotel receptionist who used Google Translate to ask a question—a very powerful tool. It also helps if people anticipate what you want. I found it curious that when I walked into a restaurant the waiters sometimes seemed to wonder what I was doing there. If not in search of a table and comestibles, why else would I walk into a restaurant?

Giner's apartments were very fine and I managed to cook a meal for myself in the kitchen, although the high-tech shower, festooned with numerous silver knobs, was somewhat confusing. I needed it as I was caught in a sudden rainstorm while popping out to shop for food and additional dressings for my foot. My wife's supply of dressings was running out, although my blister was healing nicely. Leaving Giner's in the morning was a little difficult as I locked the key in my room, not realising that I needed it to open the front door and leave the building. Reluctantly, not being able to leave or return to my room, I was forced to disturb Giner (if that was her name) by knocking on a door marked 'private' at an early hour.

After Vallada the GR7 passes through a remote area of trees and rocky hills. It started as a climb up a gorge, with layers of grey- and orange-coloured rocks, in one place forming a pillar and another a natural arch that anyone walking this way seems to photograph. Then there was some pushing through undergrowth where the path had become overgrown, the red-and-white painted stripes marking the trail were faded but still visible. That evening I had planned to stay at a 'permitted' camping area at Casa de Benali, but I could see no sign of it where I expected. Maybe it was off the trail; there was an ambiguous signpost, indicating something several hundred metres away, but I was too tired to investigate and the evening was drawing in, so I just camped beside the vehicle track which the GR7 was following through some woods, spending an undisturbed night.

The next two days were wet. I walked in cloud along a vehicle track, nothing visible beyond twenty metres. It was a strange, white atmosphere devoid of sound. Dressed in a waterproof jacket, and waterproof trousers I was comfortable enough. In the evening I camped at the site of an old house near the road. Little remained of the walls, but a flat area of closely cropped grass in the centre made an excellent pitch for my tent. Despite having seen no one, and no cars all day, I heard three cars pass by after I was safely inside. It is unlikely they saw me through the thick mist. Everything I took out in the limited confines of my tent, such as my Kindle or phone, rapidly became covered in a film of water droplets. Condensation formed on the inside of my tent. My sleeping bag was soon damp, but, maybe because it had synthetic insulation, I stayed as warm as a freshly baked bun. The next day, I saw the long reservoir of Cortes de Pallas, from high on the side of the valley, through steady rain that lasted all day. It reminded me of camping holidays in the Lake District! A path led me around the valley side. I had a moment of panic, when, faced with multiple paths and the feeling I was heading in the wrong direction, I found my GPS showing a blank grey screen, and refusing to restart. Concluding I needed to change the batteries, I worried that the rain would damage it. While the GPS was waterproof (or water resistant whatever the difference is) I was sure this did not apply when you took the back off to change the batteries. Trees were dripping water and provided no shelter, but by leaning over I managed to create enough protection to make the replacement safely. Reaching the town of Cortes de Pallas, I went into a café to ask them for one of their rooms for the night. It was full of steaming, wet workmen, sheltering from the heavy rain. Desperately hoping for a dry room, I asked if they had a *'habitación libre'*. The man behind the bar said something in Spanish and walked off. Was it a no? Thankfully not; after a worried wait of a few minutes, he returned with a key and took me to a room around the back. Soon my sleeping bag was drying over the bathroom door and other damp and washed items were spread over various items of furniture. After wild camping, my simple evening meal was really enjoyable, served by a girl who made no demands on my Spanish; I do not even remember having to go through the fuss of saying what I wanted to eat.

As I climbed out of the valley in the morning it was not fine but nor was it raining. Looking back down on the reservoir from a *'mirador'* (a viewpoint) I could see it meandering between steep, tree-lined valley sides and cliffs, a ribbon of water. After climbing up and down some hills a small restaurant at Venta de Gaeta offered a *'plato combinado'* for lunch (egg, pork and chips). I would be camping in a forest site without facilities that night and, as I carried no cooking equipment, I was limited to cold food, so a hot lunch was very welcome. It was a tiring day. At one point, around a farm, the path disappeared and I stood around looking lost. In response to the barking of multiple dogs, the owner walked up and pointed out the way ahead, up a steep hill and then right at the cliffs near the top. In addition to helping hikers find the GR7, he said they looked after abandoned dogs, as well as unwanted goats and chickens. I found a GR7 signpost among the rocks near the top of the hill he had indicated, unfortunately pointing through thickets of various varieties of thorny vegetation. I was glad I was wearing long trousers. Tired from my day's travels, I was pleased to eventually walk down into a forest campsite among pine trees. No one was around. There was a small river to wash my hands in, but on the downside, there were small insects attacking me and no mobile signal to ring my wife.

The next day, paths and forest tracks took me through pine woods, a smell reminding me of cleaning products in the air, past fallen down stone buildings; limestone country with an occasional pothole visible beside the track. A stainless steel 'message' box beside the track, made to look like a house, was presumably for suitably inclined itinerant travellers to communicate.

At El Rebollar, I had hoped to stay at a motel at a motorway service station, but the man behind the counter at the café, standing in front of a full set of room keys, said the owners had *'vamos'*, or at least I was not going to get a room. I reviewed the situation over a coffee and chocolate-coated doughnut. There was no accommodation or much else for the next day or so on the GR7, and I needed some food if I was to camp. I had found a small shop in Cortes de Pallas, hidden beneath some apartments, after asking several people for a *'tienda, por favor?'*, but there was not much suitable for a camper to buy and now stocks were running low. Faced with obstacles, there are always options. One was to walk around eight kilometres to the nearby town of Requena where I knew there was a hotel and shops, the other was to buy what I could at the service station shop and head on, camping for the night nearby. I chose the latter, which meant buying a huge round block of Manchego cheese, evidently intended for passing tourists, some biscuits and snacks. Then I walked on in the evening light past a farmer ploughing the land in the lengthening shadows, who looked like he wondered what I was doing, until I reached a small wood of pine trees, in which I hid my tent and tucked into a supper of cheese and biscuits. The Manchego cheese, made from sheep's milk, was really excellent, and has since frequently made it into my shopping basket at home. It also kept me fed the next day as I walked mainly through pine woodland, and camped hidden among trees on a rare piece of flat ground at a fork in the track, near the village of Benageber.

I also needed water. There are spouting water pipes at many of the little villages, but, possibly as a result of some EU directive, many had signs saying it was not potable. One had the 'no' crossed out, leading me to suspect that the signs meant the water simply had not been tested, and indeed, later signs explicitly stated 'not tested' rather than 'not potable'. However, on my trip across Spain, I found enough water I could be confident in to manage, or else bought bottled water. Where I was not sure I added a chlorine dioxide tablet to sterilise the water. It is claimed that these leave no taste, but I always detected chlorine.

Decamping early, under a crescent moon, I enjoyed a beautiful dawn; the clouds strung out on the horizon reflecting yellows and pinks from the rising sun, silhouetting the occasional pine tree. Western slopes of mountains were lit up with a pink glow and a platoon of distant wind turbines defiantly faced the rising sun. At one point the path dropped rapidly into a valley, before the inevitable climb, 240 metres back up the other side, the path twisting upwards besides outcrops of rock, with trees clinging to them. It made for a tiring morning, so my spirits drooped when I saw Chelva, a town promising food and a bed, but, like so many of the towns and villages in the area, it was built on a ridge above the river, which meant another descent, crossing a very fine stone bridge, and then a final, slow climb, as I struggled into town. There I was rewarded with a hotel, where the man on reception asked questions about my walk—which, being in Spanish, I failed to understand, followed by lunch in the nearby restaurant. There I asked for *'calamares y papas fritas'* as I saw someone nearby eating squid and chips and knew the words in Spanish. Many of the places I visited had no formal menus, so it was useful to know the Spanish for some type of food they were likely to have. *'Lomo de Cerdo'*, or pork loin, was a fairly sure choice. It is fortunate that I was in time for a late lunch as that evening (a Sunday) all the restaurants were closed and I had to settle for beer and crisps.

More hills wooded with pine trees followed the next day. I had hoped for some accommodation at the village of Andilla, but I walked through empty streets, everything closed up, no people visible in this village or the previous one. Maybe to be expected in February, most of the houses were probably holiday homes, their owners working in a big city. As I camped by the ruins of a farm house, high above the village, I looked down on the street lights. Normally you can see the moving headlights of a car, but in Andilla, nothing stirred.

Days of wooded hills followed, with rocky outcrops, and narrow valleys with red sandstone eroded smooth by the endless flow of water. Bejis was typical of the old established villages, built on a ridge between river valleys for defence; the ruins of a castle at the highest point. Houses were jammed together, with red pantile roofs and narrow lanes between them, plus there was an ancient stone church by a small square. Somewhere there might be a sheltered area with concrete troughs for washing clothes and nearby, a newer part of town. In Bejis I was searching for the restaurant *'El Tren'* (the train) where they had accommodation. I could see no sign of an old railway, so asked in a man in a bar. Realising I spoke no Spanish, he helpfully walked out of the bar and pointed to the establishment next door. There was no train or railway, but there was a small sign advertising the establishment. Like many such places, the motherly lady in charge took care of me, and provided a bed and food. I was similarly welcomed in the next village of Montan, where for dinner the elderly lady sat me in front of the television, to watch another episode of '¡Boom!'. A full bottle of red wine was placed in front of me and food followed. After a day's walk, it is nice to be spoilt.

Some of the walk did turn out to be on an old train line, but more interesting were paths between the grey cliffs of a gorge, cut deeply into the pine-covered mountains. One downside of walking in the bottom of a gorge is that it usually ended in a prolonged climb up its side to reach the plateau again. One night, failing to find any open accommodation, I walked off the gravel road up a little-used track that led to some abandoned beehives and a promontory. I pitched my tent discreetly among the pines beside the track as the shadows were lengthening, although it was dark by the time I had climbed a nearby summit to find a mobile signal to call home. Nearby, as I set off next morning, I found the *'ermita'* or hermitage of San Bartomeu del Boi, coloured pink by the rising sun. This religious building had been restored but the surrounding buildings were in a state of decay, windowless and with the roofs starting to collapse. Depopulation of the countryside was evident from such abandoned buildings, and the remains of terraces, cut into the mountainside, retained by walls of stone, once used to allow farming of the steep slopes, but now abandoned to the trees, their supporting walls collapsing under years of neglect.

On my walks I invariably find something of interest. As I walked among the pines, I almost stepped on a line of caterpillars, crawling across my path, nose to tail. They were pine processionary caterpillars, which are damaging to the pine trees in which they make a fibrous nest. I also passed some signs for the *'Processo de Culla a Sant Joan de Penyagolosa'*. Googling informed me it marks the route of a procession made in the week of Corpus Christi, between the town of Culla and the church of Saint Joan of Penyagolosa, a pilgrimage made for many centuries. My final climb towards Culla took me out of the pine trees and into rocky hillsides, which would be more typical of the next few days. I climbed a terraced hillside, up to areas with a light scattering of snow, and tumbledown, dry stone walls. From high points (such as at another *ermita*, that of Sant Critofol) I could now gain distant views of the sea, a silvery line in the far distance beyond lower ranges of hills. At times I was walking on ancient cattle drive ways, on stones and bare slabs of outcropping rock. Gates keeping the sheep in were often rough, makeshift affairs, made from bits of wire fencing, an old tree branch and a loop of fraying nylon rope attached to a wall or similar, which you had to lift over the top of the branch to make a gap to walk through. There were also more recent steel gates, which were no less confusing to open. Something new to me were narrow cattle grids for cyclists. It appears I was on a mountain bike trail and such grids of metal bars avoided the need to dismount and attempt to figure out how to open a gate. Towns I passed through such as Benasal and Morella were full of history with high walls, ancient churches and narrow streets. Morella in particular seemed to have attracted numerous tourists, although my perambulation of the town was shortened by sleet, falling cold and wet.

The next day, reaching the small, but old, village of Vallibona, I spotted the Hotel Restaurante La Carbonera. Much of my time had been spent as a solitary walker among remote hills and countryside, so when I saw a café, it was a good reason to stop, for a coffee at least. At such times, in addition to the coffee, I enjoyed for a few moments being in the company of the men around the bar, the television in the background, and a bit of warmth. As was common, in the bar of La Carbonera, the older men were drinking some clear spirit while I had coffee. After three weeks of walking each day, my tired legs were feeling they would like to rest a while. Although it was before lunch, the warmth of the owner, with his attempts at conversing in English, as well as the ambience of the café, made me ask if they had a room for the night. While I was offered a quince-jam-filled pastry by the owner, his wife went to make up a bed, and later made me a lunch of chickpeas and the like. Black-and-white photographs of the rugged hills of the locality hung on the wall, gentle jazz came from speakers somewhere; it was an enjoyable place to rest for an afternoon and evening, after the five minutes it took me to walk around the town, watched only by a group of cats, spectating from some steps.

The next day, as I left, the couple seemed inordinately pleased when I rounded up the modest bill slightly. I smiled to myself as I started a climb up a long gorge.

Catalonia

That was the last night I spent in the Valencia region; the next night I camped among trees in Catalonia. The landscape was more rugged, as I followed a rocky ridge with cliffs to one side. Where there was no rock there were pine trees in a forest that looked more temperate than Mediterranean, as if the weather was wetter here. That first day I saw my one and only backpacker in Catalonia (or indeed in Valencia and Murcia) coming the other way; he asked if the way ahead was mystical. I said you could say that, the morning mist among these high mountains gave them a mystical air, although, I must confess, at the time I was more focussed on not missing my step as the slope the path was traversing, between cliffs and trees, was rather steep. I was in the Natural Park 'Dels Ports', a beautiful, mountainous, forested area which I had somehow failed to come across in my research for the trip. Distant views of the coast, the blue sea blurring into a white horizon, enhanced the journey. I only passed through one village, called Caro, where I was pleased, I was able to order some food, picking out items I recognised, when the lady told me in Spanish what was available. I also found a refuge that seemed to be open in the village, something I had not come across before. However, it was just after lunch and I decided to walk on. It was around this area where I faced my biggest weather challenge. As I approached the crest of a saddle, on a steep path over loose gravel, I was hit by gusting wind. Funnelled between adjacent mountains, it was so strong that as well as nearly pushing me over, it threatened to tear off my glasses. Not wanting to lose my spectacles down the slope, I put them in a pocket after checking my GPS to confirm which direction I should be going. Then on hands and knees, I climbed onto the crest of the ridge, then headed left, spotting a waymark nearby with my somewhat blurry vision. As I left the crest of the ridge, the wind dropped—its high velocity was curiously localised.

After a few navigational difficulties (the GPS track led into some bushes, but the path was fortunately signposted) I spent another night wild camping, beside a downhill section of track behind an outcrop of rocks, which I climbed to gain a mobile signal. There was a cave a little before, which at first sight, I thought would make a romantic camping spot, mimicking our cavemen ancestors, but animals had been using it as a shelter, and their faeces did not make it an attractive area to lie down. The following morning, I arrived at the village of Paul in time for a breakfast of coffee, toast, margarine and marmalade, which the owner was proud to tell me was homemade. I then spent some time searching the old streets and asking for a shop. I found it, a small room hidden among houses, where I bought the entire supply of chocolate (i.e., one bar) as well as a few apples. I would need more for another night's camping!

Fortunately, later that day, I descended into the valley of the River Ebro, one of the larger rivers in Spain, a valley with fields of almond blossom, lines of trees laden with oranges, and spring flowers. Reaching an old railway line converted to a cycle track, I followed the red-and-white waymarks through a series of tunnels. Lights came on as I entered each tunnel, operated by some motion sensor. They went off before I left the tunnel, no doubt timed for cyclists rather than walkers. However, the red-and-white markers I was faithfully following referred to the GR99 'Sendero del Ebro', not the GR7; all GR trails are marked in the same way, so care is needed where they cross that you do not follow the wrong route (like I did). Nevertheless, I enjoyed the detour in the sunshine (outside the tunnels) before arriving at Benifallet, a town in which there was a hotel. Sadly, no rooms were available, but the kind lady in charge rang up a nearby hotel and booked me a room. Now, 'nearby' means different things to different people. What would be five minutes in a car was a five-kilometre walk uphill, taking me over an hour. However, the detour was of interest. The hotel was in a village called Ell Prinell de Brai. In a walk around the place, I found an informative sign, explaining that the area was a major battleground in the Spanish Civil War. A photograph showed the town totally flattened by artillery fire from

Franco's forces, only the church tower remained. I had been reading a book about Spain during my walk. After Franco died and democracy was restored, silence was maintained on the subject of the civil war and the subsequent repression. Only now are the mass graves being investigated.

After crossing the Ebro, I climbed over mountains, walking through an area of burnt-out trees; not the first area I had passed on my walk which had suffered from fire. Fires are no doubt one of the reasons wild camping is discouraged in Spain's national parks. Crossing a pass, I reached the church of St Blai, where a crowd of people were gathered for some purpose. Nearby there was a monument to where the first red-and-white waymark of the Spanish long-distance GR trails was painted, back in 1975. I much appreciated all the efforts at waymarking that have continued since then.

At the town of Tivissa, a campsite was advertised as being open all year. I had come across other campsites advertised as always open, only to find them looking decidedly closed. This one looked no different although a bit more official and with a telephone number outside. I rang and had the kind of conversation I often have in countries where the person I am telephoning does not speak English and where I cannot speak the local language (i.e., all countries that do not speak English). I kept repeating the phrase I had worked out ("I am at the campsite. Campsite open?" but in Spanish) but I had no idea what the reply meant. However, after the person hung up, some minutes later a lady arrived and I booked me into a chalet. I had been planning to camp in my tent but since someone had taken the trouble to turn up, and since she appeared to be offering me a chalet, it was easier to accept what was offered. When you do not speak the language, life is certainly easier if you just take what is offered rather than being picky, especially when ordering food, where you do not know exactly what you are ordering from the menu in some foreign language or its recital by the waiting staff. After she mimed what I should do with the gate keys when I left in the morning I was left with the entire, well-lit campsite to myself.

The following night I was wild camping. It had been a long day through remote mountains below cliffs protruding through the pine trees. I was rewarded with views back to the River Ebro and down to the distant coast. There was a hotel in the village of Colldejou, but it was firmly closed for the season, nor was the local bar open, so I walked on. For several kilometres there were signs to the 'Avenue of Wind'.

On my arrival as dusk was beginning to fall, I found long lines of wind turbines, lit by the setting sun. Landscape is constantly being shaped by humans, the terraces cut for farming many years ago are now being abandoned; remote churches and shrines are still scattered in the hills, but the new marks left by people on the landscape are wind turbines. These cover ridges and plains across Europe, slowly turning, turning the evening breeze into power for people's homes. As I walked below them, they emitted a low cyclic hum. People do not seem to like these modern windmills in Britain, but this 'Avenue of Wind' in particular, with its long, white columns rising to the sky, seemed to me to have a certain elegance, like the tall thin columns of a cathedral. The area was exposed with plenty of wind so I followed the path as it dropped steeply off the ridge line, finding a small patch of flat ground among the bushes to pitch my tent in the last light of day, among some low trees.

With an early start, I arrived the next day at Arboli in time for lunch at a bar in the village square whose walls were lined with rock-climbing posters. My room for the night was in the friendly guesthouse opposite, where the owner kindly rang ahead to book my next night at La Cabrera Mountain Refuge. Needless to say, I was the only guest at both places. At La Cabrera, the dogs did not seem to like me, but I enjoyed milk, fresh from the goat, at breakfast. The following afternoon, standing outside a closed hotel, I rang the telephone number posted to see if it was likely to open. I had one of those conversations, in which due to language difficulties neither party understands what the other is saying, although the proprietor of the hotel was doing his best in German as well as Spanish. Having confirmed that it would be open at some point (probably) I waited around and the owner turned up at about four p.m. At this time, I was walking across mountains on tracks through pines, sometimes in the mist. A few long climbs but nothing too difficult which allowed for pleasant reveries. At one point I passed a waterfall falling over a cliff of limestone into pools of clear blue water; distant views across the mountains increased my enjoyment. I felt a little uneasy when I saw several notices on trees stridently warning me of something. It took a while to realise they were telling me not to pick the mushrooms.

For my last four days of walking the scenery was changing, with more cultivated land, generally low hills, some scrubby vegetation, fewer pines and more deciduous trees. There were no hotels and more farmhouses (with barking dogs) making discreet camping more difficult. For two nights I camped out of sight in patches of woodland between fields.

One night as I had left finding a campsite a little late, a car stopped and the driver tried to engage me in conversation. Not having any idea of what he was saying I just kept saying *'no entiendo'*, which means 'I do not understand'. He eventually drove on. Maybe he was offering me a lift, a bed for the night or maybe telling me I could not camp in the area (something I feared) but I will never know. Conversation with passing strangers was further complicated as I was in Catalonia. Those I passed said *'Bon dia'* rather than *'Buenos dias'*—Catalan rather than Spanish. Signs were also increasingly in Catalan and there were references to a referendum on independence on the news.

One morning, after a night wild camping, two cyclists past me shouting a greeting, a man and what I took to be his father, out for a weekend ride. Spanish people are in general not hikers, but many of them put on their lycra at the weekend and head off on bikes. A little later I passed a building that my map indicated was a café; however, it was just a shack made of corrugated iron. I was about to head on thinking the map out of date, but then I noticed two bicycles propped up outside. The two cyclists I saw earlier were inside; the younger one had some English and told me to try the *'secreto'* which they had ordered. I had seen this on the menu before and wrongly assumed it was a secret dish, like a surprise speciality of the house. It was revealed to be a tender cut of pork grilled in an alcove of the hut, which made for a beautiful brunch, all the better for having started early and walking for several kilometres after some meagre rations in my tent. It was served with toast and a tomato, which you are meant to smear on the toast. I was evidently not doing it correctly, as the waitress took the tomato out of my hand and showed me how to do it properly (a little contemptuously I thought).

Between my wild camps, I stayed in a refuge in a range of mountains. This was only the second refuge I found open and its layout was similar to those I encountered later in my walk along the E4. There was one large room that served as a dormitory and, instead of separate bunks, there was a long, wooden platform to sleep on, running along the length of each wall, with another above it reached by ladders. Being early I picked a spot next to the wall, so as to ensure I was not hemmed in by people on both sides, reserving it by laying out my sleeping bag. I was possibly lucky to find the refuge open. It was a weekend and a large party of friends and their children was meeting here. The 'guardian' in charge cooked an evening meal and I sat next a lady who spoke English and wished to practise it on me. She asked about my walk and where I had been. My mind went blank, failing to recall any of the many towns and villages I had walked through. She probably either thought me a fraud or an idiot. Apart from my evening calls to my wife, I had not had any meaningful conversations in English for a few weeks, so maybe this stunted my ability to recall useful facts! It seemed like once I had been through a town, the name no longer mattered to me. She probably also thought me rather greedy. On long walks such as this one, I generally find I am not very hungry, especially during the daytime. My body seems to be saying, "let's slim down a bit, and lose some weight; being lighter will make walking easier". Certainly, I tend to lose weight in the initial weeks. But by the fourth or fifth week, while not feeling hungrier, I seem to eat a lot more. Walking all day, often uphill and with a backpack, I probably get through four thousand calories a day, so it is not surprising that my body eventually decides to up the food intake. Maybe as a result I had several helpings of the food. The main course was a spaghetti dish which my companion thought a bit heavy. I was inclined to disagree and, after everyone had their helpings there was still a lot remaining, which I did my best to clear. My companion also thought the red wine a bit too sweet, but, again, it seemed fine to me, which probably contributed to my heading to bed before the others—although getting into the bathroom early, with its one toilet and washbasin, before the main party, to brush my teeth, etc. may also have had something to do with it.

Since Arboli, I had been following the GR7 trail, but the E4 itself leaves the GR7 soon after heading for Tarragona. It eventually rejoins the GR7 in France. At the time I had not been able to find a record of where the E4 was meant to go, so I continued on the GR7. This meant I missed Montserrat, a range of conglomerate mountains, rising up from the coastal plain, which the E4 (but not the GR7) crosses, that looked very picturesque in the distance from where I was walking. On my last day of walking, the snow-capped Pyrénées were in front of me, initially tinged pink by the rising sun and gradually looming larger. I stopped at the apparently deserted *'Sanctuari del Miracle'* and looked inside the church (open unlike many others). I also appreciated the toilets after my previous night camping.

Solsona marked the end of this trip. After a good lunch, I dumped my remaining scraps of food in a bin and caught the bus to Barcelona and my flight home.

My wife had been redecorating in my absence and my thoughts were turning to what my home might look like on my return, but whatever it looked like I was smiling at the thought of some domesticity. After over five weeks of walking this had been our longest time apart in our marriage (to be exceeded later in my walk across Europe). I was satisfied with my accomplishment and ready to go home.

Chapter 5: Solsona to the River Rhône — through the mountains

Crossing the Pyrénées

Having now walked 1,800 kilometres (1,100 miles) I was feeling that it was indeed possible for me to cross Europe on the E4. My last trip had increased my confidence as I managed in less-populated areas, with fewer facilities, little visited by tourists at time of year I travelled, and had enjoyed myself, despite language difficulties and some poor weather, wild camping as and when required. However, the next section involved crossing the Pyrénées, the range of mountains separating Spain from France, including a pass at 2,800 metres. Not having previously crossed such high and rugged mountains in my long-distance walks, this was a bit of a challenge, one I was keen to tackle as soon as possible. Although I had left full-time employment, I was providing training courses and consultancy. Eager as I was, such commitments restrained me from continuing my journey on the E4 until late June. The timing was perhaps fortunate as any earlier and snow would have impeded my travels across the Pyrénées, but it meant I had a good roasting in the heat at the end of the trip as I approached the River Rhône.

I returned to Spain, catching a flight to Barcelona, then racing across the city centre by taxi from the where the airport bus stopped, to the main bus station. The lady driving fortunately caught a 'green tide' of traffic lights as we raced passed the tall blocks of the city so I was just in time to catch the bus to Solsona avoiding a lengthy wait for the next one, and a late arrival at my hotel. After checking into the Hotel Sant Roc, an architecturally interesting building dating from 1929, I spent the rest of the day wandering around the old centre before resuming my walk the next day.

The first day of walking I found hard going, up mountains, the bare ribs of the rock exposed among the scanty vegetation. As I had been busy working before this trip I was not as fit as I would have liked. Not good as the high mountains of the Pyrénées would be something of a challenge. I stopped for lunch, but made the mistake of eating a hearty meal of grilled meat, the weight of which in my stomach made the subsequent climb even more hard work. At one point the path was in a narrow passageway between blocks of rock, elsewhere I walked through pine trees. The rock was a textbook conglomerate, composed of rounded pebbles set in a sandier matrix, much of it a reddish colour. At the hotel I had booked at Saint Llorenc de Morunys, a note and my key were left on the reception desk waiting for my arrival. The owner was elsewhere celebrating Barcelona's success in the football league, wandering around the town in the team colours with his mates and blowing on a horn.

After crossing more pine-clad mountains the following day, I decided to stop early. Despite it being only my second day, I was feeling tired so, at a café in Tuixan, a small town on a low hill surrounded by towering mountains, I asked if there was anywhere to stay. Eventually a mature lady led me to the guesthouse next door offering a comfortable room for the night and a pleasant evening meal. In the morning as I paid and left the owner gave me a bookmark enclosing some pressed flowers, a sign maybe of the things to come. My final full day of walking in Spain took me over dry, Pyrenean foothills to the pretty town of La Sen d'Urgell and I admired the blue cornflowers on my way. At the first hotel I tried, a sign said 'back in five minutes'; fifteen minutes later, I left and booked into another hotel for dinner, bed and breakfast.

Leaving in the morning, after pointing out to the hotel that they had not charged me for my dinner and breakfast (so honest of me!) I walked into the tiny state of Andorra up a big valley along the main road by La Farga de Moles. There were many booths for cars and lorries at the border, but no indication of where pedestrians should go. Clearly none were expected so I just wandered across the border on the lookout for the red-and-white GR waymarks. These took me up the side of the valley. The route was along old mule tracks and small roads, past a waterfall and neat little villages with window boxes of red geraniums and views of the main road, threading its way below me to the capital, Andorra la Vella, where I also ended the day. After finding a hotel, I ate at the Mama Mama Pizzeria as recommended by the receptionist. The chef wandered over as I started to eat my pizza and instructed me to sprinkle it with olive oil, in which chillies were floating. I was obviously too tentative with the amount I put on, so he seized the bottle and demonstrated how it should be done!

Afterwards, I wandered around the town, looking at streets crowded with shops with big adverts for very expensive watches, cigars, bags and the like. Fortunately, I also found a supermarket to stock up on more essential commodities such as food—necessary as I expected to be camping or in a refuge for the next few nights.

Leaving Andorra town and climbing up into mountains far from human habitations resulted in a dramatic change in landscape. Unlike the dry mountains of Spain, there were meadows covered in spring flowers and green grass, below towering mountains of grey rock, all well-watered by streams and brooks fed by the recently melted snow. Between chunky boulders were blue gentians, opening in sunlight and closing at night, carpets of pink clover and rugs of yellow vetches and ranunculus, Pyrenean buttercups, daffodils, and numerous flowers of all colours whose names I did not know. In places bushes with red flowers that looked like azaleas proliferated. At this time of year (late June) it was a joyful experience for anyone with a love of flowers. The many brooks and small rivers were a bit of issue as they were too deep to cross without water coming into my boots, so at first, I took my boots off and waded through in my sandals, but I soon became lazy and just got my feet, socks and boots wet.

There was a scattering of walkers on the trail. I passed a group led by a guide and asked about the route ahead. He warned me of a thunderstorm expected later in the day and suggested I stayed at the refuge at the top of the valley. Wise advice as late that afternoon I looked out from the veranda of the refuge and heard the thunder move around the mountains surrounding me. The refuge was a simple affair, a long building built of stone from around the site. There was no 'guardian' this time; you just helped yourself to a place on the sheets of perforated steel that extended the length of the dormitory. There was a table where you could eat your food in another room and outside a pipe brought fresh water from somewhere, maybe the reservoir above the refuge. Some workmen doing something on the refuge, and they slept in a separate room. Around half a dozen hikers were staying the night. As I looked out at the lake in front, through the slight rainfall, I chatted with a Belgian hiker. He was walking the GR11, a popular and I am told very scenic route that runs the length of the Pyrénées. By seven p.m., some of the other residents were already in bed, not that there was much else to do other than read from my Kindle. They were up before me at five a.m.

I was only slightly later and had the joy of climbing the final 330 metres to the highest point on my trip so far, the Collada dels Pessons at 2,814 metres. I took a 'selfie' to celebrate and from the rock-strewn summit, admired the vista of mountain tops poking through the clouds in the pinkish morning light. The trail then went down over boulders to a greener area at the top of some ski runs, where I was advised by two young men (mountain safety volunteers?) of a further impending thunderstorm in the afternoon. It was early and I reckoned I could cross the next pass before midday. So I thanked my advisors, assured them I would be fine and headed up the trail... unfortunately not the right trail. Suitably humbled, I slunk passed them again and carefully followed my GPS to the next pass and the northern border of Andorra with France. I was reading a novel where the main character smuggled goods across the Pyrénées and I could easily imagine I was doing the same as I crossed the invisible line between one country and the next, high in remote mountains with no one nearby. The rain that I had been warned about looked about to start as I reached the small ski town of Porte Puymorens, so instead of heading for its campsite I tried a hotel. It looked closed, but I was in luck, for someone answered, gave me a room and fed me spaghetti Bolognaise. Our conversation was all in French, but I kept forgetting and using words of Spanish, so it took me a little time to establish when dinner and breakfast were...

The next day I walked up another beautiful Pyrenean valley, full of flowers, to a second major pass. Although it was lower at 2,400 metres, it posed more difficulties than the previous day due to snow. As I approached the summit of the pass, what looked like a vertical wall of snow faced me, flanked by steep crags or large, loose boulders. I tried approaching from two directions but in neither case did it look attractive. Now maybe close up it was not actually vertical; with crampons and an ice axe it would probably have been safe to climb, but I had neither, not even a trekking pole to give some extra purchase. Looking at the map on my GPS there was a more roundabout route to reach the pass. So I retraced my steps, and viewed the alternative trail from a distance. I could see a snow-free path to the skyline so I headed up, successfully reaching the pass by this route, but then I had to get down on the other side. While there was snow, it was fortunately not too steep at the point I needed to descend and I moved between the snow and boulders which I could clamber over, all the time moving carefully and slowly to avoid my leg getting trapped between boulders or breaking through the snow. At the edge, where snow meets rock or boulders, its thickness is often reduced by melting underneath, between the base of the snow and the rock. One's foot can suddenly slip in such places, causing loss of balance, injury or in my case, a face full of snow.

To cover the five kilometres up to the pass and down the other side took me some four hours with my various attempts to find a safe way up, and left me feeling tired and looking forward to a night at a refuge, which I understood had a 'guardian' in charge and offered food. I was therefore somewhat dismayed when I saw a large party of school children. They were staying at the refuge, which meant it was going to be exceedingly full. Fortunately, the 'guardian' let me camp on the grass outside, while still being able to have meals and use the shower inside. I changed into my sandals before going for a shower, but this footwear proved inappropriate and I was firmly told off by the refuge staff and advised to use the indoor shoes provided. After a wash I was able to buy a carafe of red wine and, at the appointed time, sat down at a table for dinner. The wrong table as it turned out—it was for the teachers. I was allocated a place with some fishermen from Toulouse, who were planning to catch fish in the high Pyrenean lakes. They had brought their own, homemade *pastis*, strong aniseed-flavoured alcohol, and one was somewhat drunk, promising eternal friendship, etc. while we ate a filling meal. Tired after a strenuous day, I was soon in bed, glad I had a separate tent, slipping into sleep to the sound of school children singing around a nearby campfire.

As I headed for breakfast early in the morning, the Toulouse fishermen passed on their way to fish, although without their most bibulous comrade, who was no doubt still sleeping it off. Having checked with the guardian's assistant about my planned route (he said long but doable, but easier to start from the opposite direction), I started my day's hike. It involved loosing seven hundred metres in height, dropping into a valley populated with cows, their bells creating a cacophonous clanging, which nevertheless buoyed one's spirits. Then I had to regain all the height I had just lost and some more to cross my final pass of the Pyrénées, although with waterfalls and beautiful wild flowers, lakes and distant views across the mountain tops, it was not too much of a hardship. The only annoyance was being told off by a fellow hiker for trying too hard to avoid a patch of snow that dropped steeply into a lake, but then I did not fancy a cold bath.

Reaching the Canal du Midi via some unconventional lodgings

The following days between the Pyrénées and the Canal du Midi were over wooded hills and past fields of ripening wheat. I stayed at a few interesting places. Signs leading to one village advertised a hotel, but on arrival, I found it had closed long ago, its name still visible in sadly peeling paint. As I pondered my next step, probably wild camping in nearby woods, a lady approached and asked if I needed help. Now my French is very limited but, as I studied it at school for five years, it is considerably better than my Spanish, or any other language that I do not speak. So I was able to say I was looking for a hotel. She said there was none in town but there was a place I could stay nearby which she very kindly proceeded to ring and arrange a room for me. After I declined a lift, thinking she had done more than enough already, she directed me along a road and told me it was at the blue house. Following instructions, I arrived at a house, which was indeed blue, and enquired about the room. They had no knowledge of me but after some discussion I was invited to part of a complex of buildings. It was actually a Buddhist retreat. After a long, tiring, hot day walking, the ripe peach and herbal tea with which I was welcomed was surprisingly delicious, though not something I would normally enjoy. Joining in the evening meditation, I was fortunately offered a kind of seat to support my back as I have trouble maintaining a cross-legged position even when I have not spent all day walking. A (very good) vegetarian meal followed and the person who had received the call from the kind lady in the village popped in to say hello. I was also told a lot about their approach to Buddhism, or rather a way of life influenced by Buddhism. Regarding payment I was asked to give whatever I thought my stay was worth. I find this very difficult, not knowing what is expected, not knowing what value to place on things. I gave fifty euros as it was a round sum, a single note of some value, and similar to what I was paying elsewhere at that time.

Another night when I asked about accommodation at a local tourist office, they suggested a convent, which struck me as strange as I am a man. However, this was where the GR7 and one of the pilgrim routes to Santiago (called the 'Way of St James' or the Camino de Santiago) followed the same path for a while. The red-and-white GR waymarks were joined by scallop shells, either real ones, nailed to a post, or symbolically depicted by yellow lines on a blue sign. The convent provided rooms for pilgrims. It took me a while to find the door, as it had a sign stating it was closed at the hour I arrived but, thankfully, a nun with a cheery, red, round face, framed by her wimple, let me in and showed me to a room. A simple meal was provided later for a modest sum, but the friendly nun was a little disappointed that I had no pilgrim's passport for her to stamp. My fellow guest was a more serious pilgrim and I lent him my phone so he could speak to his wife.

I also stayed at few campsites, including one with the dreaded squat toilets. I am not very stable squatting, and holding position, balanced on my toes, my leg muscles taut, while being relaxed enough to do the necessary is a challenge, so I only venture into such facilities if it is unavoidable. Fortunately, there were also some hotels, including at the town of Mirepoix, with its historic square in the town centre, where half-timbered buildings and covered arcades contained shops for tourists. Chalbre was another attractive town.

The paths in this section were tracks through trees, or by wheat fields, over low hills, easy walking. At one point the route followed an abandoned train line (including a lighted tunnel); at another a narrow path. There were meadow flowers to admire, a snake, some unusual sculptures made of mannequins, old bikes and the like, and a few castles. In Puivert castle, a re-enactment was being prepared, although being on a walk, the pull of the road meant I did not wait for it to start.

Walking through mountain streams meant water had filled my boots on more than one occasion, softening my nails, and now bits of my big toenails had fallen off. Nevertheless, I was now making good time and crossing a final section of flat land I reached the Canal du Midi. The GR7 briefly follows the towpath of this broad waterway lined with trees.

Montaigne Noire and the fight against the Cathars

When I left the Canal du Midi, my path took me past fields of sunflowers, their yellow faces all looking towards me, and wheat, just being harvested, before climbing into the wooded hills of the Montaigne Noire. I camped at a site at La Cammazes after a long day's walk, then followed an aqueduct which supplied water for the canal. Water from the hills trickled down this channel, winding around the contours of the mountains, shaded by trees. That evening I stayed at a small, simple campsite run by Arfons' Mairie (town hall). I am sure the white-haired man at the Mairie mistakenly charged me for two nights, but I enjoyed a coffee and beer at the little shop in the village and there was an ancient weighbridge by a funny turret-shaped building, and buildings with walls covered in slates.

Walking through forest tracks among beech or pine trees, admiring the view where gaps existed, past meadows of grass, I encountered several wrought iron crosses, a sign of local religiosity. Religion had an important place in the area's history. I walked down into the town of Mazamet, following a winding road, steeply descending through the picturesque village of Hautpaul. This was the site of a siege in the 13th century, part of the fight against the Cathars. I visited a museum in Mazamet to learn more about this religious group that existed in the area between the 12th and 14th centuries. Cathars rejected the Roman Catholic Church, the authority of the Pope and the material world, believing in a good God and an evil 'Satan'. Rejecting animal food, they were vegetarian, and believed women could play leadership roles in the church. Needless to say, this was completely unacceptable, and the Pope arranged for a crusade to eradicate this challenge to his authority. Many Cathars died in the subsequent wars or were burnt at the stake by the Inquisition, established to root out the last of their number. A bloody history of intolerance for such peaceful countryside, I was to find more examples of such barbarity in the name of religion later in my walk.

Woollen mills, in various states of decay and ruin, lined the road as I left Mazamet, a sign of an industry now gone. This left me in a sombre mood which lifted as I walked through forests, over the mountains and meadows of purple knapweed and white yarrow, on woodland tracks and sunken lanes. I walked rather longer than I expected to reach Labastide-Rouairoux, having misunderstood some diversion of the GR7, and the alternative I traced out on the small screen of my GPS proved lengthy.

Haut-Languedoc

For the next four days, I hiked through the mountains of the Haut-Languedoc, through pine and deciduous forests on vehicle tracks, with views of small waterfalls tumbling down over rocks. Outcrops made of gneiss, a metamorphic rock, attracted my attention with thin layers of silvery mica, sparkling in the sun, wrapped around crystals of white feldspar. Flowers: pink; blue; white, and yellow of all shapes and sizes made me smile as I walked along, admiring the occasional butterfly, orange with black markings. On a narrow path I traversed slopes covered in pink heather and outcrops of rock. Inevitably, areas of large white wind turbines marked the current progress towards renewable power catching the wind on the higher ground. A memorial to those who died in the Resistance in the Second World War saddened my mood. A sign showed how many people died in the war: 1.5% of the population of France; 1% of the British population; an astonishing 18% of the Polish population; most of the dead were not in the military and many were Jews. One night I spent in a simple refuge, the only person there, for which the part-time 'guardian' asked for a very modest sum, despite providing me with coffee for breakfast before he went off to deliver milk or some such thing. Another night I camped by a hut. The evenings were light until very late at this time of year and, after settling in my sleeping bag, I was disturbed twice, initially by some people on a late hike, then much later on I again heard movement outside. Whilst normally confident when camping alone on a hilltop, the stepping around my tent went on for some time, making me worried that someone was checking out my tent for some nefarious reason. I quietly unzipped my flysheet and peered out. There, silhouetted against the twilight sky, was a mouflon, a kind of timid wild sheep not normally seen in daylight. One of a herd, they evidently fancied the lush grass growing around my tent. I very quietly zipped up to avoid disturbing their nocturnal grazing.

In the morning, after admiring the view of the valley below from some outcrops, I walked down to Lamalou-Les-Bains, a town with a number of sanatoria for improving your health. I settled into a hotel for a late lunch and a pitcher of cold rosé. That evening after dinner, I ventured into the main square, where a band was playing popular pop songs from the last fifty years. Rows of chairs were set out and most of those seated in them were the older side of sixty. I was surprised to see them dancing in the area in front of the stage—at least one in a wheelchair, another on crutches, all enjoying themselves as the band belted out '(I Can't Get No) satisfaction'. I was even more surprised when they played 'Gangnam Style', at that time, a recent hit from South Korea. The dance area filled up and everyone did the actions just like the singer Psy, sometimes described as mimicking riding a horse. Surreal, or maybe it's me and my preconceptions of old age and disability?

The next day took me on a lengthy walk, through lower hills. A long day but with the historic village of Dio, a chateau, an old church, some vineyards and views into a nearby valley among other things to admire. Unfortunately, the sole of one of my boots split and I could see the other was not far behind. I had made the mistake of taking a half-worn pair of boots with me on this trip. Fortunately, the manager of the Hotel du Nord at Lodeve pointed out a sport shop nearby and a good French restaurant. They (the sports shop) duly sold me a new pair of boots at a modest cost. Unfortunately, a long-distance walk on a new pair of boots is not such a good idea and over the next week I developed some nasty blisters on the balls of my feet. Painful!

The Causses and the limestone gorge

I climbed out of Lodeve, past another derelict factory (and a modern retail park) to Saint Martin de Castries. I am not sure I was too welcome at the only auberge there, where the gist of the conversation in French with the lady in charge was that she was very busy, so I said I would wait (possibly not taking a hint or just not understanding). Whilst I was loitering in hope of a positive outcome, an elderly white-haired customer told me about Languedoc, the area of France I was walking through. Apparently, it means the language of Oc, an ancient language spoken in the area. Oc actually means 'yes'. He said much more besides until his wife said it was time to go. I made a second attempt at securing a room and this time I was successful.

The next day I walked across one of the 'Causses', a dry area of limestone, without the trees common on my walk to date; instead, straw-coloured grass with the occasional blue thistle. The highlight was walking into a deep, dramatic gorge, along which a precarious path took me past cliffs of gently folded rock to the scenic village of Navacelles. I stayed at the Gite d'Etape. A Gite d'Etape provides inexpensive dormitory accommodation, and I was the only one staying there, despite the other accommodation in the village being full. It was co-located with a crêperie at which smiling staff served salads and pancakes. At the bottom of the valley a river ran over outcrops of rock by an ancient arched bridge. The weather was by now rather hot and people in their swimming costumes were sunning themselves on towels beside the river or wading through the water to get cool. In the morning I walked up the steep road out of the gorge. Looking back at the village, its adjoining fields and the winding river, I could see where the river had changed course in its history, leaving an abandoned meander where the once-flowing water had cut down deeply into the rock, forming the steep sides of the valley. Shadows cast by the morning light highlighted the depth of the valley. A place I would not want to have missed.

Cévennes and the tale of a donkey called Modestine

At the town of Le Vigan, I stayed at the Mas de Prairie hotel. A reviewer had commented on the soft toys on the beds and I was pleased to see what might have been a stuffed dog waiting for me. I could have saved some money by staying at a campsite but I was feeling hot and tired. My extravagance was rewarded as a splash in the hotel's cool blue swimming pool proved very refreshing. I do not like to look too scruffy so for the evening meal on the terrace I put on a very lightweight, long-sleeved hiking shirt. The waitresses thought this very funny as, due to the heat, everyone else was in tee shirts, but then a gentleman has certain standards to maintain.

Refreshed by a good night's sleep I tackled the mountains of the Cevennes, stopping whenever there was a café or restaurant for some refreshment. The path took me up through pines achieving a total ascent of 1,800 metres for the day, which I thought pretty impressive, reaching the weather observatory on Mont Aigoual, from which lines of sharply defined, green, wooded mountains extended out into the blue distance. After securing a place in the attached Gite d'Etape and refreshing myself with a *'grande bierre'*, I had a look at the exhibition in the observatory. At the end was a shop where I bought a homemade honey cake and some local, cloudy apple juice. The ingredient list on the cake package indicated that more than 50% of the cake was indeed honey. It tasted OK, but I blamed the apple juice for a subsequent attack of diarrhoea, which meant I left a smelly toilet which I doubt the other residents of the Gite d'Etape appreciated. I departed early in the morning avoiding having to face my fellow travellers and managed to buy coffee and a breakfast at the next Gite d'Etape.

It was a day of walking through woodland and high pasture on gravel tracks. I admired the blue harebells and the silvery schist, the mica of the rock shining in the brilliant sunlight. I spent the night at another Gite d'Etape at Barre des Cevennes. I again had it all to myself once I had managed to work out which door to knock on to gain entry. It was Bastille Day, the National Day of France, commemorating the storming of the Bastille, a fortress and prison, by citizens in 1789, starting the French Revolution. In the evening there were celebrations. A theatre group did something (incomprehensible to me) in French, the mayor walked around shaking people's hands, including my own, coloured lights were strung across the street and the French and European Union flags were much in evidence. A band played Latin music (somewhat incongruously I thought, but maybe the mayor's daughter liked it). Lots of people were around enjoying themselves, which meant the waitress at the crêperie was struggling.

Up to now I had been walking on the GR7 through France which may not always correspond to where the E4 might be meant to go, but is a pretty good route. The *Grande Randonnée* of France are well marked, but the "E" routes are not. Now I moved onto the GR72. Part of the route overlapped with 'Le Chemin de Robert Louis Stevenson'. While I remembered Robbie Louis Stevenson for books such as *Treasure Island* and *Dr Jekyll and Mr Hyde*, he also wrote a travelogue called *Travels with a Donkey* about a solo hike through the Cévennes with a recalcitrant donkey he called Modestine. He made the trip in 1878, a pioneer of the type of long-distance walk I was now undertaking, but, unlike him, I had no donkey to carry my baggage. However, inspired by this well-known writer, others were walking the route with a donkey, leaving a trail of donkey 'doo' marking the path. It seems there were companies from which you could hire one. I met a few people with pack horses instead, which might have been more biddable. The landscape of rounded hills, wooded or covered with heather, with easy paths, made for excellent donkey-walking country.

I stayed in a guesthouse in Pont de Montvert, a small town surrounded by bare hills. People were bathing in the river on this very hot day and the town had a happy air of people enjoying themselves. It was not so in 1702. The people of the area were staunchly Protestant Huguenots, Christians not accepting the authority of the Pope. Inevitably there was conflict between them and the Roman Catholic religion of the French state. On 24 July of that year, Francois Langlade, Abbe of Chayla, imprisoned and tortured a group of Protestants in the town. A band of rebels asked for their release. When this was refused, they killed Langlade and two priests. There are many old Protestant 'temples' in the area today, although the flowers growing out of the steps of some of them suggest religious fervour is not what it was. I felt glad that people no longer killed each other in the name of God; however, in this I was wrong. A few days later a sign in a field said *'Je suis Charlie'* in several languages (although curiously not English) a reference to the recent murder of several people in the office of the *Charlie Hebdo* magazine for publishing a carton of Muhammed, by people who decided they could judge people on behalf of God or Allah. This crime made an obscure

French satirical magazine famous throughout the world, substantially boosting its sales and influence.

Leaving Pont de Montvert, I climbed over mountains admiring the granite rock with its large pink feldspar crystals. The trail was through a mixture of woodland and open grassland enjoyed by cows; in places following a river, which at one point was crossed by an ancient and much-photographed granite arched bridge. I arrived at Villefort; like many of the towns I had passed through it had a prominent war memorial dating from the First World War.

Ardèche and the summer heat

I now entered the Ardèche: a region of hills wooded with small trees, oaks and the like. In places the path followed the top of limestone cliffs and I looked down on the River Ardèche below, sometimes in a dramatic gorge. At other times I followed stony tracks through the woods, by old buildings now in ruin, but once carefully constructed from nearby stones without the use of any mortar, new trees growing out of their walls. I left the GR72 at Villefort and joined the GR44, later moving to the GR4 and then the GR42 and GR429, a confusion of GRs!

The hotel I stayed at in Le Vans was my first experience of a computer check-in. I entered my details at a computer screen by the gate and gained access to a room. In the morning there were staff at reception, but I guess it meant that the hotel could avoid paying staff at night and so make the rooms cheaper for me!

Now the weather changed from warm to unpleasantly hot. Leaves on young birch saplings were wilting in the heat. Wearing just a thin tee shirt and shorts there was little I could do to cool down as I climbed over hills. If I dispensed with the tee shirt my rucksack just chafed at my shoulders. I tried exposing my belly by hitching up my tee shirt, but what looked good on young ladies was not a good look on me! As I walked through the hot afternoon I lusted after a cold beer. It was my first activity on reaching a campsite for the night, before bathing in their pool or showering. Sometimes I made do with an ice cream and a Coke when I passed a wayside shop or café, although the sweetness of soft drinks made them less than refreshing. I made the mistake of buying a bar of chocolate at one shop, which was a molten mass within a few moments. My last few nights of the trip were spent at one or other of the many campsites in the area, full of families enjoying themselves. By contrast, at one point I encountered a memorial to a massacre in the Second World War where all the families in a small settlement were shot as a reprisal.

I ended this section of my travels at the River Rhône, a major river I would cross more than once on my next trip. In the ancient, stone town of Viviers, the campsite I stayed at was not clean and this depressed me, but I revived after a meal in the village, then wandered around making a guess at where the bus I needed to catch the next day would stop. Back at the campsite, I woke late in the night when a party of noisy people decided to pitch their tent right next to me (why do people do that?). On my final day I successfully guessed the right place to catch the bus into the pretty town of Montelimar (home of nougat), then it was a local train to Lyon and a fast Eurostar to London. It was the first time I had travelled on a Eurostar train and the speed at which it devoured the French countryside was a stark contrast with the speed that I had been walking across it, making it seem unreal outside my air-conditioned carriage, as if on a television screen. At Lille station, the disembarking, border checks, lengthy waits and re-embarking, rather made a mockery of the high speeds.

Chapter 6: From the Rhône to the Rhine — a tale of two rivers

From the Rhône to the Isère

I resumed my walk across Europe on the E4 Long Distance European Path in mid-September. Flying to Lyon proved cheaper than travelling by Eurostar and after a train to Montelimar from the airport, then a bus to Viviers, I was back on the trail, raring to go. Not wanting to carry any extra weight, I threw my spare British change, pennies and the like, into a rubbish bin, not finding much else to do with it. Seemed a bit sacrilegious, but what can you do? On the evening of my arrival, I crossed the wide River Rhône on the road bridge, a not quite modern suspension bridge, and made my way to the campsite at Chateauneuf du Rhône. The office was empty so I pitched my tent under a shady tree and paid later when the lady in charge returned. Not sure all the other campers were quite so honest…

I left town through an ancient stone gatehouse and after looking back at the jumbled old, red roofs of the town, climbed into the mountains of the department of Drôme. The mountains looked as if formed of giant, tilted slabs of rock. There would be cliffs on one side of each valley, above a steep, tree-lined slope, and a more gradual wooded incline on the other side. It soon seemed to me that whenever such a cliff came into view, the path would turn and head up to it. From a distance it would appear that you would need to be an experienced rock climber to scale the cliffs and reach the top; however, at the last moment, some passage would appear between the crags offering me an easy way up. As a reward there were long sweeping views from the top. The valleys were farmed and contained old villages built of stone with rivers running through. These settlements had attractive old, stone-paved alleyways and steps, with the occasional cat observing all who passed. Village roofs were typically clad in pale reddish brown, curved pantiles, slightly varying in colour, giving a mottled appearance. Windows had shutters. Isolated churches (including a ruined one) and shrines added interest to the walk. Sometimes I would be following a narrow path, sometimes a forest track.

On my second night I wild camped near the top of a mountain, admiring the appearance of lights in some distant town as night fell. A few hours later my sleep was disturbed by people arriving, presumably to admire the same view. Their voices expressed great surprise when they came across my tent in a hollow near the top, sheltered on one side by a few trees. Friend or foe? I just kept quiet and they moved on. Next morning, I enjoyed one of the great pleasures of France, eating a croissant with a coffee for breakfast in the town of Dieulefit after an enjoyable morning walk down a ridge to sharpen my appetite. I copied the locals and bought my croissants at a bakery, along with a sandwich for lunch, and then ate it at a pavement café with the coffee I bought there *("une grande café au lait, s'il vous plaît")*. The town also had a nice public toilet in which to do my morning ablutions. I found the French local bakeries very attractive and, if the opportunity arose, would invariably purchase something for lunch. *'Tarte aux poireaux'* (leek tart, better than it sounds) was my favourite but these rarely lasted until lunchtime as I found these little quiches too tempting. I tried buying two of them, but that just meant I had two tarts before lunch!

The following night I pitched in an official campsite by the river in the village of Bourdeaux (different from the similarly named city on the Atlantic coast). A car rally was in progress, the roar from exhausts echoing off the walls of houses lining the streets as they passed me. After a healthy meal (loin of cod) I settled into bed, but my night was again disturbed. Heavy rain caused the material of my tent to expand and sag, collecting a pool of water on the flysheet above my feet. Little of the water came in but I felt it necessary to go outside to tip off the water and tighten up the guy ropes to prevent a new puddle forming. In the process I became wetter than I would have if I had just remained in the tent and kicked the roof to dislodge to the collecting water.

I was now on the GR9 path that would take me to Switzerland. It climbed from Bourdeaux high into the mountains. I passed a hunter, waiting by the path with his shotgun, dressed in a camouflage jacket, and trousers of muted greens and browns, his attempt to blend into the landscape somewhat undermined by his luminous orange waistcoat or *'gilet'*. Hunters in France accidentally kill about twenty people a year, usually each other, and I felt somewhat exposed without any bright clothing (a mistake I corrected on later trips with a brightly coloured buff). It was September and the hunting season had just begun. Anticipating distant panoramas from the mountainside, I was mostly disappointed to find my view obscured by trees (a common problem), but was later rewarded by a section along the top of a series of jumbled, limestone cliffs. Broad valleys stretched beneath me. In one place there was a hole, like an arch in the rock, where I could see down to the valley below. After a long descent I turned around to look up at the same hole; it seemed a long way above me. Trees, cliffs, views and some high pasture, were not the only things to add interest to my amble, for example in one place in the woods there were strange metal cylinders, ancient stills I thought perhaps?

That evening at Sallians, I could have stayed at a campsite but rain was threatening and I managed to gain a room at a hotel (after a little wait for the owners to return) and a pleasant meal nearby reached by scurrying through the rain. I felt a little guilty going for comfort rather than being 'tough' and camping in the rain, but why should I have to prove anything? I had enough money for the less-expensive hotels so I might as well enjoy them. Indeed, one of the joys was to experience all types of accommodation, in almost all price brackets.

The next day, a view of distant cliffs high above the trees presaged a long climb of some 1,500 metres and a walk of some thirty kilometres following the red-and-white markings of the GR9. Longer than I expected as a hotel in Beaufort sur Gervanne, where I had hoped to stay, failed to answer its doorbell or phone. A café next door provided a *'jambon'* (ham) sandwich for lunch, and I was pleased to see an E4 sign, rare in France: *'Sentier European 4 Pyrenees-Jura-Neusiedlersee'* it stated, omitting the Spanish part and everything beyond Austria, but it was my first reference to the lake of Neuseidlersee which I would cross eighteen months later. That night I camped in woods by a small stream. As I nibbled on some cheese and biscuits for tea, I thought I was a long way from civilisation, only to hear the sound of a nearby car as I settled down to sleep.

As I followed the forest and farm tracks, the mountain scenery was dramatic, but I also liked visiting churches in the valleys, dwarfed by the terrain, such as the simple church at Lioncel where there was a painting, a triptych, of the Madonna and child, all gold and haloed like an Orthodox church icon. After crossing a cliff-bound valley I climbed up to Bouvane le Bas and a hotel where I was a lonely resident. It took some time to find the lady in charge when I arrived; entering through the open door, I eventually found her in the kitchen. The next day I climbed over the Col de la Machine, a good name I thought as I walked through trees past great cliffs of rock. It seems I took the more difficult option to return to the valley, on a narrow path along a cliff, but not too scary. It took me to the town of Pont en Royan, another scenic town, in which houses were balanced right on the edge of a cliff overlooking the river.

On the day I left the town, a storm was forecast. The weather was hot, so I just wore a light rain jacket over my bare skin and waterproof trousers over my underpants. Initially the rain held off as I climbed the steps out of town past the inevitable recumbent cat. However, as I began to climb the steep, narrow path up the side of the valley, heavy rain began with thunder and lightning. Fortunately, much of the path, although steep with loose stone, was among trees, which I tried to console myself would provide some protection from lightning (or was it more likely to attract it!?). Only three people are killed by lightning in Britain each year, and I doubt many more are killed in France, but most of those are male, and I was not fancying my chances. By the time I reached the top of the climb and a high plateau, I was soaked. Much of the water inside my waterproofs was no doubt sweat from the steep climb. No longer climbing up the steep slope I soon found myself becoming very cold. A refuge appeared, like a wooden alpine hut with overhanging eaves. Deserted, it had wooden bunks on which to sleep and a roof providing immediate and welcome respite from the rain. I went in, opened the shutters, and changed into dry clothes. It seemed a good place to stay the night and as the rain stopped and the sun came out, I draped my wet clothes over some rails outside, laid out my sleeping bag and settled in for a late lunch.

As the afternoon was turning to evening a girl put her head around the door and asked if she could stay there. I replied that it was for anyone to use. She left and returned with half a dozen young men and women, some with distinctly 'new age' garb, piercings, coloured clothes and long hair. They were soon at home as the evening closed in. I was somewhat perturbed when they later produced silver foil, candles and other stuff they hid from my view and I thought it best to retire to my sleeping bag. When I went out to pass water in the early hours, they were still awake, one on a bench, one outside by a fire they had lit, the others scattered around, peacefully contemplating something. I left early in the morning when they were asleep, passing what I took to be their van parked among the flowers at a point where the forest track was becoming impassable for ordinary vehicles. I reached the hotel where I had originally planned to stay and bought a breakfast of coffee and croissants. By contrast it was full of middle-aged motorcyclists.

The next night I spent in much more salubrious surroundings at the Hotel de la Poste in Autrans. Arriving early, I sunned myself on my balcony after lunch, draping my drying washing over the railings, which somewhat detracted from the display of red geraniums on view to the visitors. I needed the rest as the following day was a long one, taking a circuitous route into Grenoble. It followed the high ground and I looked across great distances from the wooded mountains to the River L'Isere and the fields and villages beyond, their tiny houses way, way below me. Eventually I was looking down on the city of Grenoble. It seemed so close, but it was only after many more hours of walking that I arrived at the cheap hotel I had booked for two nights, to give me a rest day. The owner was keen to watch some rugby or football match, and several messages on my phone were trying to alert me to this. However, I walk with my phone switched off to save battery power for emergencies, so knew nothing of his anxious attempts to contact me. Maybe despairing of me arriving, he had left word with a couple staying at his establishment that he was to be phoned once I arrived. By this strategy I gained a room, although not before unsuccessfully, as it later turned out, explaining that there was one of me staying two nights, not two of me staying one night. He was surprised I was still there on my second morning, unlocking the door and walking into my bedroom without knocking. I am still not sure why he could not understand not only my French but also the fluent French of the couple also staying at the hotel. After he had departed for his sporting fixture, I enjoyed a beer and a pizza with the other couple, one of whom had been a photographer working all over the world until the internet had destroyed his trade, so now he made furniture.

River Isère to River Rhône

After mastering the tram service, I left the suburb in which I was staying and wandered around the streets of Grenoble for my rest day looking at the museums and markets. It was all very scenic with the old buildings, the cloud-topped mountains surrounding the city and the river running through. A folk group of mature people in colourful traditional dress were dancing by the cathedral, no doubt for the benefit of the watching tourists. I had hoped to find some local French cuisine but most of the restaurants were Italian. I had lunch in a Brazilian place, but I found something 'local' in the evening in which cheese (suspiciously Swiss tasting) featured prominently. Leaving Grenoble, it was a sustained ascent up past some fortifications with progressively better views of the city spread out beneath me and the summits of mountains beyond peeping out over the haze that hung above the town.

I was finding the GR9 a rather serpentine route, weaving back and forth to pick up all the mountains, and it was starting to frustrate me. Would I ever reach Switzerland? On my second day out of Grenoble, above the sheep pastures, I reached a point where the path took a turn up a steep slope of rock outcrops. A chain was provided to help the passing hiker. I looked up and could see a party climbing a ladder attached to a vertical cliff high above. It rather unnerved me. Walking alone meant if I fell there would be no one to help. In addition, I knew that I found climbing upwards a lot easier than climbing down, so that if I reached a point at which I did not feel safe to climb any higher I might also find it difficult to descend. Although in retrospect, the ladder on the cliff was probably not part of my route, at the time I decided that safety was the priority and I picked an alternative route along a valley, which I enjoyed as it was a change to constantly climbing up mountains.

That evening, over dinner at a hotel in the village of St Pierre d'Entremont, the lady in charge told me that heavy rain was forecast for the following day, and indeed low cloud already obscured the mountain tops. She suggested I stay another night. Bravely, I declined the offer. Consequently, I spent much of the following day in the rain. Fortunately, the climbs were not too great as I walked up a small river and then circumnavigated a mountain, so I was able to wear my waterproof jacket and trousers without overheating. Upon my reaching a village called Les Echelles, the persistent heavy downpour made me reluctant to stay at the campsite as I had planned so I asked the girl in the tourist information office if there were any other options. She rang some places (there being no other customers to distract her) but to no avail, so after she had directed me to the campsite and recommended a traditional French restaurant, I headed off. The lady in the campsite office looked at the rain pouring down the window as I booked in and said, *"Bon courage"*. Fortunately, she also said there was a common room I could sit in. After I had pitched my tent in the rain, the weather cheered up slightly and my mood was also greatly improved by the fine meal I had that evening, so I was not too upset that a camper van had parked right in front of my tent. Did they actually see it, I wondered? I slept very well (maybe the result of the good French wine) and in the morning as I climbed into the hills, the low, wet, ethereal misty clouds among the trees in the valley looked very French.

After a day spent walking among the pasture and woods, with trees starting to turn an autumnal yellow, bunches of mistletoe in their branches, I reached my destination for the night. Unfortunately, my intended hostel was closed. I climbed into the nearby village and looked at signs for various accommodations. A lady engaged me in conversation and was trying to advise me where to stay at great length and speed, but sadly my French was not up to it, so I smiled and said, *"Merci,"* and headed off in the direction of one of the signs. After a walk somewhat longer than I anticipated I reached a Pilgrim's hostel, where I stayed for the night. I was again crossing the 'Way of Saint James' and my two female companions at the hostel were walking it in stages, a few weeks each year, with the aim of eventually reaching Santiago de Compostela. After giving us a sample of some liqueur, the genial hostel's owner invited us to help ourselves to food, wine and beer. Payment was voluntary by putting money in a box and I later stuffed in fifty euros.

After failing to persuade my companions to include me in their meal preparations, I found some spaghetti and a tin of Bolognese sauce and made my own dinner, then settled in a bed well away from them. I rose early the next day, hopefully not disturbing them as I left.

The day brought fantastic views over the River Rhône, which I had crossed weeks ago at the start of this trip. It looked a little like the view approaching Grenoble (although that was a different river). Low, cotton-wool clouds initially covered the valley as I walked through the trees, but the sun burnt these off as the morning progressed. Later I dropped into the valley among the many vineyards. It was the *'vendange'*, and I passed small groups of people out picking grapes, before I spent the night near the river at a campsite by the village of Chanaz.

River Rhône to Switzerland — at last!

The next day I crossed the Rhône for the last time, the far side of the river hidden by the mist as I walked over the road bridge. Then a climb into the alpine mountains. I was to the north of the very high French Alps where Mount Blanc lies, but I could see them to the south; snow-covered peaks poking above the clouds which I admired while enjoying a blueberry ('myrtle') tart with Chantilly cream at a wayside, mountain restaurant. As I walked along the grass-covered ridge beyond it I met two men and a dog. One spoke English (not the dog) and expressed surprise at my walk and asked why I should do such a thing. I am always struck dumb by such a question and just indicated the beautiful view around me. He also asked where I would sleep that night. My plan was to stay at a refuge. I am never sure what to find at a refuge; sometimes these huts are locked, sometimes open for anyone to use; sometimes they have a guardian and food available. Arriving at this refuge, I found it occupied by a party of people. They looked at me quizzically and, in answer to my query, told me all the beds would be full that night. So I said I would camp outside. While looking for a spot to pitch, two of them came out and drew my attention to a map showing two other refuges not so far away. I divined that I was not welcome; maybe they were planning a wild drug-filled party at this remote spot, or maybe they just did not like me, so I headed off in the pleasant, early evening sun. At the location where the map indicated another refuge there was a small cottage sporting a prominent 'private property' sign. Unperturbed, I walked a little further and camped, hidden among some trees, so that even a passing vehicle on the nearby track would not be able to see me.

I was similarly unlucky the next night as the hotel I had planned to patronise in St Germain de Joux was full.

"Complet?" I said to the receptionist, surprised as it was not exactly high season.

"Complet," she said, sounding surprised as well although I suppose it *was* a Saturday night. She did not know of any alternative accommodation nearby. I rang a guesthouse in the village of Giron, but there was no room available (at least I think that was the gist of what a lengthy piece of French meant—sometimes one prefers a simple *'oui'* or *'non'*). Finally, I looked at where a Gite d'Etape was meant to be. It looked very closed up so I wild camped a second night hidden in some woods on an overgrown forest track, glad I always walked with a supply of food and water. My reward early next morning was seeing a beautiful pink moon setting over tree-covered hills, the sky coloured in bands, dark blue by the horizon then pinky blue, pink, bluey-white and pale blue. The low, rising sun then started sending sun beams through the trees beside the track I was following. As an additional treat there were some excellent, large, clean public toilets at Giron to spruce up, and a playground in which to enjoy a late breakfast!

The path wound around, up and down and over hills, with woods, grazing and occasional houses until I reached a point which said the path was closed due to some disagreement with the landowner, as far as I could tell. I had heard something of a dispute where landowners were claiming that they had never given permission for the *Grande Randonnée* footpaths to cross their land, so maybe this was part of that? Consequently, I diverted up a quiet road through a gentle valley. The diversion saved me a day compared with the more correct route followed by my predecessor, the blogger John Hayes. I cannot say I was too upset. The winding GR9 route, taking in every mountain in sight was getting tedious. The hills and mountains, views and rocky outcrops, grassy pastures, rustic houses and old farms were all beautiful, but I had seen quite a bit of them by now. I was keen to reach Switzerland and at times it seemed like I would never get there. I descended into the village of Mijoux on a path through the woods and was fortunate to find a hotel with plenty of room for me, there being only two other guests. Tomorrow I hoped to be in Switzerland.

First, I had a steep climb out for the valley to the top of the ski lift, then I followed the Balcon Du Leman trail along the tree covered ridge towards Switzerland. This went through the *'Canyons des Neige'*, which consisted of curious, narrow canyons in the hillside, bounded by cliffs. Unlike most such features they ran parallel to the ridge and not downhill, and the paths through them followed them down and then up. Finally, I left the woods, crossed a field and arrived at the Swiss border. There was a stone marker and sign saying you had to have the right documents to cross the frontier. There was no one around to check and I felt a bit like a refugee in the Second World War, reaching Switzerland, having walked from Grenoble.

Switzerland — home of walkers and fondue

Switzerland immediately looked different from France. There were simply more cows, heavy with clanging bells, and more grass pasture for the cows, instead of trees. Indeed, if you are afraid of cows, this trail cannot be recommended. In Switzerland, the E4 follows a route called the Chemin des Crêtes trail in the western, French-speaking part of the country, or the Jura Höhenweg in the eastern, German-speaking areas. It is also known as the Jura Crest Trail for English speakers, or footpath Number 5 for those with little imagination. It follows the Jura Mountains, a ridge of limestone that curves over the northern part of Switzerland. A gentler landscape than the high Alps to the south for which Switzerland is more famous. Between the Jura Mountains and the Alps lies a flatter area containing large lakes such as Lac de Neuchatel and major cities like Bern. Due to this geography, views across to the snow-covered Alps, forty kilometres or more away, were a pleasant feature of my walk. Yellow diamonds marked the route, replacing the red-and-white stripes of France and Spain. In my travels from Spain through France to Switzerland, the number of walkers I encountered had, in general, increased. Hiking was evidently a popular pastime for the Swiss, but rather unusual in Spain except for foreigners and weekend walkers in suitably scenic spots.

From the border with France, I climbed up through grass-covered mountains, dotted with groups of pine trees, to the peak of Mount Dôle, where I saw my first mention in the country of the E4 as a *'Sentier Européan'* from the Pyrénées to Jura to Balaton (as in Lake Balaton in Hungry). One day maybe the signs will cover the complete E4 from Tarifa in Spain to Cyprus. I walked down to the town of St Cergue where a very helpful lady in the tourist office found me a Bed & Breakfast for the night and reserved me a bed for the following night. The lady at the B&B spoke several languages, none of them English, but we managed! I tried the raclette for dinner, being in the general area where such dishes are eaten. I have ordered the dish a few times; it involves heating cheese and applying it to potatoes, but each time the contraption used to heat the cheese seems to change and I required extensive instruction. The apple strudel and cream for dessert was divine!

One of the famous Swiss trains passed me at a level crossing as I left town, after I had received a single very large denomination note in Swiss Francs when I tried to obtain money from a cash machine. Back in hills again, I admired at close quarters the placid bovines, big bells hanging on leather straps around their necks clanging as they grazed. The yellow diamond waymarks and occasional signposts led me across grass and by trees into the mountains. I spent some time trying to photograph the rocky snowy peaks of the Alps, in the hazy distance some thirty or forty kilometres to the south, the other side of Lake Geneva, which was lost in the mist and clouds somewhere below me. Not so easy, as the colour of the pale blue sky blended in with the bluish mountains, with the snow only a slightly whiter shade. That evening I stayed in the dormitory accommodation at the top of a hillside hotel, rather than pay for a room of my own. Prices in Switzerland can be pretty high, but many of the hotels on my route had much cheaper beds in dormitories in their attic. At this time of year, except at weekends when they could be full of families, I generally had these dormitories to myself so the hardship was not great. Of course I then ate at the hotel restaurant so the hotel still made its money from me. Possibly because I was single, I found a tendency for them to try and put me in a less congenial bar rather than giving me a seat in the restaurant, at which I was somewhat offended.

The next day, the first day of October, started misty but soon turned into a blue-skied sunny day as I followed the rolling ridge with its lines of limestone rock and dry-stone walls with the occasional summit marked by a metal tripod. I stayed at a campsite at Vallorbe that night but the following night treated myself to a hotel in the tidy town of St Croix. The hotel had a large selection of bottles of absinthe. I thought this alcoholic drink, 'the green fairy', was no longer produced, as it tended to result in hallucinations and the like in the days of the French Impressionists and Emile Zola. Guided by the hotel's manager and after a careful consideration of different brands, I tried some as an aperitif. It was a bit of a performance dripping the stuff through a cube of sugar. I do not recall any ill effects!

I continued on my walk up and down the Jura ridge among grass and trees, following paths which had little turnstiles to guide you through barbed wire fences. The route is close to the German border and the anti-tank defences of concrete blocks or metal stakes seemed well-maintained. I had some glimpses of chamois deer but the most impressive sight was the ridge continuing ahead of me, cliffs on one side, more gentle slopes on the other. Even the farms were pretty, their window boxes filled with bright red geraniums, the Swiss flag on display and the inevitable herd of contented cows. At Le Soliat, there was an impressive semicircle of limestone cliffs, with a plateau of pasture above and scree then trees on the steep slope below. Nearby was a busy and fairly basic refuge where I stayed. This one was run by half a dozen Spanish ladies and, possibly because it was a Saturday, was full of families and friends. Fortunately, I arrived early enough to place my sleeping bag at the wall end, and on the lower level, of the long sleeping platform, so I was only sleeping beside one other person and could easily go outside to reach the toilet at night. Cheese fondue was the default dish for dinner, but I felt that a fondue really needs two of you and maybe some romantic candlelight, so I had the alternative cheese-and-ham dish. Breakfast was enormous with more ham, cheese and bread, or perhaps they thought I was one half of a couple or family group and provided enough for a few people. I finished it anyway.

Leaving the refuge, I walked down the steep slope into the valley, through trees, by rock outcrops, to the village of Noirage, then climbed an equally steep slope up the other side of the valley—pleasant nevertheless among the trees, the deciduous ones just turning to a golden brown beneath the blue skies. As I reached higher parts, I looked down to Lake Neuchatel and beyond it, above a line of clouds, the snowy peaks of the Alps. In the days that followed, there was a mixture of trees and bare ridges of grass, with the occasional cross on a summit and in one case a television mast that looked like a red-and-white rocket about to take off, and always great views. Occasionally I came across mountain top cafés and *'buvettes'*, patriotically flying the Swiss flag and providing welcome refreshment. The machines used to cut trees were quite impressive with hydraulic arms extending in all directions to hold onto the trunk, cut the tree and stack the tree trunks. Tree-cutting operations could be an issue at times as the track would be blocked off with stop signs, necessitating a detour through the trees. In one case, where avoiding the track was going to be lengthy and difficult, I ignored the signs as there was no noise nor other indication of any activity and came across two foresters having a snack. After recovering from their surprise at seeing me, they gave me a telling-off. At least, I imagine that was their intention. Despite the language barrier, their facial expressions were fairly unequivocal.

At the point where I moved from the French-speaking part of Switzerland to the German-speaking part, a sign pointing west stated *'Chemin des Crête'* next to a sign pointing east directing me along the *'Jura Höhenweg'*. People started giving me unexpected greetings; in the French area, *'Bonjour'* was typical, and I was expecting 'Guten morgen' or similar in the German area, but no, the most common greeting was *'Grüezi'* from the many walkers I passed. I asked at a hotel what it meant and the receptionist, perhaps thinking me a little obtuse, waved her hands and said it was something like "greetings". A hand-painted sign asked you to close a gate due to a mother cow with calf. Written in German, it ended in the French, *'Merci'*.

While most nights I stayed in hotels, in their dormitory rooms if they had them, in the small town of Hauenstein, I spent the night in a *'Schlaf im Stroh'*. This involved sleeping on straw in a concrete barn. I was the only one staying there that night so I could spread out, dry some clothes and use the toilet in the farmyard without bothering anyone except the chickens outside the barn who made a racket whenever I left or returned.

Dinner was in a local restaurant. I declined a dish which I loosely translated as "head to tail of a cow" in favour of the *entrecôte* as a safer bet. Breakfast, provided by the farmer's wife and young daughter, was really good. I stayed at a youth hostel at the town of Brugg, an historic stone-built building with shutters brightly painted with red-and-white stripes, similar to others I had seen nearby. I was told by a genial older man sharing the dormitory that I was near the castle where the Hapsburg dynasty originated, before they went on to rule the Austro-Hungarian Empire, which curiously did not include their original castle.

After Brugg, the ridges I had been following petered out. The *Jura Höhenweg* ended at Dielsdorf without any great ceremony, just a sign pointing in one direction only. I continued on what I believed was the E4 through a busy landscape of towns, farms and woods. Towns on my route such as Baden were, however, pleasant to walk through, with historic buildings with spires of multicoloured tiles and old mills. Bells rang out from church steeples. It was clearly a prosperous area, with many tall offices and blocks of flats and also apartments built into the hillsides in a sympathetic manner, the gardens of one house seeming to be the roof of the one below. Unlike the mountains and woods, I had been walking through, there were busy roads and railways, but also places to buy a coffee, pastry or a hotdog. Dogs were well looked after and, as I walked across flatter farmland, I was surprised to see doggy poo bins, with a supply of poo bags, beside the fields in out-of-town locations. Points of interest included: a covered bridge (stone piers, wooden walls and a tiled roof); farmed fields of lilac-coloured flowers with serrated leaves of a type I had not seen before, and another hotel staffed by a computer.

At last, I reached the River Rhine, crossing a bridge decorated with flower boxes across the broad expanse of water to reach the touristic town of Stein am Rhein. I walked up to the campsite with the aim of keeping accommodation costs down, but the reception was closed. I called the phone number on the sign but could not understand what the person answering the phone number was saying. So I thought, *sod it, I have walked five hundred miles this trip*, so I treated myself to a hotel in the town, the most expensive so far. Its outside walls were painted with pictures of fish, an organ, birds, a dancing girl, and a semi-naked man among other things. It was by no means the only building with images on its walls from some bygone age. Now late in the season the pedestrian, cobbled main street with its arch at the end had few people around, and I enjoyed fish from the river for dinner. There were a few other guests present.

My last day's walking of this trip was among the fields, orchards and vineyards above the water where Lake Bodensee emptied into the Rhine. I walked through villages with window boxes of flowers decorating little railway stations, picked up some chocolates to take home to my wife from a factory shop and then caught the train from Kreuzlingen to Zürich After a night at the backpacker's hostel, a walk around the city, and the purchase of more chocolate with imaginative ingredients, I caught the plane back home. While my wife enjoyed the chocolate, she suggested that on my next trip, perhaps not quite so much!

Chapter 7: From the Rhine to the Danube — two more rivers with some high ground between

Back to Switzerland and a walk around a lake

Owing to a wonderful, round-the-world trip with my wife (a long-held ambition) I did not return to Switzerland and the E4 until the end of August 2016. Flying into Zürich, the efficient train service whisked me back to Kreuzlingen. I set off walking immediately and camped for the next three nights at sites conveniently located on the banks of Lake Bodensee. An easy walk along the lakeside, there was even an option for wheelchair users. I admired the boats and sunsets over the distant shores. People were enjoying themselves swimming off jetties in the warm afternoons, or enjoying a beer at tables beside the water, the setting sun reflected in the golden contents of their glasses. Arriving early at one campsite, I followed the *'Apfelweg'*, a short walk through the surrounding apple orchards. Towns dotted the lakeside, with promenades, railway junctions, marinas, restaurants, buildings old and new. On my third day of walking around the lake, the trail took me over a hill and then down into a delta where the Rhine entered the lake. Above one of the channels draining into the lake I crossed a bridge from Switzerland to Austria, unchallenged by the customs officer. I guess my rucksack looked too small to interest him. An embankment led me past lakeside reeds on one side and flat land on the other. A lady on a bike stopped and told me of her walk on the Jacobsweg to Santiago de Compostela. Mosquitos buzzed me at the flat, busy campsite by the lake, but on the plus side, coffee was available early in the morning to help me on my way.

After crossing various river channels my route turned inland. There were now two alternative E4 routes. The 'low' or northern route follows the Maximilian Way through the Bavarian Alps whilst the 'high' route takes you through the Austrian Alps and is advised for more experienced Alpinists. Not counting myself as an experienced Alpinist, I chose the low route, although it soon became apparent that this was a bit of a misnomer, as there were many days with total ascents of over a thousand metres (by 'total ascent', I mean all the upward climbs in the day added together, it may be that by going up and down hills, you do not reach any great height, but by adding all the 'ups' together, you have actually climbed a large (and tiring) total ascent). The day I left the lake had plenty of climbing, including a steep climb up to the top of Brüggelek, although a mountaintop café (complete with an E4 footpath sign marked 'Pyrenäen-Jura-Neusiedlersee-Balaton') provided me with refreshments. My meal at the Gasthof in Lingenau, was very welcome at the end of a long day. The next day, a walk among bright green fields took me through a village bedecked with flowers. Several sights that typified this part of the E4 started here, including: flower-filled window boxes; little wayside chapels; churches with bulbous spires; fields of cow pasture in the valleys; tree-clad slopes, and houses and barns with overhanging eaves.

Maximilianweg, the not-so-low, low route

After traversing a covered bridge and enjoying cheese on toast for lunch, I crossed the border from Austria to Germany. Beside a road, a couple were making tuneful noises on Alpenhorns, a sound evocative of the Alps and a fitting accompaniment to my walk which mingled with the jangle of cow bells and parents encouraging their children as they cycled up a valley into the mountains. There followed a very steep, if short, climb up to Stauffer Haus. This was one of many mountain huts that I slept at on this trip. I had joined the British section of the Austrian Alpine Association, especially to gain discounts at the huts in Austria and Germany (gaining free insurance in the process). Their huts were staffed and offered food and dormitory accommodation. Stauffer Haus was located near the top of a ridge close to a cable car terminus. Nearby was a wooden framework like a door frame with prayer flags that claimed to be a transition to a mystical, sublime world, but I walked through and found both sides to be the same. The evening meal on offer at Stauffer hut was Sauerbraten, i.e., roast pork with dumplings and gravy, a dish I would become very familiar with over the coming weeks, but was nevertheless always appreciated after a day's walking. Every bed at the hut that evening was taken. On arrival I could see that the warden would have preferred to send me on my way, but I had booked and pointed out my name in her diary. There was music, by a small band, in the dining room in the evening but I was disappointed that every seat was taken and I could only listen outside, watching the sun set, pink below streaks of orange clouds. It was hot in the dormitory that night. The large group I was sharing with had foolishly decided to close the only window and I found myself sweating in my silk 'hüttenschlafsack'. A 'hüttenschlafsack' is a sleeping bag liner (the words for 'hut', 'sleep' and 'sack' are joined together as in many German words); you bring your own and it is used in huts beneath the blankets they provide. I had brought mine especially for the trip, although on this night I dispensed with the blankets due to the heat. At some hour deep in the night I heard a whispered conversation and gave silent thanks when someone opened the window. While some huts were very popular, others had few other occupants. On one occasion I shared with just one, young couple, which was more embarrassing than sharing with a full room. I was usually among the first up in the morning, all the better to use the bathroom facilities before a queue formed.

The following day was a longish walk along a scenic ridge, a great slab, grass covering one side, cliffs on the other, a continuation of the Jura Mountains I had walked along in Switzerland. Blue, delphinium-like flowers, an iron cross and distant views of the mountains I was to cross in the coming weeks held my attention as I climbed up and down to the various summits. A popular walk, many people exchanged greetings with me. A common greeting I had not heard before, was 'grüß Gott', God bless.

After a night in a campsite in Sonthofen the weather changed from the fine blue skies of the previous day to low clouds in the valleys, black clouds above and heavy rain. Stopping early, I was grateful that the cheerful lady at the Hotel Anneliese in Unterjoch could accommodate me. Waiting for a room to be prepared, I sat on a chair by reception with a cup of coffee, dripping steadily and was embarrassed to leave a big puddle of water behind. The rain stopped once I had settled in and had a shower.

I again crossed into Germany after a brief excursion into Austria, hiking along a steep-sided ridge that marked the border. On one side I looked down on an Austrian valley, on the other across the Bavarian lowlands, with its neat towns, green fields, lakes and trees. Where there were no cliffs, the ridge was thickly covered with trees. Falkenstein Castle stood at a high point on the trail, romantically perched on a clifftop. That night I stayed in the Füssen youth hostel among a group of Chinese visitors with their suitcases.

Many come to the area to see the fairy-tale Neuschwanstein Castle. Built by mad King Ludwig II, as a homage to the composer Wagner, and an inspiration for Disney films, I had visited the castle before. On this occasion I was unsure whether the E4 climbed up past the castle or continued on lower ground for a while. An E4 signpost suggested the lower path, but the signage petered out, so I headed upwards at the cable-car station, following the path, with many others, to the summit of Tegelberg. Unlike the last few days, the weather was fine with blue skies and a few clouds dotted over distant mountains. As I climbed nine hundred metres up a steep, switchback path, a vista across Bavaria opened out beneath me, while around me an alpine flower meadow bloomed yellow, blue and pink, giving me an excuse for a periodical rest as I admired my surroundings. This meant I passed and repassed the same people, and a golden Labrador dog. A mountaintop restaurant sat at the summit where I had lunch. Many of the patrons arrived by the cable car. This was very much a trend for the days to come. I would toil up a mountain (with, I must add, many other walkers out for a day trip) and find a restaurant or café serving refreshments at the top, reached by a cable car or mountain railway. Most days I would climb a total of over a thousand metres. The paths, marked by regular yellow signposts, were colour coded. Blue trails were easy, red were more difficult and black routes needed a head for heights. After Tegelberg I had a choice, either a more difficult high-level route by rocky peaks or an easier lower-level wooded route. I took the easier route, reaching Kenzenhutte for a dormitory bed and an evening meal. Many of those in the hut were a similar age or older than me. Evidently hiking in the mountains is a much more popular pastime in this part of the world than it is in Britain. One of the men who spoke English shared a carafe of red wine with me. While

I am not naturally gregarious, he was a chatty bloke, and I learnt quite a lot about this and that, including his work in Greece, where he had learnt to speak English.

The next day dawned with a misty drizzle which promised rain to come. Those up and getting ready were discussing where to go on a day such as this. Again, I had two options: a low and a high route. Playing for safety I took the lower route down through trees to the grounds of the Linderhof Palace. I entered on a narrow path, possibly avoiding an entrance fee. There were a variety of rotundas and pergolas, grand stairs, empty pools and buildings in white stone with rounded grey metal roofs. People, less well dressed for the rain than me, wandered around under umbrellas and took photographs of each other. I climbed away from the palace to August Schuster Haus, a mountain hut perched in a dramatic location on top of a ridge among cliffs and trees. There I enjoyed a typical Bavarian sausage for lunch. Then it was down to the valley below, pausing to admire the small chapel near the bottom with its miniature 'onion' dome, baroque paintings and architectural curves. It was one of the many such shrines I encountered, some with dedications to family members. I had not realised that this part of Germany was Catholic rather than Protestant. In the town of Unterammergau, there was an attractive building, its windows embellished by paintings and with the inevitable window boxes of brightly coloured flowers, very typical of the region. Then it was a climb back into the mountains to a bunk and meal at Hornlehutte, a very quiet hut.

The Maximiliansweg, which the E4 follows across Bavaria, is supposedly the route King Maximilian II of Bavaria travelled to view the boundary of his country in 1858. I confided in a couple staying at the hut that I was aiming to walk to Lake Walchensee the next day following the Maximilian Way. They seemed sceptical and reminded me that King Maximilan had a horse. As they surmised, the day was indeed a long one at thirty-seven kilometres with a total ascent of almost 1,500 metres (for those who might not be familiar with long-distance walks, I can assure you this is a lot!). As the afternoon was waning, I reached the peak of Heimgarten after a long climb up the steep, wooded slopes of the ridge. Refreshing myself at the inevitable mountaintop café, I had a choice. A 'black' trail along the top of a sharp, narrow ridge that led to a hut that might have a bed, or an easier trail down to the town of Walchensee, where there was a campsite and multiple guesthouses. Tired as I now was the black trail looked a little risky and I headed down to the lakeside town on the easier path. In Britain, September is 'low season' after the school holidays end, and accommodation is usually available, but here the month seemed a busy time of year. The campsite was full, and two or three guesthouses also turned me away. Finally, the owner of one place took pity on me and gave me a room she had been keeping back as they were so busy, provided I left reasonably early in the morning so she had plenty of time to make up the room for the next night's guests. Very thankful, I collapsed on the bed and stayed there all evening, largely immobile, eating my emergency rations rather than walking to one of the (very busy) restaurants.

Another tiring day followed, although on a beautiful path, up through woods and then along a ridge. Initially there were a lot of people and children around. I stopped for some buttermilk at a café by the mountain of Jochberg, admiring distant Alps to the south. Approaching Tutzinger Hut, I again had a choice: drop down into a valley to a hut that might well be full, given the number of people about, or continue over the summit of Benediktenwand. I choose the latter. There was some kind of empty cabin on the summit where maybe I could have stayed the night, but I decided to head onto the next hut. I was now walking alone along the long ridge in the evening light, admiring the views, the crowds having headed to some other place for the night. Unfortunately, on arriving at the hut, I was told the place was taken over for a wedding party. The place was full of guests celebrating the happy event. Thankfully, as it was now getting late, the warden, with a resigned look, led me to a large, empty dormitory, told me to leave it exactly as I found it, and fed me the ubiquitous Sauerbraten for dinner, some of the food the wedding guests were also eating. I tried to be discreet, eating it in a corner away from the party, and left for an early night.

Climbing up and down mountains was the essence of the Maximiliansweg. So next morning it was again a climb down into a valley beside the ski lifts, across a river at the town of Lenggries (after stopping for a 'kaffee und kuchen') then up the other side, through some mountains with rocky paths, then down again to Bad Wiessee on the banks of the Tegernsee lake. 'Bad' is a prefix that always amused me but of course it does not mean naughty; it is German for 'bath', 'spa' or a place associated with water. I treated myself, booking into the Gasthof zur Post. Dressed in petunias overflowing from their boxes in pinks and whites and blues, the windows were further embellished with paintings and shutters, the eaves extending several feet beyond the walls. It looked altogether the epitome of an alpine hotel, in a pretty lakeside town enjoyed by tourists.

The following day I caught the ferry across the Tegernsee, climbed up another mountain and down the other side into Schliersee (another lake, you have probably worked out what 'see' means). En route, I passed a small chapel that caught my attention. Inside, above the altar and the Madonna, was a picture of a soldier tending a wounded man with the Alps in the background. It seemed to be a family shrine, maybe a relative had died in wartime. On the door, '20-K+M+B 16' was written in chalk. I had seen such chalk markings before. Apparently, on the Christian Feast of Epiphany, chalk is blessed by the church and used to mark places with a prayer. K, M and B refer to the wise men Kaspar, Melchior and Balthasar, who visited the baby Jesus.

After an excellent breakfast at Gastehaus am Kurpark, I climbed through the mist and cloud over wooded hills to the village of Fischachau and then continued on towards the summit of Wendelstein. Wreaths of cloud scurried up the hillside through the trees. During my walk through the higher mountains, I had heard whistling and was not sure where it was coming from until I saw a marmot. This small, furry, brown-and-grey creature was sitting up on a rock with its front paws before it, as if begging for something, whistling no doubt as a warning call to fellow marmots that there was a hiker about. Quite a brave creature, it did not run off as I walked by. Near the summit of Wendelstein, a mountain railway terminated at a café. After a coffee and snack, I climbed up the steps to the mountaintop, among the aerials with their drum-shaped microwave transmitters. Owing to the mist, the aerials were about all I could see. Climbing down from the mountain, once again below the clouds, I gained a better view of the rack-and-pinion railway with its multiple tunnels and yellow "Wendelstein bahn" electric train, and indeed slept beside it in the Mitter-Alm Hutte (served by its own train station). The warden tried to sell me a more expensive bed in a room of my own, but I stuck to my choice of a dormitory; as it turned out, I was the only one using it so saved a few euros. The brown beer was very good and there was an excellent view down the pine-tree-clad valley to my next range of mountains.

As I left early in the morning, the sun was out, burning off early, wispy clouds in the valley. I descended the mountain, following a small, rock-strewn stream sparkling among a display of wild flowers and admiring the sharp shadows the trees cast across the forest track. After a slow crossing of the broad valley of the River Inn, it was another day climbing up a mountain, this time to the summit of Hochries. I had hoped to stay at the hut there but its sleeping accommodation was closed for some reason so, after a Coke, it was down the other side. A similar situation pertained at another hut on the way down, followed by a guesthouse, also closed, as it was a Wednesday. I looked in at what looked like a hotel in Hohenaschau but no one was around. As it was by now getting late, I concluded that I would have to wild camp, which I understood to be illegal in Germany. However, as I walked out of town, I passed a *'ferienwohnung'*, a small guesthouse. Spotting a lady outside tending the garden, I asked if there was a *'zimmer frei'* (a free room), which there was, so I was legal that night (and enjoyed an expensive but very tender cut of meat at an empty restaurant in town).

Before me the following morning was the mountain of Kampenwand. A blog by a previous E4 walker, referred to a difficult descent of this peak holding onto fixed ropes. Erring as ever on the side of safety, I choose a path around the main peak. The strategy was not entirely successful as there was still a steep rocky section of the path where a steel cable was provided to assist one's descent. A day later I accidentally followed one of the dreaded 'black' paths. Fortunately, it was not so bad and I survived, although somewhat sobered by the occasional memorial or shrine to someone who had died in the mountains. Such steep terrain did, however, yield some spectacular views, of which I accumulated many photographs with which to bore others on my return!

I was now very much in the rhythm of climbing up and down a mountain or two each day, stopping at some mountain café or restaurant for refreshment and admiring the flowers and distant views. Each day was different but yet the same. Pine woods alternated with grass-covered hillsides, rocky summits and tidy valleys with their neat towns. I was far from alone among the many people out walking for a day or more.

Two nights in hotels followed my climb over Kampenwand. The second, Hotel Wittelsbach at Ruhpolding, had a particularly pleasant, smartly dressed host, rooms decorated with modern, bold colours, a good selection of gins and real English Breakfast tea in the morning. Outside Britain (or even in it!) tea can be a risky choice, and can take the form of a cup of lukewarm water turning up with a tea bag, possibly herbal, so a proper pot of tea was most welcome. Later on, during my trip I also came across a 'Teestube', which served a choice of teas. I had first flush Darjeeling, with a slice of divine gooseberry cake, the layer of gooseberries just moistening the surrounding cake and the tartness of the gooseberries offsetting the sweetness of the sponge.

I decided it was time for a campsite to contain costs. One was a located a little north of Bad Reichenhall. I decided to deviate off the Maximillianweg to approach it more directly on a path shown on my map around a mountain which towered above the town. While the path certainly existed, it was on the side of a steep slope, crossing sections of loose scree, Bad Reichenhall spread out beneath me. Not the best routing when one is tired, late in the afternoon, although as always, a beer and meal in a local hostelry revived me in the evening. That was my last night in Germany.

Austria on the Weitwanderweg 04

Salzburg is a beautiful city, which I had been lucky enough to visit twice previously and, this time, I entered its tourist-filled streets through an imposing city gate. From previous visits, however, I had no recollection of the mountain in the middle of the city that I had, perforce, to climb over en route to the campsite on the northern edge of the metropolis. So, by the time I reached my destination, I was tired. Although the campsite owner gave me detailed instructions on how to return to the city centre nightlife by bus, I had seen enough for the day, electing instead to dine on rotisserie chicken at his campsite.

Leaving Salzburg, the route was now following the Weitwanderweg 04 (WWW 04 or the Austrian long-distance path 04) to Vienna. The first part was through the Salzkammergut, a region of mountains and lakes, much-loved by tourists on account of its scenery. It began with a steep climb up to the summit of Gaisberg with some panoramic views back to Salzburg. Then it was a walk among trees. I spotted an occasional pothole in the limestone and a group of figures made of straw dressed in ladies' clothes, with some flowers and a watering can at the entrance to the village of Faistenau, but my most vivid memory was a worker cleaning a church tower by abseiling off the top of the spire. The owner of the guesthouse I stayed at asked about the E4 as she was planning to walk the start of it in Spain in a few weeks' time. I hope she enjoyed it; her enquiry surprised me, as not many people have heard of the route, and I gave a bit of a flustered reply to her question about the length of the first day's walk.

After a short day, walking to the town of St Gilgen, I ate an ice cream lying on the grass by the lake and sunbathed until the youth hostel opened, but the following day was more tiring. First, a long climb up to the summit of Schafberg. On the way I admired the little train carrying tourists to the top (illogically I did not think of myself as a 'tourist' like them, more an adventurer). Below me, a small white biplane circled the lake and near the summit, people prepared to paraglide off the mountainside in colourful if insubstantial kites. I was concerned about the route down the other side taken by the E4, a 'black' route, but the only alternative was another 'black' route. So I reconnoitred the path; if it looked too difficult I could return the way I had come and make a long diversion around the mountain. The designated E4 route was called the Himmelspfortenweg (Heaven's Gate Trail) and began with an arch and a sign warning it was for experienced Alpinists only. A group of Japanese tourists were taking photographs of each other in front of it. Viewing the path down from a nearby promontory, it did not look too difficult, a zigzag route down the back wall of a corrie, so I decided to give it go, preparing myself mentally for a steep return ascent if I came across something too difficult. I kept waiting for that 'too difficult' section, but it never came. It would have been a challenging descent in wet weather or snow, but on a fine, dry day it was straightforward, although not advisable for tourists arriving by train in flip-flops or otherwise unsuitable shoes. I guessed (or hoped) I was becoming a more experienced alpine hiker.

That night I intended to stay at Weissenbach, a lakeside village. Two campsites were marked and there were other accommodation options. The first campsite seemed to be a residential site for longer-stay residents. There was no reception and no one answered the phone number that was posted, so I continued a few kilometres to the next site. It, too, was unattended and, although there was a phone number, large portraits of Marx, Lenin and other communist heroes at the site made me decide to try the local hotel. This was full except for a large suite which was outside my price bracket. By then it was getting late. I should have negotiated on the price, pointing out that it was now unlikely to be booked that evening. After failing at another place, I elected to wild camp. This is illegal in Austria too but I reckoned that if I followed the E4 up the next mountain for half an hour it would be dusk, no one would be around and so no one would know. I climbed up, passing people coming down, looking for a place to pitch my tent. Unfortunately, I had neglected to take into consideration the steep side of the mountain which offered no flat spots, until I reached a picnic table beside the path. This appeared to be the only flat area I was likely to find, small though it was. Hikers were still coming off the mountain, so I sat at the picnic table and had some food watching the gathering dusk over the lake below. Then, in almost complete darkness, I pitched my tent and climbed in. Still, I had not escaped attention; as I prepared to sleep more people passed, their head torches scanning my tent. Nevertheless, no one disturbed me or my sleep.

I was rewarded in the morning by an amazing view. I looked down on clouds that covered Lake Attersee. Above the clouds, the rocky tops of the blue-grey mountains were highlighted in pink by the rising sun, still invisible to me. High above, the skies were blue. As the path climbed over rocky slopes, the stones now highlighted by the low sun, my water supply gave out. I had foolishly forgotten to fill up at Wesissenbach the previous evening. Nevertheless, I knew there was a mountain hut ahead of me, where I was in time to catch breakfast: cheese, ham, bread, coffee, and the like, and very welcome after my emergency rations of the night before. The warden filled my aluminium water bottle, commenting that its many dents showed it had done quite a few kilometres, which made me very proud for no very good reason.

The mountain range I was crossing now had few trees of any size, a result of the dry, limestone geology. Any rain water would rapidly disappear into the cracks and potholes I crossed in the rock, only low shrubby pines remained. Views were spectacular down the steep slopes to lakes set in the forest a long way below. I slept that night in a mountain hut built among bare rock and a limestone pavement. A girl staying there bemoaned the end of summer. Waking down the mountain I was concerned that the various red warning signs in German with exclamation marks were informing me of some hidden danger that I needed to be aware of. Careful work on my phone with Google Translate informed me that the signs said, "Do not drop litter and keep the mountain clean"!

I was now leaving the highest mountains, and walking through slightly lower ones. As the girl predicted, summer was ending and it was raining as I walked through trees, by lakes and rivers, or over cow pasture. Fortunately for the next section, I was well supplied with guesthouses; in my waterproofs, I was not uncomfortable and there was always something of interest, like how to photograph rain so it looked like it was raining. The circles made by rain drops hitting water in a lake seemed a good way. Walking up a path through trees I saw my first fire salamanders, black reptiles with yellow spots, not that rare but new to me and rather pretty, slow to move, maybe as it was getting colder. Maybe due to the weather there were not many walkers around, although, on entering a mountain hut, it was full of older people enjoying lunch and a beer or two, their wet clothes dripping in the lobby. A dog lay in a bed below some shelves, and the English-speaking 'guardian' sold me a welcome bowl of hot bread (!) soup and some cake. Later I came across an unusual hut, more of a shed, on a hill in a grass field with a picnic bench outside and no one around. Inside was a vending machine. I put my money in and out came a bottle of cider (of the alcoholic variety). Judging by the empty bottles, maybe a secret cider club?

At Maria Neustift, I briefly joined the Mariazeller Wege, a pilgrimage route, which the lady in the guesthouse thought I was walking. Instead, I was heading east into gentler landscapes of large green fields, frequent farms, areas of woodland and more villages and towns, such as Waidhofen an der Ybbs, nestled among the hills. I arrived early in this town of onion-domed spires and visited the museum in the castle (Schloss Rothschild) beside the River Ybbs. Gresten was another town I walked through, staying at an inexpensive, if a little rundown, residential campsite. In the absence of a reception, one of the residents took me to the older lady in charge, who accepted a very modest payment. Gresten was dominated by the Welser engineering works. I enjoyed a pizza in a café there. Maybe they do not get many visitors because there was some interest in me and I explained that I was walking across Europe on the E4 and that Hungary was my next country. They said the food was better there! In the morning I had breakfast at a pension. The owner, miming sleeping, was curious where I had slept and was surprised when I said *'campingplatz'*. But, as I had explained to the guys at the pizza place, my next night would be in a real castle. This was the 800-year-old Burg Plankenstein, built on a rocky outcrop, entered via a bridge over a ditch and through a fortified gateway. Rooms and passageways in the castle were odd shapes; evidently it was not built as a hotel! Close by was a church, with the characteristic metal onion dome on top of its tower. Inside there were paintings on the ceiling with a modern looking Adam and Eve being admonished by God, their modesty concealed by carefully disposed arms and legs. Outside, a red-and-white Austrian flag fluttered and a sign indicated that this was the crossing point of the E4 and E6 *Europäischer Fernwanderwegs* (European long-distance paths). The following night was in my last mountain hut of the trip. I called ahead to reserve a bed and fortunately the lady who answered spoke English (it is always a fear when ringing that I do not understand what is being said). She was worried a party in the floor beneath my bedroom would disturb my night, but if there was any jollity, I slept through it, waking to a beautiful sunny morning, the geraniums in the bedroom's window box a brilliant red, low cloud hiding the valley floor.

Now I was walking across rolling, green hills and through occasional woods. The scenery was not as dramatic as the high, rocky mountains of earlier in my trip but various items caught my attention, such as a curious sculpture marked the *'Panorama Höhenweg'* and a seat made of metal bars inside a section of pipe. Large, hand-drawn signs announced a birthday (with photos of the lucky person) and the arrival of a baby at a nearby farm (complete with wooden stork carrying the baby). Pale purple colchicums (like crocuses but autumnal) with delicate yellow stamens dotted the grassland on the hillsides, together with yellow dandelions and purple knapweed. I did wonder where all the cows were to enjoy this pasture; perhaps kept in barns and fed cut hay. Quiet on weekdays, at the weekend the paths had plenty of walkers, gathering at a hilltop restaurant for a good lunch.

I was now reaching the famous Vienna woods. In places where the path took me through the forests, I was impressed by the tall beech trees rising above me, atmospheric in the morning mist or when a blade of sunlight cut diagonally through the trees to light a patch of the low, green undergrowth. After a few nights in hotels and coffee and cake at various cafés (including one call Muck, where I had a Black Forest gateau) I arrived at a ridge on which a concrete tower and steps had been constructed so that you could see over the top of the trees to the River Danube lying in a broad area of flat land beyond, a major milestone on my trip, and in my mind the start of Eastern Europe. A wooden boardwalk took me down a tree-filled valley to a field where I had my first sight of Vienna, its skyscrapers just visible around the hillside, although that night I stayed at a campsite, by the Danube at Klosterneuberg. I was in time to visit the ancient monastery in the town, a landmark with its twin green spires and dome that I had seen many times as I approached the town, gradually getting bigger.

My final day of the trip took me over hills, the many channels of the Danube spreading out lazily before me, Vienna in the distance, its tower blocks rising through the grey haze each side of the river. There were many vineyards. I passed a *'heuriger'*, empty at the time, but a place where young wine is served. It reminded me of a business trip to Vienna many years before, when our hosts took my colleagues and me to such a place. They said the wine was not strong, and I ended up drinking too much of it in a general atmosphere of *'gemütlichkeit'*. Little food was served and inevitably my performance suffered at the meetings the next day. My father, on a quite separate business trip to Vienna, had a similar experience, finding it a little difficult following the tram lines back to his hotel.

The latter part of the day was spent walking beside the Danube, swapping from one channel to another, admiring the locks and large barges steaming up and down the river. Each of these barges would invariably have a car perched on its stern, with a little crane, presumably to lift the car on and off. At one point I came across a group of skyscrapers. One looked as if the architect had lost his ruler as one side was wavy. At my business trip *'heuriger'*, many years ago, my hosts had talked of naked women, cycling by the river. I gave it little thought, until I came to a section of riverbank populated by naturists, enjoying the sunshine with no clothes on. In Britain this often seems an activity only enjoyed by middle-aged men, but here there were men and women, walking on the footpath, sunbathing or swimming in the river channel. It was a hot and sticky day, I had time to kill before catching a train for my plane home and it seemed impolite wearing clothes when everyone else was naked; there was time for at least a little sunbathing on the banks of the Danube…

Chapter 8: Vienna to Budapest — lakes, forests and volcanoes

A surprisingly flat part of Austria

Eager to return to long-distance walking in 2017, I flew back to Vienna late one evening at the end of February, starting my walk, in cool sunshine the next day. On leaving a hotel room, hostel or campsite, I have a strict practice of looking at all the surfaces in turn to make sure I have left nothing behind, but maybe my childlike excitement at starting off a new trip made me less thorough on this first morning. The casualty in this case, discovered some hours later, was one of my water bottles, maybe left in the hotel bathroom. No great loss, as I had another and could use a mineral water bottle instead, but annoying nevertheless.

For much of my remaining hike through Austria, the E4 followed the Weitwanderweg 07 (WWW 07). This makes a wide loop down the Danube to the Slovakian border, before turning back on itself to cross Lake Neusiedlersee, then taking a more obvious route to Hungary. Prior to Neusiedlersee, much of the route is over very flat land. One might be tempted to miss out this loop, but I was glad I took the time, finding it a rewarding walk. There were no dramatic mountains to climb, although white-topped mountains were visible in the west, rising above the plain which this section crossed, but there was history, a different type of scenery and a serene sense of peace.

My path for the first two days would be largely through the Danube Forest National Park (or the Donau-Auen National Park) on the north side of the river, but first I had to reach it. I crossed the Danube on a hydroelectric dam to rejoin the E4. Some of the quieter Danube channels still had a thin coating of ice (including where naturists had swum on my earlier trip). Mistletoe was common in the starkly bare, leafless trees. Industrial areas skirted my path, not without interest. One steel storage tank had a face painted on it, the nose being a pipe leaving the tank. However, I was glad to reach the woodlands that lined the Danube here.

In 1984, there was a plan to build a hydroelectric plant on the river, similar to many elsewhere on the Danube. This would have destroyed one of the last natural, free-flowing sections of the river. Extensive protests meant that instead a national park was created to preserve the forests and wetlands of the floodplain. My walk took me through these forests on tracks and paths, sometimes among the trees and by reed-lined lakes, sometimes on the top of flood-control embankments somewhat away from the river, and sometimes on the riverbank itself. Lit by the low wintery sun, the white bark of poplar trees contrasted with the blue sky and golden reeds. All were reflected in still lakes. The paths were well signed and of good quality, avoiding some swampy areas. There was a fine looking, yellow, stately home and several river barges to admire, pushed from behind by a tug. I wondered how the tug steered the barge in the right direction, which must be difficult when pushing from behind, or maybe someone was sat on the barge operating its rudder. An example of one of the many curious thoughts that pass through my mind when walking. Leaving the forest, I crossed the Danube to Hainburg and what I thought would be a riverside hotel for the night. It was indeed by the river, but an elevated train line between me and the water blocked the view from my (very elegant) bedroom. In compensation, Hainburg was a beautiful and historic town to wander around, with gatehouses, ancient-looking shop signs and a castle which I was too tired to climb up to. Dinner at the hotel was very fine, carp with beetroot and trimmings. Unlike Britain, where I have never seen freshwater fish like carp and perch offered in restaurants, on my travels from here to Serbia such fish were often on the menu (at least in places with more diverse choices).

The next day the path was a scenic riverside walk around a mountain that stands next to Hainburg. Slovakia was now on the other side of the river and I would be close to its border for the next two days. I climbed a hill by a ruined castle to an observation tower at the top then descended into the small town of Kittsee. Arriving early, I visited a few sights: the Schloss (not open to the public); a Jewish cemetery (I peered at it through the metal gates) and the chocolate factory shop (where I was obliged to purchase a few of their products to evaluate quality).

Following my stay in Kittsee, I walked for three days across the flat, agricultural plain of Eastern Austria, which extends into Hungary and is called the 'pusta' or 'puszta'. I walked along quiet tarmac roads or cycle paths, often lined with trees. The fields each side, large and open with no hedges, extended into the distance, the horizon broken by faraway trees. I tried and failed to capture their immensity in photographs. Some had short dry grass, others were ploughed, brown earth which hares seemed to like. I saw many such creatures crouching in shallow hollows or hopping away. Maybe I saw them as there were so few other people about. I only saw one group of older men walking. They greeted me, surprised at my presence, and maybe a little unnerved as I had my warm hat pulled down and my buff, or neckerchief, pulled up over my mouth and ears to protect me from the cold wind ripping unimpeded across the plain. Maybe I looked like some refugee who did not want to be recognised, all my belongings in the rucksack on my back. This was relevant as the other people I saw were Austrian soldiers, sitting by tents and shelters looking out at the Slovakian border. At a time of widespread concern at the refugees sweeping across Europe, they perhaps wanted to stop them entering Austria on some quiet country track. Another distinctive sight were the formations of giant wind turbines, rising high above the trees, blinking with red lights at night across the endless plain. Scattered villages had single-storey houses lining their streets, with large doors to one side for the entrance of tractors into some courtyard behind. Painted in pastel colours, behind trimmed grass verges, all was neat and ordered. Larger towns had churches with onion-shaped spires and clocks reading the wrong time, schools and maybe a stately home (of which one had a sculpture park). There was also accommodation and sometimes places where I could buy a creamy cake to go with a coffee. Between the towns, small shrines showed people's religious devotion.

My first major obstacle was Neusiedlersee, a large lake. Ferries plied routes across in summer, but not before April, and I arrived at the very beginning of March. I had arranged a water taxi by e-mail with one of the ferry companies and walked down to the jetties by the lake hoping it would turn up. A little before the appointed time a ferry arrived that could take a hundred people or more. I was surprised to discover this was my water taxi. The two crew were also surprised there was just one of me, they thought I was three. They brought the ferry rather than something smaller as it had two engines, so they could keep going if one failed, there being no one else on the lake at this time of year to rescue them otherwise. Having a large choice of seats, I was not sure where to sit. I started on the top deck and watched the seagulls follow the boat as we headed out of the golden-brown reeds that surrounded the lake. As the lake is landlocked, with no way for the water to leave other than by evaporation, it is somewhat saline. Having admired the view, I joined the crew on the lower deck. They said a week or so ago the ice at the harbour was still thick enough for people to skate on.

Leaving the ferry, I walked to the nearby town of Rust, a tourist town with smart, coloured houses, shops and cobbled streets, but at this time of year the tourists were conspicuous by their absence.

The next day I climbed into low hills beneath a blue sky, passing vineyards and looking back at the lake with its fringe of straw-coloured reeds. I crossed the Sultan's Trail, a long-distance walking route to Istanbul that I would follow for a few days later on in my trek in Bulgaria. My last day in Austria took me by two castles and into extensive woods. There was no formal accommodation nearby so I wild camped. Wild camping being, in theory, illegal in Austria, I hid among the trees, pitching my tent on dry beech leaves.

Hungary and the Blue Route

The next day was spent walking through more forests to reach Hungary. A white, square stone inscribed with an Ö for Austria and a date of 1922 marked the border, which was the only sign that I was walking through the woods from one country to the next, across where once the Iron Curtain, with its watchtowers and border guards, stopped the movement of people across Europe. Earlier an Austrian gentleman out walking discussed Brexit with me; unlike the majority of British people, he believed in a closer union of the countries within the European Union. A lack of harsh border controls was certainly a benefit of greater European integration. Soon I was in Kőszeg, the first town in Hungary, using my phrase book to try and ask for a room for the night in Hungarian. My pronunciation (or lack of it) caused blank-faced incomprehension on the part of my hosts, but once I reverted to English, my bed for the night (and later a bowl of goulash) was soon arranged.

For the next two and a half weeks I was following the Blue Route to Hungary's capital, Budapest. The Blue Route, or Kéktúra, is the oldest, long-distance walking route in Europe (if you put aside the medieval pilgrimage routes) dating from 1938 and runs through the low mountains that span the northern part of Hungary. It gained its name from the waymarks which consist of blue-and-white stripes. The waymarks and signs are frequent enough to make the route easy to follow. If you wish you can get a 'passport' to stamp at various places where a rubber stamp is provided, to prove you have completed the route. I did not, you will just have to trust me. If you think of the E4 heading from Austria to Serbia and Bulgaria, then the route it takes through Hungary is unnecessarily long, running three quarters of the way around the circumference of the country. It follows the Kéktúra, or more precisely the Országos Kéktúra, from west to east close to the northern border of Hungary, then the Alföldi Kéktúra from the northeast corner of Hungary to its southern border. In theory you could miss out many, many kilometres by just following a third route, the Rockenbauer Pál Dél-dunántúli Kéktúra, which runs from the north- west to the southern border of Hungary. Then again, if you wanted to cross Europe quickly, you could catch a plane.

The first four days of walking in Hungary took me from Kőszeg, through Sárvár to Sumeg. Each of these attractive towns had a castle and there were cobbled squares, hotels and cosy restaurants. Between them I walked through farmland, grass, young crops or bare, brown, ploughed fields and a large number of trees. Sometimes the forest tracks or quiet tarmac roads went through trees in a straight line for several kilometres. While monotonous at times, the numerous snowdrops provided some compensation. In places I again crossed the Mariazell pilgrimage route which I first encountered in Austria; here wooden, purple arches marked the route, a bit more elaborate than the few lines of paint marking the Kéktúra. Outside the towns, I wild camped. In Hungary this is legal in state forests, due to some ancient law. One of the enjoyable aspects of wild camping in the woods is waking up to birdsong, and the fresh, earthy smell of a new morning. As in nearby Austria, the village streets were lined with single-storey houses, with red-tiled roofs, although maybe a bit more faded. Unlike Austria, they all seemed to have dogs behind their fences. In villages a wave of excited barking would follow me as I walked through.

Continuing through forests into low hills, I reached a large Buddhist stupa among the trees. Not what you expect in the Hungarian countryside. Prayer wheels lined the circumference of the white concrete, domed building, which I spun while walking around trying to repeat the suggested mantra. Prayer flags fluttered in nearby trees above picnic tables. In the village of Zalaszántó, there was a small museum, not uncommon in Hungary. I visited its modest collection which was associated with a water wheel and admired an old, single cylinder engine on display. Unfortunately, the lady in charge only spoke Hungarian and there were no English signs so the educational value was limited. The village had a handpump painted in bright blue gloss, beside the road. Such blue pumps or taps, seen in most villages, once provided the village with its water; now people have supplies in their own houses, so these pumps are more valuable to hikers wanting to top up their water bottles. I was told they are gradually disappearing as local councils cut costs, so they do not have to pay the water companies to supply them. After Zalaszántó I climbed up to the castle ruins at Rezi and looked back across the valley to yesterday's stupa.

My next big milestone was reaching the expanse of Lake Balaton, which I did at the town of Keszthely. A popular town with a baroque palace, pedestrian streets and tourist facilities, it sits on the edge of the lake, which was so large I could not see the other side. The area is famous for its spas. I booked into a hotel advertising a spa thinking that lying in hot water would provide welcome relaxation for my muscles after covering a few hundred kilometres. Sadly, I was disappointed. The spa was closed for the season; in retrospect, not surprising, as I was the only one staying at the hotel. My irritation was perhaps too obvious to the man on reception in the morning as he offered me a voucher for a lake heated by a thermal spring at the town of Hévíz. However, I had walked through Hévíz the previous day and had no intention of retracing my steps. Undeterred by my early morning misanthropism, the receptionist proceeded to explain how I should pronounce 'angol', meaning English, which is what I said apologetically if anyone tried to talk to me (in Hungarian of course) on the trail, although until this point my bungled pronunciation was just gaining me blank faces in response. I was very slowly picking up a few words, the main ones being *'jó regelt'* and *'jó napot'*—good morning and good afternoon, common greetings among walkers and, of course, *'köszönöm'* (pronounced 'kursunum') for thank you as I try to be polite. A sign I saw often enough to check what it meant was *'Magan Terület'*, which means private.

For the next week I walked the Kéktúra's indirect route towards Budapest, winding erratically across the countryside as it made sure I saw all the sights. In this area, these include old volcanoes, pretty towns, castle ruins and many trees. The volcanoes, while extinct, were not old when considered on geological time scales, so they still had a clear comical shape, rising, often isolated, from the plains. As I climbed up and down them through the trees, I was pleased to see occasional outcrops of dark-grey basalt, the vertical columns of rock looking like organ pipes, proof that these hills were indeed formed by lava from old volcanoes. The trees were bare of leaves at this time of year but some of the lower ones had attractive yellow blossoms, their vivid brightness a sharp contrast to the surrounding dull greys of the trees. Seeing my photographs my cousin said they were witch-hazel trees.

In forested areas, trees have a habit of obscuring the view. Fortunately, in Hungary they have many *'kilátó'*. These are observation towers you climb up to see the surrounding countryside over the treetops and represent one of the ways the Hungarians help ramblers. Another way is using waymarks to show where certain trails go; for example, the routes up mountains are marked with a pyramid waymark, paths to springs with a circular waymark and ruins are indicated by an L-shaped mark. As it was difficult to leave the country during the Cold War, hiking was very popular in Hungary and, on the main Blue Route I was following in the north of the country, walking is still popular. Even in March I regularly exchanged greetings with fellow hikers.

Castle ruins were common on this section, evidence of wars fought across Hungary, most notably with the Ottoman Turks in the 15th and 16th centuries. For the rest of my walk along the E4 in Europe through Hungary, Serbia, Bulgaria, Greece and Cyprus, the Ottoman occupation, for many centuries in some of these countries, dominates their history, although surprisingly few remnants of Ottoman rule remain. At school in Britain, I learnt little of this Muslim invasion despite its importance in this part of the world. These ancient monuments, whose crumbling walls I climbed up to and walked among, now proudly fly Hungarian flags of red, white and green. Curiously, the flag sometimes, but not always, has a coat of arms in its centre. As I neared Budapest the Kéktúra went by a monument to the battle of Pusztamarót, when the Turks killed twenty-five thousand people in 1526, soldiers and refugees fleeing after defeat in an earlier battle. Later in my trip I saw a memorial to a more recent event, slabs of polished rock commemorated sixty years since the failed 1956 uprising against communist rule. Soviet tanks entered Budapest to suppress the revolt and the ensuing deaths persuaded many intellectuals in the West that they should no longer support the Soviet Union. The will of the people in Hungary, wishing to follow a different strand of socialism, was clearly secondary to the power of the politburo in Moscow.

I visited a baroque monastery in the town of Zirc on a rainy afternoon. An impressive amount of gold surrounded the altar of the church, apparently hidden behind whitewash for many years. I would have learnt more but the tour was conducted in Hungarian. An earlier town of Tapolca was one of my favourites, although maybe because I drank too many glasses of the very pleasant white wine, while admiring reflections in a still mill pond of the yellow-painted buildings opposite and amusing myself by exchanging jolly texts with my wife. The area I was walking through had many vineyards, often small affairs on the lower slopes of the old volcanoes. At this time of year, the leafless vines, like tangled wire, were being pruned and the cuttings burnt. Wine, beer and food are among the pleasures of my walks. Hungary did not disappoint. I enjoyed the Balaton Bumm, actually a type of chocolate bar. Cakes or tortes at coffee shops, more cream than cake, were another pleasure in Hungary; a lot of calories, but, with several hours' walking each day, carrying a rucksack, using up to 4,000 calories, the odd cake (every day ideally) can be justified. One dish I tasted that I now regularly reproduce at home is chicken paprikash. It uses a lot of paprika, spoonsful of it, a classic Hungarian ingredient, plus sour cream, to produce a rich, full-flavoured sauce. It was usually served with small dumpling type things, for which, at home, gnocci are a perfectly adequate substitute.

Of the many places I stayed, Karolyi Kastely stuck in my mind. A stately home built in the 19th century in a grand, classical style, it was owned by the aristocratic Karolyi family, but after the Second World War it was confiscated by the communist regime and later housed orphans. With the fall of the Iron Curtain, it is now again managed by the Karolyi family as a hotel and conference centre. A family member gave me a tour. Despite the grandeur, the price for half board was very reasonable. It could have done with a few more guests however. I wandered around the grounds, by a lake, thinking of the efforts of the family to retain a link with their history.

Before reaching Budapest, I caught a train from Dorog for a short journey off the trail to visit Esztergom. My inspiration to visit this town on the Danube was Patrick Leigh-Fermor's account of his walk across Europe in the late 1930s, described in his book, *Between the Woods and the Water*. I did not have quite the same experiences as he did, but the view across the Danube to Slovakia from the grand Basilica, the sun turning pink in the evening sky, has stayed in my mind. The Basilica, like the Karolyi Kastely, was built in the 19th century in a grand classical style.

From Dorog, I walked to Budapest in one day, not my original intention, but sometimes at the end of a trip, fit from weeks of walking, I just wonder, why bother stopping! The day took me through the wooded Buda hills—the first green buds just about visible, among the witch-hazel blossoms and spring flowers. The last few kilometres were through the suburbs of Budapest until I reached the Children's Railway. It was closed, but apparently it is run by children. Nearby was a tram station, and, after some fiddling with the ticket machine, it gave me a 24-hour travel ticket. As the tram trundled into Budapest, I peered out of the window into the darkness looking for a hotel. Spotting one somewhere near the centre, I left at the next stop and booked in. The first plane home was in the evening of the following day, so I spent the morning walking a short section of the Kéktúra, through the wooded Buda hills above Budapest. It was a sunny weekend and joggers, dog walkers, families and groups were out in brightly coloured jackets for a stroll, enjoying the views back down to Budapest and the Danube. In the afternoon I made up for the lack of a working spa at my hotel on Lake Balaton by visiting one of the steaming thermal baths in Budapest. Succumbing to an expensive tourist package, I tried pools of various temperatures, from very hot to very cold before a man stuck his thumbs deep into my muscles for a massage. A relaxing way to end my trip.

Chapter 9: Budapest to Debrecen — across the hills to the endless plain

The Northern Mountains

On my return to Budapest, my first two days of walking on the Kéktúra took me across mountains enclosed by a very large loop of the River Danube. It was now June and the trees were a vivid green; wild strawberries could be found alongside the path and cherries hung from trees. I walked in sunshine on paths through the woods, leaves creating flickering patterns of sunlight on the path. Here and on other parts of the route there were little memorials to those who died in the Second World War. On one side of the hills enclosed by this river loop, I looked down on Budapest, cut in half by the Danube but connected by multiple bridges. On the other side I looked down on Visegrád, a much older capital of Hungary. It had several ancient buildings to visit, such as the 14th century Citadel, on a hill overlooking the Danube, and the 14th century palace. The town fell to the Turkish Ottomans in 1544 and the palace was buried under earth for many years until it was rediscovered in the 1930s. I arrived at the palace at 4.45 p.m. and, as it closed at five p.m., the ticket lady sternly told me I had only ten minutes. To compensate, I paid the rate for a sixty-two-year-old, although the cheeky woman, implied I could have passed for seventy and receive an even lower rate! Maybe I misunderstood…

The next day, I crossed the Danube on a barge pushed by a tug with a moustache painted on its bow. It landed at Nagymaros, a town on the opposite bank. The ferryman had to shoo the waiting, smiling children off the landing ramp before we could moor. As the Kéktúra takes a wide loop to the north through a forested national park with limited accommodation, I expected to be camping in the woods for the next two nights, so I stocked up on food. I chose some Granny Smith apples (not my favourite) as they could withstand being knocked about in my rucksack without too much bruising. This caused the lady at the checkout to burst into a stream of Hungarian and she was forced by my incomprehension to find an English-speaking colleague. It seemed that the Granny Smiths were an extortionate price (about sixty pence each) and I needed to be warned. Not knowing the correct price of apples in Hungary and considering the long queue behind me listening in, I assured her that was fine (me being a stupid Englishman with more money than sense). Armed with my apples, I followed the trail up the mountains to a viewpoint from which I could see the River Danube both to the north and south as it looped its way around.

I continued up to Nagy-Hideg-Hegy (which means "big cold mountain") where there was a Turistahaz (or Tourist House) signposted, allegedly offering food, drink and a bed. Such places were established for hikers by the state in the time of socialism in Hungary, hiking being an activity of which the state approved. Sadly, I have had little success with these establishments to date. Either they have been abandoned since the collapse of the state socialism, or they are closed with a telephone number on the door which I dare not ring with my non-existent Hungarian. In my most successful case a lady directed me to a nearby *panzio* (pension). The first two Turistahazs I passed today were overrun with children running around and noisily enjoying themselves. While beer was advertised, the bars appeared to be closed. The final Turistahaz of the day was on the top of Nagy-Hideg-Hegy. After a long climb, with many false summits, I was tired and sweaty so on reaching the place I was hoping for at least a beer. Things looked promising, the doors were open and a sign indicated that the bar was open but nobody was around. I rang the bell beside the bar and waited. As nothing happened, I rang it again for longer. This resulted in loud pop music being turned on. I waited some more, while reading the posters (apparently, I was intersecting the Jacobsweg again, the local name for the Camino de Santiago). Despite the loud music, no one turned up and after shouting a few 'hellos' through the kitchen hatch I gave up and went to look at the view from the mountain top. A kilometre or so away I camped among the trees and enjoyed some food I had brought with me at a nearby viewpoint with a large section of Hungary and Slovakia laid out in front of me.

As evening approached the following day, I reached the village of Szendehely. A crowd had gathered by the church so, curious, I wandered up to see. Shortly a small group of musicians processed across the street, playing accordion and tambourine, leading a wedding procession. There was the bride (in white), the groom and what I assumed were bridesmaids in lilac accompanied by their beaus. In the crowd of villagers, cake and refreshments were being passed around and I was fortunate to be offered a plastic cup of dry cider and two (very welcome) slices of cake. These unexpected occasions make my walks special. That night I camped by some sinkholes in the limestone hills leading to an extensive cave network. I was careful not to wander around too much in the dark in case I fell in one.

I had been walking through forests of beech and oak, up and down hills, with the occasional ruined castle, through small villages with single-storey village houses often with attractive verandas. Now there were more open fields and meadows with bright flowers such as harebells and cornflowers in great profusion, bees buzzing around them. Food, as ever, was an attraction. I had sour cherry soup and chicken with prunes one night when I stayed in some rooms in a village. Cake, or rather the expectation of cake, had a strong pull. A café, advertised with pictures on signs along the trail, caused me to hurry on, only to be disproportionately disappointed to find it closed. Somewhat grumpy, I had to make do with a Coke and ice cream from a nearby shop which would normally have been a great treat. Sometimes the coffee and cake were hidden in places behind frosted glass windows; you had to look at for the word 'Cukrászda'.

Holloko, a 'museum village', was on the route, with another ruined castle and a series of folk museums, restaurants and cafés, housed in traditional houses with whitewashed walls and tiled roofs, lining a cobbled street. A major tourist destination, at least for Hungarians. Little English seemed to be spoken or on display in the museums I tried (my fault of course for not speaking either Hungarian or German). However, in the printing museum, the curator earned his entrance fee by showing me through gestures, practical demonstrations and sheer enthusiasm how printing machines have evolved. Together we made a print on a hand-operated Gutenberg press.

For the next eleven days I walked over many mountains, on paths and tracks through the trees. I agreed with a pair of German hikers that there was a lot more climbing on the Kéktúra than we expected. Although there were some rocky outcrops, the mountains were rounded and not particularly high, and the trail in itself was easy to follow (except when made slippery by rain). It was simply the number of ascents and descents that tired the thighs. There was beauty in the walk, the bright green of the trees, oak, beech, pines on higher ground, and also locust trees, a species with which I was not previously familiar. Beneath the trees, golden-brown leaves gathered, left from last autumn. Where enough light reached the forest floor, fresh green growth brightened my way. Between the woods and in valleys, meadows of long grass grew interspersed with flowers, and, later in this section of my trip, there was grassland and fields of golden wheat. The flowers were a delight; white, yellow, shocking pink, blue, red, purple and white, ox-eye daisies lining my path through the meadows, yellow foxgloves in the woods, all kinds of flowers, of which I could name but one or two. I met some forest rangers, one of whom spoke English. He pointed out that as we were in a national park, they had a duty to preserve the variety of flowers as well as the birds and wildlife. The rangers asked how I found the Hungarian people. A difficult question to answer as, with my lack of Hungarian, social intercourse was difficult, especially as I am not by nature a conversationalist. In consequence, I inevitably miss a lot of things.

Sometimes, language is not required. In one village a cheery villager pointed upwards. Following his direction, I saw a stork in a large nest on top of a telegraph pole with a baby stork (a storklet?). Other wildlife I spotted included a deer, a baby wild boar, and later a small herd of wild boar hurrying out of my way. On several occasions there was the sound of something crashing through the undergrowth as I approached. One day a red fox crossed into my path, paused to look at me (while I tried to stay still pretending to be tree) and then headed off, unconvinced by my tree impression. This happened twice, the most foxes I have seen in a day since walking through London on the Thames path (Britain has a lot of urban foxes). Orange-spotted butterflies were fascinated with my black rucksack, collecting on it, for reasons best known to themselves and a pleasure to watch, prettier than the fat snails which appeared on the path when it rained and which I tried to avoid crunching.

As well as the joy of walking quietly through trees and meadows, with the occasional kilátó to climb and look out at the massed, mountains ahead, there were ruined castles and churches to visit. Castles invariably had a dramatic location with views over the surrounding countryside. Regec castle ruins were among the more spectacular, following the line of a ridge. Churches or holy places would appear in the woods, such as St Laszlo's pilgrimage site (he was apparently an 11th century king of Hungary) and a sizeable, but simple stone church once attached to a Cistercian monastery. I also came across a Jewish cemetery, one of a few I have seen on the E4 since Vienna, all lacking any post-war gravestones, a vestige of a Jewish community that no longer seems to exist.

Being limestone country there were also caves, of which Aggtelek cave was most famous. Arriving early after a night camping I enjoyed a morning coffee and a hamburger from a nice couple in the *'bufe'* by the car park, before proceeding on a guided tour of the caves as recommended by 'German Tourist', a famous blogger. The caves were good with some nice, broccoli-shaped stalagmites, and I liked the music they played in the 'concert hall' cave, although some coloured lights and laser beams would have helped the light show. I also should have taken a jacket as it was rather cool…

For accommodation I either stayed at rented houses, guesthouses or small hotels, or else camped either in official campsites or among the trees. On one occasion, expecting a few options and unsure whether I would reach the village that day, I had not booked anything. Unfortunately, all the accommodation was either closed or full. The lady at one took pity on me while my dry throat really (really) enjoyed a cold beer after a long, hot sweaty day, finding me a room at a nearby sports academy. I had dinner among ladies from Turkey's judo team, some powerful-looking young Serbian men and various other athletic-looking types. Clearly state-run, I had to sign eight pieces of paper to get a bed while the patient lady at reception typed in extensive details of my life history. When renting a house, a glass of *pálinka* was sometimes offered by way of welcome. This is a spirit, a clear plum brandy. You down it in one, it seems. Although quite strong you don't realise that until later…

after the third shot, one of my hosts was giving me a bear hug before his wife took him away. Owners did not always speak English, and, while there are some obvious transactions that gestures can accommodate, getting out your wallet to pay, handing over the key, being offered a glass of *pálinka*, unexpected topics can present a problem. On one occasion a lady tried to explain that if I wanted to eat anything that night, I needed to visit the village shop in the next ten minutes before it closed. Increasingly worried, she called in a neighbour with a few words of English to help. Accommodation was commonly self-catering, especially on the latter part of my walk on the Great Hungarian Plain section, and in the villages, there were usually no restaurants. Consequently, I would pick up a can of something at a shop to cook. Never quite sure what I was buying, the writing being Hungarian, my only clue was the picture on the front. I would empty the can into a saucepan and heat it until it started boiling and then assumed it would be fine.

When camping, mosquitos were an issue on hot, still days, forcing me to zip myself up into my inner tent in the evening, despite sweating in the heat. Then in the morning, I hurried to get packed up as the mosquitos buzzed around no doubt singing, "I smell the blood of an Englishman". As the dawn chorus started at four-thirty a.m. at this time of year, with its short nights, I was often up early. One of my more pleasurable experiences was rising early, walking through the trees for a few hours in the cool, soft morning light, listening to the birdsong (a loud symphony of tweets and twitters) and then having breakfast at a small village guesthouse, the walk having intensified my appetite. I chose ham and eggs to eat, mainly as they used the English (or possibly American) words 'ham and eggs'; everything else was only on offer in Hungarian. I did not have to worry too much about overeating. Signs posted along the trail informed me that the Országos Kéktúra was 1,159.82 kilometres long and I would need a massive 197,035 kilocalories to walk it—the graphics seemingly equating this to eating 646 hamburgers, 2,074 apples and 450 slices of what might have been bread.

The Great Hungarian Plain

The first big town for many days was Sátoraljaújhely, a name I was unable to pronounce when asked where I was heading for. An important milestone, nearby I left the main Blue Route (the Országos Kéktúra) shortly before it finished at Hollóháza, and joined the Great Plain Blue route or, in Hungarian, the Alföldi Kéktúra. For my walk it was also a dramatic change in landscape from the hilly landscape of the main Blue Route to the pancake flat of much of the Great Hungarian Plain. I would have no more hills to climb until I reached Belgrade in Serbia, 1,500 kilometres of walking on the flat. I began by thinking this could be a little tedious, but I was wrong, although it was a very different kind of hike, ideal for people who do not like walking uphill. Instead of wooded hills to look over I now saw huge fields stretching into the distance.

My guidebook was a bit dismissive of Sátoraljaújhely, a border town next to Slovakia, not far from Ukraine, but it had a sort of faded grandeur, with occasional buildings decorated with classical motifs and missing rendering. I ate a meal on the main, tree-lined pedestrianised street, watching the local girls and boys sitting on benches on opposite sides of the street, joshing and giggling (to my mind the lads had the sharpest haircuts, some barber around here was handy with the clippers). The Alföldi Kéktúra was created in 2000, much later than the main, much better known and more popular Országos Kéktúra I had been following, and, despite signs for it (and the E4 which it forms part of) outside the local tourist office, the people inside appeared unaware of its existence, or maybe I did not make myself clear when I asked if they had any information on accommodation along its route.

My first day on the Great Plain Blue Route began with a long walk along a busy road—fortunately not typical of the trail, which mainly follows tracks across farmland, through forests and on embankments beside rivers. As I walked south on that first, hot day, the mountains I had been walking across for the last few weeks grew gradually smaller as I looked back at them across flat, fields of green maize, golden grain or grassland with a few cows. The fields seemed enormous and the weather still, hot and sweaty. I stopped at a wayside bar for an alcohol free, lime shandy, called Radler (actually German for cyclist), much more refreshing than the sweeter Coca Cola or Fanta. I camped that night by a stand of trees, just on the edge of a field of long grass to avoid the mosquitos circling in the woods, listening to the sound of motorbikes racing up and down a nearby track. In the morning, after struggling through some overgrown and clearly rarely used sections of trail at the edge of fields, I reached one of the straight drainage ditches that were presumably responsible for changing the landscape from swamp into large areas of farmland. These drains, the straight tracks beside them, the big fields of wheat with no hedges and the occasional copses reminded me of the Fens in Britain. One difference was a flock of sheep cropping the grass on the banks of one of the drains and looking fat and healthy on it. They were escorted by a shepherd and his two dogs of indeterminate breeding which raced up to me barking aggressively. I stood my ground, turning to avoid them getting behind me, various sources had indicated that such sheepdogs can be very protective. The shepherd shouted commands at the dogs, waved his stick and walked towards me. After the usual exchange in which I indicated I was a stupid English person who did not speak Hungarian I checked (with hand gestures) that it was OK to pass through his flock so as to continue on my route. He said, "Egen," (yes) so I slowly moved through trying not to disperse his sheep, then moved steadily away while the dogs mounted a rear-guard fit of barking. Shortly after, I disturbed a deer which ran off, then stopped and turned around as if to check what I was, before trotting off. Later, walking beside a drain lined with poplar trees I disturbed a brood of storks which took to the air. I also disturbed herons. Birdsong filled the air. As I was to discover, the Great Plain is a paradise for bird watchers.

Barely half the land was agricultural on this section. There were extensive forests of poplar and locust trees growing in sandy soil, home to light brown deer with large antlers and white bottoms outlined with dark brown stripes. The white poplars looked particularly beautiful, the wind fluttering their leaves, showing off their white undersides like crowds of flirtatious maidens. An old, narrow gauge forest railway, now used by an old diesel train to bring picnickers from the city of Debrecen, ended in a forest clearing. From the top of the nearby kilátó, or observation tower, I could see just how extensive the forest was, not surprising as I had spent a few days walking through it. There were reed-lined lakes, drainage channels, noisy with the sound of croaking frogs, and rivers, including the great River Tisza, which I would later follow in Serbia.

Almost entirely flat, any change in height was normally imperceptible; however, in a few places low, sandy hills stood a few metres high, maybe ancient sand dunes? I 'climbed' to the highest point on the Great Plain, Hoportyo, on a slight rise above the surrounding land, a concrete post marked the summit, but the trees obscured any views.

South of Debrecen I crossed expanses of rough grassland between areas of conifers, maybe the soil too sandy for crops. Large birds of prey perched on the branches of some trees. Traditional wells had a distinctive arrangement to help lift the water out of the well. One length of raw timber formed a vertical pole, its top acting as a fulcrum for another length resting across it. At one end of this beam there was a rope for lifting buckets of water, and, at the other, a wooden counterweight to make the lifting easier.

There were plenty of towns and villages on the agricultural parts of the plain, usually with a small hotel or a holiday house to rent, and an opportunity to buy a coffee, Coke or cake, or else food for lunch or a meal in the evening. Arriving early at a small lakeside cabin I had booked, I called the owner and said I would wait in a nearby *'bufe'*, basically a small bar, usually a bit rough looking with mismatched chairs. Here I managed to get a beer and even better a free *pálinka*. The men seated in the bar were curious about what I was doing (few if any British people must reach this area), so when the helpful cabin owner arrived, who spoke some English, I answered various questions he translated: where was I from (England I said, strictly I am from Wales but that has less name recognition), how far did I walk each day (23 kilometres on average) and how heavy was my rucksack (quite heavy as I was carrying the means to make an evening meal, but usually around 15 kilogrammes)? Some nights I camped. On such occasions I had been hearing 'barking' in the crepuscular hours—not a dog but something else. Keen to find its source I peered out of my tent one night. On looking down a row of oak saplings I saw a deer against the twilit sky. After a few minutes it must have seen me too and slowly wandered off, still barking.

Many towns and villages had something to look at, a church (Reformed or Catholic), a park, or remains of some castle. The most unusual sight was a MiG-21 fighter jet rising out of a rose garden in the village of Gyulahaza, beside a bust of Yuri Gagarin, the first man in space. It was to celebrate the first Hungarian astronaut who was born here. I caught a bus into Debrecen for one night, an attractive and lively place with a large Reformed Church and an important place in the history of Hungary. Here, in 1848, there was a failed revolution against Austrian dominance.

The final few days were through farming country with huge fields of sunflowers in bloom, their yellow heads all pointing the same direction. Fields of maize extended south to where I knew from my GPS the Romanian border lay, just a few hundred metres away. Soon it was my final day of walking on this trip, to reach the village of Nagykereki, where I would catch a train back to Budapest.

A few kilometres down the farm track to Nagykereki from the village of Kismaria, I ran into problems. A man appeared behind me, shouting something, I presumed to his dog. Then he came up and grabbed my arm and refused to let go, dragging me back towards Kismarja. Aggrieved and resentful I protested, but he did not understand English and I did not understand Hungarian. He was then joined by a second man talking on his phone. They made it clear to me that I had to follow them back towards Kismarja. I indicated I was going the other way. I caught the word 'Romania', which made me think they were in some way concerned with refugees crossing the border (rather than robbing me) so I showed my itinerary and pointed to the word 'Nagykereki', and at the blue-and-white Kéktúra waymark on a nearby tree, but without effect. I then showed them my British passport—no help either. They did not offer any ID to me. At this point a car appeared and the men flagged it down. I was instructed to get into the car and the driver returned me to Kismarja, asking where I wanted to be dropped as we approached the village.

I headed off walking back to Nagykereki. Having hiked the E4 Long Distance European Path, of which the Alföldi Kéktúra is part since Spain, I was not going to be stopped at this point, but for my own safety, this time I walked along the main, tarmac road. After a few kilometres some police stopped me, checked my passport and asked what I was doing and where I had been. I explained last night I had camped in some woods, and showed my track on my GPS, proving where I had been that day and that I had not strayed into Romania. I gave the officer (who acted in a very professional manner) my itinerary for the trip and he rang his superior. He began reading out my lengthy itinerary, but did not get far. I heard the word 'GPS', and after a while it appears I was given the all-clear. They checked I had enough water for the rest of my walk and sent me on my way. I tried to determine what the problem was with the guys earlier, indicating they had grabbed my arm, but language difficulties limited our conversation. I gathered that the proximity of the Romanian border (the current border of the Schengen zone) was an issue, but not much more. With refugees trying to enter Europe in large numbers as a result of the Syrian civil war, and poverty or repressive regimes in their own countries, people were jumpy, not wanting this tide of humanity to arrive in their country.

While I have no problem with police checking on people, being manhandled by (I presume) civilians while peacefully walking a national and international footpath was disturbing and I found my hand shaking as I wrote down my address for the police. I was happy to catch a local train from Nagykereki, soothed by its 'bonk bonk bonk' sound as it slowly bounced along the old line to Debrecen, followed by a much faster train to Budapest and a flight home.

Swiss Jura: The E4 crosses many beautiful areas. In the above, the path follows the Jura Crest trail along the ridge of mountains in the northern part of Switzerland.

Pindus Mountains: In addition to crossing mountain ranges popular with walkers, such as the Bavarian Alps and the Pyrenees, the E4 took me through the Pindus Mountains in Greece, an alpine region in a country better known for its beach resorts and ancient ruins.

Catalan coast: There are many distant views from the E4, here down to the Catalan coast from the mountains of the Park Natural dels Ports.

Navacelle Gorge: Several gorges are visited by the E4, above is the limestone gorge of Navacelle in France.

Iron Gates: The Iron Gates of the River Danube feature on many river cruises, but the E4 gives a better view of this boundary between Serbia and Romania, note the barge passing through.

Vienna Woods: I walked on the E4 through many woods and forests; shown here are beech trees of the Vienna Woods in Austria.

Austrian Pusta: Not all of the E4 is through mountains and woods. A good chunk is across flat plains, as in the picture above, where the E4 crosses the "pusta" of Eastern Austria. Walkers are more familiar with the more mountainous areas of Austria such as Snow Mountain seen in the distance.

Sunflowers: A field of sunflowers on the Great Plain of Hungary. Beyond the field lies Romania.

Road with cypress: The E4 follows a variety of paths, tracks and roads. Here in Andalucía it follows this quiet road lined with cypress trees for 10 kilometres of easy walking.

Koncheto Ridge: At the other extreme, the E4 follows the crest of the Koncheto (or Marble) Ridge in Bulgaria. The wire rope visible in the foreground is provided to assist but just gets in the way. It is actually easier and less frightening than it appears (at least in good weather).

Great Hungarian Plain: A track on the embankment of a canalised river (out of view on the left) through farmland makes for gentle walking in Hungary.

Overgrown path: Sometimes the paths the E4 follows have become overgrown, as can be seen here in Spain. Note the red and white waymarks on the trees.

Camping: The accommodation available varies greatly, but sometimes camping is most convenient, as here in Spain.

Hotel: On other occasions I stayed in picturesque hotels, as here in Vercors, France.

Lovna Hut: Mountain huts provide a place to sleep in popular walking areas, as in the Lovna hut in Bulgaria, however you can find yourself sleeping rather close to other hikers in this dormitory accommodation when they are busy.

A day in the mist: Clear sunny skies cannot be guaranteed, here I was walking through the clouds in Spain.

Camping in snow: The "Beast from the East" struck Serbia as well as Britain in 2018, leaving me camping in the snow (not as cold as you might think).

Rain in Bavaria: Rainy days, here in Bavaria, are to be expected when walking the E4 or indeed any other long distance walk.

Cold front: A cold front approaching. Wind and rain followed as I camped on a ridge in Serbia.

Bear prints: Bear prints alongside my boot in Greece. Before I walked through the country I did not realise there were any bears there. They avoid humans, so you are unfortunately unlikely to see one.

Fire salamander: Most wild animals ran away before I could photograph them but this fire salamander was concentrating on its earthworm.

Furry cows: Cows, sheep, horses and goats were a common sight, but these cows in Bulgaria looked kind of cute, or maybe I had been too long on the trail!

Stork: Storks in Hungary beside the E4, I also saw them in Portugal.

Morella: Villages were a source of food and accommodation, but those in Spain were usually sited on a hill, topped by a castle, requiring a climb at the end of the day when I was feeling tired. The photograph shows Morella.

Chalbre: Villages in France always looked attractive, this is Chalbre.

Topli Do: In many places villages are falling into disrepair as younger people move out and older people die. This village is in Serbia, where posters of the departed are common.

Kinizsi Castle: As I walked the E4, I came across a lot of history and historic buildings. Kinizsi Castle is in Hungary.

Pindus bridge: This is an example of one of the ancient stone bridges in Greece, with a graceful arch across the river.

St Ioannis church: Numerous religious buildings (and also religious conflicts) are encountered on the E4. This is the interior of a mountain church in Greece.

Mountan top shrine: Little shrines and memorials are common; this one in Greece was on a mountainside above the clouds.

Bavarian shrine: A shrine in Bavaria in a Baroque style.

Votive Church: The Votive Church in Szeged, Hungary, built in thanksgiving after a flood of the city.

Kikinda Oilfield: A nodding donkey producing oil in Serbia in a field of maize beside the E4.

Wind turbines: Increasingly Europe is turning to renewable energy as in this "Avenue of Wind" in Spain, the E4 passes many wind turbine and solar power installations.

Flowers at the edge of a cornfield: Flowers brought joy to my soul whenever I saw them, these beside a track in Hungary.

Flower meadow: There were so many flowers I could not identify. I particularly liked the pink "dandelions" that I saw in Peloponnese meadows. Mary and George at Anavryti lent me a photo album which named them as Crepis Rubra.

Chapter 10: Debrecen to beyond Belgrade — a flat bit

Continuing across the Pusta

In September I returned to Nagykereki after a night in Debrecan, where the hotel keeper thought I was Ukranian as I put UK for my country on the registration document. At three-thirty a.m. I had an attack of diarrhoea and another at six a.m. I assumed it was the stuffed cabbage and Debrecen sausage I ate the previous night. A local dish, probably only requested by rare tourists. Drinking lots of water, I decided to forgo food until the evening, so it was just a small black coffee at the station before I caught the train back to where I left off last time (and a panic about where I put my phone). Leaving Nagykereki station I tried to be discreet as I walked through the village to avoid an incident similar to that on my previous trip. Not so easy when you are carrying a rucksack and a dog at every house barks long and loud to announce your presence. A group of men stood waiting for something. They stopped talking as I approached, I said a polite, *"Jó napot,"* and passed by without breaking my stride. Soon I was glad to be walking on a farm track through large fields of maize and sunflowers. The seasons had moved on since my last trip and the maize had turned from a luxuriant green to a dull, dry straw colour and the sunflowers no longer had sunny yellow flowers, instead hanging sad, grey heads. A lot of the walk was beside drainage ditches and there were thousands of little flies forming large swarms in the sky, constantly changing shape. In places the house martins were out eating some of them. Elsewhere a stork flew with lazy wing beats and a small lizard crossed my path.

I do not normally use a walking stick (or maybe I should call them trekking poles) but I did this time as a book advised it as a defence against dogs when walking in Serbia, a country I would reach later on this trip. It proved helpful here as well when a black dog raced up to me barking with bared teeth. He was clearly not wanting a pat! Fortunately, waving my stick helped keep him at a safe distance as I walked on, although he followed me for a while, waiting for an opportunity to strike.

Reaching Berettyoujfalu, a village where I had booked a room for the night, I was thirsty so stopped for a Pepsi at a bar. A couple drinking there tried some conversation but my lack of Hungarian made this difficult, so I showed them a card I had made with a translation provided by the author of the best website of the Kéktúra, Béla Horváth. I had asked him to write: "I am an English tourist walking on the Alföldi Kéktúra, I am not lost, I am not a refugee". His Hungarian translation was: *"Angol túrázó vagyok. Az Alföldi Kéktúrát járom. Nem tévedtem el. Nem vagyok menekült. Köszönöm!"*. They thought it very amusing. I was using Béla's account of his walk along the Alföldi Kéktúra as a guide. As it is written in Hungarian, I used Google Chrome's translation option to render it in English. This gave rise to some amusing translations such as, "Melon, the outlaw universe!", a response to being sold mineral water instead of being given tap water. Google also translated place names which could be confusing, so the village of Nagykereki became "Big Wheel".

Next morning, I had a culinary treat for breakfast. A stall at the edge of the village was selling *'langos'* and coffee. *Langos* is a deep-fried dough, slightly salty, and delicious, sometimes offered with cheese. As on many parts of this trip, I walked some of the day on the embankment beside a drainage canal. Possibly it was once a river that had been straightened and enclosed between embankments to prevent flooding, connected to a system of ditches that kept the land drained. Sometimes there were abandoned meanders, full of stagnant water left by these large-scale engineering works. On each side of these rivers were fields of crops, but the embankments themselves had grass cropped close by flocks of sheep guided by shepherds. Often willows grew beside the water. Later that day I followed a road through extensive flat grassland with distant groups of cattle. At night I stayed at some rooms *('szoba')*. The owner's daughter spoke good English and showed me pictures of her sister working on a cruise ship.

As I started along the embankment of a sizeable river, I was hailed by a man at the bottom of the slope. Recalling my previous experience and wanting no trouble I went down to see what he wanted. Although difficult as he had no more English than I had Hungarian, I understood he did not want me to proceed as I was heading towards Romania. He showed me his ID which indicated he was in the Polgárőrség, or civil guard organisation. I showed him the card that Béla Horváth helped me make and indicated I was going to the villages of Biharugra and Geszt. This seemed to work and he allowed me to proceed along the Kéktúra after telling me how he had been in London in 1999... or maybe that was when he tried to learn English and that I should learn Hungarian. Anyway, I smiled and was glad to proceed.

A kilometre or so later I was again called down from the embankment by some men on the riverbank by what I took to be a green, army jeep. It was not military but instead belonged to some fishermen, and, instead of another interrogation, they were offering me a welcome cup of coffee. Even better, they spoke English. They explained, among other things, that I was on a direct refugee route from the Romanian border. The refugees were told by people smugglers just to follow the river into Hungary and it would soon lead them to Budapest but in fact the waters eventually flow into Serbia, many days' walk away. The coffee and their friendly attitude gave me a boost and they reassured me that with my British passport I should be able to follow the Kéktúra safely along the border zone.

Soon after, I left the river and followed an abandoned railway line to the village of Körösnagyharsány. The station sign was still there although the line is much overgrown. Then it was across grassland on another embankment for a long stretch with Romania just a few hundred metres to the south. I was again waylaid by a man on a motorbike checking I was not going to Romania. Eventually I reached the road for Biharugra after edging past a flock of sheep. According to the map, the road passed next to lakes known for their birds, but they were well hidden by tall reeds and trees. However, at one point there was a side road to a raised observation platform with a sign describing the birds you could see. I could not see any of them. Possibly it was the wrong time of day for bird watching as in the evening I heard hundreds of geese on a nearby lake.

By a smaller lake at the edge of Biharugra, the border police interrupted me while I was halfway through a peach at a picnic table.

With sticky hands, trying not to drop my juicy peach, I dug out my passport. All was in order and they left me to finish my lunch. Then it was a long walk on open grassland followed by a large lake invisible behind the reeds. The map implies that you walk on water across the lake but (fortunately) it is misleading; the path, although overgrown for a short section, is largely dry and surrounded by reeds. Reeds were being harvested at one point: one man on the top of a lorry piled high with a mountain of reeds looking vaguely unstable and another man passing up further bundles.

On reaching the village of Geszt after a large field of maize and sunflowers, I hoped to visit Tisza Kastely, a stately home owned in the past by two rather important Hungarian prime ministers. As I entered the grounds, a security guard stopped me, told me it was private and that I had to leave. We then sat down as he explained its history, dating from three hundred years ago. It was currently being restored and was covered with scaffolding. Leaving town, the Kéktúra passes through a cemetery, somewhat overgrown, with a few bare bones showing! Many of the cemeteries I was passing had wooden boards to mark the graves, but this was of a better class with proper stone gravestones.

I walked across grassland with distant flocks of sheep, herds of cows and drifts of purple flowers, known as Hungarian statice. They are the type of flower you might use in a dried-flower arrangement. Often on this trip, the statice gave the grassland an attractive purple hue, looking a little like an impressionist painting. I set up camp that night in some woods, far away from anyone so I thought with only the sound of honking geese on the nearby, but invisible, lake. But soon my peace was disturbed by barking dogs and the sound of a distant engine. The immigrant issue and the hunting season (Béla warned me to be careful) was making me jumpy!

For the next ten days I walked across the Great Hungarian Plain, by fields, across grassland, beside canalised rivers and drains and through small towns and villages. In the huge fields large, lime-green machines laboured to harvest the maize and sunflowers, periodically filling lorries that pulled alongside them in a well-co-ordinated routine, leaving only rough stubble behind. Contrasting with this modern agribusiness, there were occasional smallholdings where an older couple might be handpicking the corn cobs. Although in general the farming is highly mechanised, there was still room around farm tracks and drainage ditches for wild flowers to bloom. Unlike in Britain there were no hedges or permanent fences, grazing livestock being controlled by a rather temporary looking, single wire electric fence, or else a shepherd or cowherd.

As I walked on the river embankments, I could count the kilometres with the white stone markers placed every 200 metres. A heron might rise from the water, or a V-shaped formation of geese fly overhead. Fishermen often dotted the river banks. It was by no means boring. There was something to see most days, the meanderings of the Kéktúra made sure you did not miss anything. One day it was an archaeological park, with artefacts from Neolithic times through the copper and bronze age at progressively shallower depths in the preserved excavation of a low hill—the hill itself seemingly created by the accumulated remains. At the top, the remains of the last period were of a medieval church and monastery. On another day it was the great bustard reserve, where these birds are being saved from extinction (the last native bird of this species in Britain was shot in 1832). I visited the grounds of Karoly Kastely, now an old people's home, but once owned by the Karoly family, one of whose grand houses I visited on a previous trip. One night I camped by a thermal spa, the hydrogen sulphide smell from the baths most offputting…, why would anyone think it healthy? Yet it seemed to attract middle-aged campers (some of the men with bigger bellies unwisely wearing rather small swimming briefs). To reach the historic and attractive town of Szarvas I needed to cross a river on a ferry; unfortunately, it was out of service, so I hitched back to the last town in a car with a friendly family and caught the bus to reach it by a more roundabout route. Later in my trip, approaching the village of Tompahat, a number of handsome horses and traps passed me. They were from a fête underway at the village. There I was treated to songs, music and a demonstration of ballroom dancing by local children, a magician and, as it became dark, fireworks, and a performance by a professional crooner. A short shower did not dampen the mood of the crowd, and the beer tent struggled to keep up with demand. Tired after my walk I went to sleep in the village's dormitory accommodation as the extravaganza continued.

In the mornings of my trek, I would seek out a bar, finding one even in the smaller villages where a small, strong coffee would revive me. I would see many people on bikes, taking children to school, shopping or off to work. I reflected that using bikes was far preferable to the polluting cars and 4 x 4s that crowd the street by the school near my home. Then I felt guilty as people here probably use bikes as they cannot afford a car, and one should not want people to be poor. Nevertheless, I felt sad that in years to come as Hungary increases in prosperity such villages will probably become clogged with cars on the school run, and the health and fitness of the inhabitants will suffer. In the hot afternoons, I would drop into a bar for a Pepsi, although in larger places I could maybe indulge in a cake, or in the evening enjoy a meal—a pizza, hamburger or sometimes something more Hungarian. On the walls of some bars, and also seen elsewhere, a map of Hungary would be on display, showing the country as it is today, set within an outline of Hungary as it was before the First World War when it was much larger, extending into Romania, Slovakia, Serbia, Slovenia and Croatia. These lands were lost as part of the Treaty of Trianon, dictated by the victorious allies of the war. Such maps, illustrating their former greatness, seemed to show people's nostalgia for when Hungary was a more powerful, more important country.

Prior to setting out I had consulted my podiatrist as I had been getting hard skin and blisters, particularly on the outside of my heels and she had diagnosed a problem with pronation, i.e. a tendency to start my stride with the outside edge of my heel. In hopes of correcting my wayward gait, she had supplied me with insoles with wedges attached. Sadly, these seemed to cause the blisters to form even more quickly and, after several days' walking, the wedges parted company with the insoles so I dispensed with them and was much more comfortable.

I left the Alföldi Kéktúra at Mindszent. After a hearty lunch in the town, I headed down the embankment of the Tisza River towards Szeged; it was a river I would follow deep into Serbia. Most days of this trip had been sunny, with blue skies and white fluffy clouds, but today the afternoon sky broke into thunder, flashes of lightning and heavy rain. I walked under the trees lining the river in the hope that the lightning would hit them not me. Fortunately, it had stopped by the time I picked a picturesque spot by the wide river to pitch my tent, a low mist collecting on the still water, the trees lining the banks, reflected in the water, their leaves starting to turn yellow. The next day I walked into Szeged and spent the afternoon looking at the splendid classical and art-nouveau architecture and squares of the city. The paintings inside the Votive Church impressed me. Echoing the fresco paintings of the Renaissance, they were clearly modern, dating from the 1930s when the church was built as a result of a vow taken by survivors of a great flood. That evening I enjoyed one of the best meals of this trip: turkey, sour cream and tarragon soup followed by catfish in paprika sauce, eaten while watching people walk by in a square.

Crossing Vojvodina — a province of Serbia

The next day was a milestone, when I walked down the side of the Tisza River to the border post with Serbia. I saw no traffic passing through and I am sure British people were rare as the Serbian border guard focused on the front cover of my passport slowly reading the words, "United Kingdom of Great Britain and Northern Ireland". Anyway, he let me through and I continued along the embankment of the Tisza, passing on my way a sign for the Iron Curtain (bicycle) Trail or Eurovelo number 13. The sign promised that cyclists would master "the line between reality and dreams" as you followed the line of the Iron Curtain through Europe. I would meet this trail again!

In each country the E4 was different, and presented its own challenges. In Serbia the challenge was to find where the route was intended to go. It was loosely described in a booklet called "Rambling through Serbia at a slow pace", but the maps were hardly detailed and, except in a few small areas, there were no waymarks or signs. Detailed maps suitable for hikers seemed to be unavailable in Serbia except in certain popular tourist areas. The electronic maps I acquired were best. I bought two from different cartographers for my GPS, which showed some of the footpaths, and Google Maps also helped. Prior to my trip I spent some time with Google Earth tracing out where the route must go, using the satellite photographs to follow it along farm tracks, and along the two faint lines left by vehicles driving along river embankments. It helped to look at various historical views, as tracks stood out better in some lights and photographs than others. This generally worked well except in wooded areas, where either the trees hid smaller paths or features I thought were paths were some other landscape feature.

My friends expressed more concerns about my walking through Serbia than any other country. This was understandable as Serbs were involved in atrocities in the recent Balkan wars (as were other ethnic groups) and appear as the bad guys in a number of films. Initially, the people I met showed an expressionless, inscrutable exterior, unlike the vaguely friendly smile or greeting one might expect in Britain. However, this was misleading, although it often needed a *"dober dan"* (good day) from me to break the ice. Although there were exceptions, in general I found Serbians the friendliest of all the nationalities I met as I walked across Europe, especially on my second trip in the southern part of the country, a complete contrast to their general depiction. In part, I suspect it was because I was so unusual and people were curious. There are many long-established Serbian mountain associations which organise group trips into the countryside; however, there is no tradition of long-distance walking unlike in neighbouring Hungary, or indeed of walking alone. *"Sam?"* they would say, meaning "alone?". Outside the Belgrade area I met very few people who were not Serbian in some sixty days of walking, and only one person from Britain. He was there as he had married a Serbian woman, so someone walking long distances, alone, and a foreigner was definitely of interest.

As I always do before a trip, I checked Britain's foreign office travel advice. According to the website, crime tended to be in larger cities and it did not indicate Serbia was of a higher risk than other European countries. I found some advice about "not mentioning the (recent Balkan) war". In general, I took this advice but on the one or two occasions I broached the subject. There was a feeling that Serbia was unfairly treated compared with other Balkan groups whose war crimes had not led to high-level individuals being punished, and a sadness for friends and relatives lost in the fighting. Important parts of their history took place in Kosovo, which was felt to be part of Serbia.

For my first three days of walking through Serbia the way was easy to find as it was on one or other embankment, of the tree-lined River Tisza. This led me to my first night's accommodation at a small guesthouse beside the river, set in a park by a yellow suspension bridge, in the small town of Novi Knezhevac. One of the challenges was learning a bit of Serbian and trying to understand the Cyrillic letters. Having practised a few key phrases in Serbian, I tried some out in this my first town. No doubt my pronunciation was terrible as I was not understood and people replied in Hungarian! Maybe, I should not have been surprised, as this area was once part of Hungary, and in the northern part of Serbia Hungarian is, I discovered, widely used as the first language. Fortunately, as I sat down to dinner that night, another guest at the hotel spoke some English and I was able to agree to the food that the guesthouse owner was suggesting. This included a *'shopska'* salad, with which I would become very familiar as I travelled through Serbia, Bulgaria and Greece, where it is renamed Greek salad. It consists of tomatoes, cucumbers and a white cheese similar to feta, plus any additions the chief might select, such as sliced onions or peppers. My fellow guest told me the alternative was Serbian salad: tomatoes, cucumber and peppers, sometimes quite hot. The guesthouse owner took my passport away, returning it with a slip of paper registering my presence with the police as a foreigner here.

I continued down the Tisza, passing farmland similar to that in Hungary, although the harvesting machines seemed a bit older and more varied. I noticed hay bales were of the old rectangular type rather than the larger, modern circular ones. The landscape was flat. Together with the Great Plain of Hungary it forms part of the Pannonian Plain, which extends almost to Belgrade. As in Hungary, flocks of sheep were led along river embankments, and also herds of cows. On my second night in Serbia, I stayed in the town of Senta. A place worth visiting for its (Hungarian) Art Nouveau architecture. The people in the tourist office were very friendly and seemed pleased to see me, booking my next night's accommodation for me (in Hungarian). When I returned to a coffee shop for breakfast next morning the waiter welcomed me back. It rained as I walked down the Tisza to the next town of Ada. When I asked the hotel receptionist if there was anything to see in the town, she said there was nothing, although I thought the riverside park would have been pleasant on a sunny day. Today it was raining. I had dinner in the hotel's socialist era dining room: large, with attempts at grandeur, fancy lighting and a highly polished floor, more ballroom than dining room for a small number of guests. I was attended by a tall thin man; grey hair, dark jacket and trousers, white shirt with no tie, an attempt at old-world smartness from something of a bygone age.

As I left the town in the morning, people were picking walnuts off the pavement where they had fallen off trees. Walnut trees seem common in this part of the world. Following the maps in *Rambling through Serbia*, I left the River Tisza and headed east across the treeless plain to the town of Kikinda. Initially it was along what the map indicated was a farm track, but which was now a modern, two-lane tarmac road, not busy but with some very fast cars. Later it was along the side of the Kikinda canal.

Approaching Kikinda I stopped to view an oil well in a field of maize, having earlier seen a drilling rig, its mast rising high above the plain. I had started seeing gas wells in the southern part of Hungary, and they continued in Serbia, usually smartly painted in yellows, blues or reds. While the gas wells were just a collection of valves on top of a pipe coming out of the ground, oil wells were more distinctive with their slow moving 'nodding donkeys', more correctly called beam pumps. Some were nicely painted in the local company's colours of blue and red. Seeing them appear in the mist one morning later in my trip, I found them attractive, sitting in the crops, their regular movement up and down reassuring and somewhat soporific.

Reaching Kikinda I found a festival filling the main pedestrian area of this major town. Between the cafés and bars and the pastel-coloured classical buildings there was a stage with a singer, lots of stalls, balloons, a funfair and children dressed as something rustic with sunflowers, pumpkins and sacking. A harvest celebration maybe? After some refreshment I headed to the guesthouse I had booked on the outskirts of town. Unfortunately, it was not at the location indicated by Google or the online booking site. In addition, no one answered the phone number supplied with the booking and the local people I asked did not recognise the street name. I kept being directed to the Hostel Kruna. Arriving there for want of my chosen destination, the very helpful proprietor directed me to where her competitor really was. Once there, an hour or more later than I had indicated when booking, there was of course no one to let me in. Eventually I gained entry, and then wearily went for a pizza at a handy place across the road.

I continued along the Kikinda canal next morning. These canals, or canalised rivers and their embankments date from when it was part of the Austro-Hungarian Empire. Although used for land drainage, they were also designed for navigation and I saw quays for loading and unloading. Maybe there were more barges on the river in earlier times. I only saw a few on my walk and they were not working, and there was no sign of any tourist boats. Many fishermen were enjoying the Saturday sunshine at spots nearer the town. Later I met a cowherd who tried hard to engage me in conversation in a few languages, which did not include English. Several times people I passed said a word sounding like *"peshachenyai"*. I thought they might have asking me if I was a fisherman thinking of the French word for fishing *(pêche)* but eventually I discovered *'pešačenje'* or, in Cyrillic, "пешачење", meant a hike or maybe hiker, so after all, a simple yes, or *"da"* would have sufficed. Dogs were a nuisance and a worry. On a number of occasions, they rushed me, barking. They were either all black or all white in colour, of medium size with a furry coat. One never knew whether their mad barking would escalate to biting. Serbia was classed a high-risk country for rabies (possibly due to the lack of data) and although I had received a course of the rabies vaccine almost twenty years ago, my doctor's surgery advised I would need two boosters if bitten. At a minimum this would seriously disrupt my trip.

The night after leaving Kikinda I had been planning to camp, it being too far to reach the next town. According to my map, among the acres of farmland, a few trees surrounded the ruins of some medieval church, duly signposted as "of the utmost historical importance" and to which I headed both to see this monument and in the hope of camping there. The church had been burnt down by the Turks in the 16th century and never rebuilt. An atmospheric place, there were a number of people around when I arrived, so after a look around I kept going, camping in a field of stubble beside a little used farm track as the sun set, big and blood red on the horizon below low clouds. I hoped the sharp stubble would not damage the thin groundsheet of my tent, a new one for this trip— fortunately, it passed the test.

In the morning I crossed a nature reserve with (apparently) a salt lake that was hidden by the surrounding rushes, reaching the town of Novi Becej for a morning coffee. There was a bust of another member of the ubiquitous Karoly family, descendants of whom I had become familiar with on my walk through Hungary. This particular representative was still remembered with wreaths, the ribbons in the colours of the Hungarian flag on the plinth. The town had a pleasant promenade beside the River Tisza which I briefly re-joined before following the DTD (Danube-Tisza-Danube) canal out of the area. Leaving the canal, I crossed the Rusana grassland national park, disturbing a sleeping cowherd and his charges, to reach the spa town of Melenci. The motel I was targeting for the night was closed but there were several signs for rooms (*'sobe'* in Serbian). With the help of a passing neighbour, who shouted for the owner, I managed to gain a small apartment for the night in the owner's garden. Fortunately, the owner's young son spoke remarkably good English for his age. After checking in I wandered down to Banya Rusanda, at the edge of a nearby lake. This was a health facility, and clearly popular, with plenty of people in wheelchairs or with walking aids. The lake itself was largely mud; of the birds it was alleged to shelter there was no sign. The tap water smelt strongly of hydrogen sulphide (a bad-egg smell) no doubt associated with the thermal springs in the area. As my guidebook stated, Serbian tap water is safe to drink but you may prefer mineral water.

Zrenjanin was the next town, and it rewarded my day's walk beside another section of canal. It appeared that I had booked a suite at the Hotel Vojvodina, the best hotel in town, which overlooked the pedestrian square near the centre. Although costly by Serbian standards, it was inexpensive to my British wallet, as were most things in Serbia—a good reason to visit. The square had fountains lit at night by various colours and surrounded by august, but attractive, buildings, many dating from the 19th century and tastefully painted. At the tourist office the two staff were most helpful and seemed excited to see me, taking a lot of effort to book my next few nights' accommodation. This was not so easy as the tourist offices in Serbia only seemed to have information on their local area. They had to ring the tourist office in the neighbouring town to help find me suitable lodgings.

Following the Becei River out of Zrenjanin, I paused to watch men fishing off a bridge with nets about one metre square on the end of a length of rope. Their buckets suggested they were catching some edible-sized fish, possibly carp. Fish featured prominently at my hotel that night, located as it was next to fish farms at the edges of a lake. I chose the perch for dinner. It tasted fine, but separating the fine bones made eating a slow process. It reminded me of fishing for perch from the Grand Union canal in my youth, which we returned to the water after catching them.

Opposite the hotel was the Carska Bara nature reserve. I followed some of its paths among trees and reeds beside a shallow channel disturbing ducks and a heron, spotting what might have been a great egret through the rushes.

Continuing across the plain I zigzagged on farm tracks, overgrown paths and small roads tarmacked or cobbled which was my best effort at trying to reproduce the route illustrated in *Rambling across Serbia*. After camping one night among bushes, beneath some night flying birds, I reached the village of Uzdin, with a church reputed to be the most beautiful in the area. However, I preferred the retro café that looked unchanged since the 1950s where I bought a duplo espresso and drank it while watching a Serbian black-and-white film on TV with local men reading their papers over coffee and three schoolchildren drinking milk.

The next day, I was in Padina where I had a room booked in a traditional house. In this area the houses that line the broad avenues were single-storey, detached with tiled roofs; their windows often outlined with paint or brickwork. The older ones sometimes had fancy curved frontages or patterns worked into the exterior plasterwork. There would be gates leading to a courtyard and there might be a storehouse made of slatted wood, for storing cobs of maize. The lady of the house I stayed at tried her hardest to speak some English, referring to a phrasebook that gave questions she might ask in English. Unfortunately, they omitted to provide translations of any answers, so she arranged for a student living nearby to come and talk to me in English while a large dinner of sausages, roast potatoes, salad and bread was prepared for me. In addition to some background on Serbia, the student also told me I was not the first person to follow the E4 across Serbia, a French person having come before me, who complained about the lack of a clear route. Was I only the second person to follow the E4 in Serbia I wondered?

Breakfast next morning was so generous that the leftovers also served me for lunch and supper. The landscape was beginning to change to one of slight undulations and dry valleys. These low hills seemed to be dunes of windblown loess (silt). In places the track cut through the soft sediment. There were a couple of old wells with a large, wooden capstan-type arrangement for lifting the water. I was surprised the water level was so deep. Google showed a hotel in the town of Alibunar where I hoped to stay, but it did not exist or had long since closed. The tourist office had also closed, at least for the day. After posing for selfies with some passing kids, a group of youths with some useful English and a good knowledge of British Premier League football teams pontificated on the accommodation options in Alibunar and after some discussion among themselves, agreed there were none. It was however agreed that the grass and tree covered low sandy hills of the Deliblatska Peščara would be a good place to camp if a bit far away to walk. So, declining an offer of beer as it was late in the afternoon, I headed off, being careful not to cross the zebra crossing unless the 'green man' was illuminated, having been warned that the police were very keen on prosecuting people for jaywalking. After crossing fields busy with harvesters, I reached the Deliblatska Peščara close to sunset. This area is composed of ancient sand dunes, now covered with rough grass, small trees and holiday cabins. I camped on some tussocks of grass, around which I shaped my body to sleep, soon after reaching the area and before night fell.

Continuing over these fossil dunes in the morning I discovered my first red-and-yellow E4 signs and waymarks in Serbia, which caused me a disproportionate amount of excitement! Further excitement followed as I was able to buy breakfast at a nearby restaurant. This set me up for a long forty-nine-kilometre day, first a pleasant walk across the dunes, then along roads, or tracks across farmland to my hotel at Pančevo. A much appreciated 'Lav' beer followed (probably not the best name for a beer).

The next day I reached Belgrade (or Beograd as it is known). After failing to find the route through some riverside woods, I followed a cycle path, crossed the River Danube for the final time on my walk across

Europe, and walked beside roads into the centre of town. In 1981, when I was a student, a few of us drove to Greece in an old Hillman Hunter car which broke down every few hundred miles. We drove through Belgrade, stopping to change some traveller's cheques. At the time, it seemed grey and unwelcoming. Since then, it seems greatly changed with busy pedestrian areas, pavement cafés, buskers and artists selling their paintings. That evening I strolled along the promenade of the Kalemegdan gardens by the old fortress, to view the sun setting over the River Sava with the selfie-snapping couples and happy, family groups. It is at romantic times like these I miss my wife not being with me…

Down the Danube from Belgrade

I wanted to walk beyond Belgrade on this trip so that my trek to Sofia would be more manageable on my next visit, so I spent the next eight days following the E4 as it loosely tracked the Danube downstream. Very different from my walk across the great Pannonian plain, there were low hills as well as river floodplains as I walked through urban areas, apple and cherry orchards, vineyards, grassland and trees. There were moments of great beauty, such as low mist overflowing the banks of the River Danube in early morning and the walls of Ram Castle rising up from the river in the blue sky. There were also some pretty ugly bits: fly tipped rubbish piled up beside the track; industrial areas, and strip mining, although such things are not uncommon where I live in Wales.

I started by threading my way south through a series of pleasant parks, the outskirts of Belgrade with its red-roofed houses, and some rough ground with Michaelmas daisies to reach the highest mountain on this trip, Avala. At the top of its wooded slopes there was a memorial to the Unknown Soldier which I tried to visit but was stopped by policemen. It seems the president of Greece was visiting and had not been told to expect me. So instead, I visited the nearby TV tower, bombed by NATO in 1999 (I was informed of this more than once by various written sources) and subsequently rebuilt to look a bit like a rocket at its base. I bought the "viewing station plus beer in the tower's café" ticket. The beer tasted good after sweating up the mountain and sitting in the bar high up in the tower was a warmer and generally more pleasant way to view the scenery compared with the lookout platform, although a heavy haze rendered the outlook somewhat indistinct.

Lunch the next day was on a boat moored on the Danube during which I watched long barges, low in the water, travel up and down the river as cormorants dived for fish and gulls gathered in floating groups. The Neolithic archaeological site nearby had a small museum containing clay figures with oversized sexual attributes. Heading down the river, sometimes close to its banks, sometimes on a ridge beside it, I again crossed the Sultan's Trail. Apples were being picked and, in the yellowing, evening light, elderly tractors returned to houses in a village near my lodgings with trailers full of fruit and apple pickers. I saw one lady even sitting side saddle on a tractor's bonnet; a more relaxed (if less safe) attitude than in Britain (where roll-over protection would be required). Some village houses had fences, gates and arches decorated with purple, pink and white ribbons, presumably celebrating a wedding or birth. I visited Smederevo's 15th century castle. A fortification of impressive size, it would have been a formidable barrier to the Turks, something I contemplated over a slice of Opera cake at a café beside the Church of St George in the town's main square.

After Smederevo, the E4 takes a circuitous and somewhat underwhelming route heading east, south-west, south, north-east, and finally north, crossing the floodplain of the River Veliki Morava, the extensive twists and turns in part necessitated by a notable paucity of bridges over the river. Eventually, however, my peregrinations were rewarded by an iron truss bridge comprising a single-lane road shared with a railway line. Old brick buildings beside the bridge with gun slots suggested its strategic significance. Reaching the Viminacium Roman site, anticipating some cultural input, I was disappointed that the tour on offer did not fit in with my timing. I had hoped to see what had once been a major fortification and city for two legions, its mausoleum reputed to house the remains of a Roman emperor. The archaeological site was surrounded by an open-cast mine and large draglines could be seen in the distance. Much of the archaeological work was completed ahead of the remains being destroyed by mining.

My final full day walking on this trip was perhaps the most beautiful. It started cold. As I rose early from my wild camping spot, a low mist was clinging to the ground beneath blue skies, softening the lines and obscuring the base of trees, giving everything a grey wash and an otherworldly feel until the sun rose high enough to light up the yellowing leaves of the trees by the river. Ducks ran and flapped into the air as I passed. Gradually Ram Castle revealed itself on a promontory in the river beside a hill. The castle was closed so I climbed the hill behind to enjoy a breakfast of drinking yoghurt and chocolate. There was an excellent view back up the river to a U-shaped island left by the higher water level created by a dam some distance downstream. Higher up the path, the view was hidden by pine trees so I took a diversion off my planned route to view the river downstream. The river looked like silver in the reflected light from the morning sun, appropriate as I was heading for a place which in English means 'Silver Lake'. Sunlight was also reflected off flakes of mica in pieces of schist in the track—schist being the type of hard rock that forms the hill here, forcing the Danube into a narrow valley. Romania was now on its opposite shore. Going off track through the trees to regain my planned route, I dropped down to the village of Zatonje, briefly joining the Eurovelo Cycle 13 Iron Curtain route as I did so.

The next day it was an early, and overcrowded, bus from Veliko Gradište back to Belgrade. The driver was having a good laugh with the girl next to me while also answering his mobile phone as we passed places that I had visited on foot a few days before. As at the end of each trip I was looking forward to seeing my wife again, marvelling that I again had managed to walk such a distance (945 kilometres or 590 miles).

Chapter 11: Beyond Belgrade to Sofia — a sunny welcome in snowy Serbia

Through the Homolje Mountains

In the spring of 2018, the 'Beast from the East' swept in from Siberia bringing heavy snowfalls across Europe. My flight to Belgrade was booked for 20 March. In most years the city would be snow free at this time of year but, before I left, the forecast indicated snow falling for the next two days. I should have delayed my trip, but refused to consider it. My mother had died at the beginning of the year. The last few weeks of her life had not been easy for any of my family, so, after the funeral and such matters as needed to be arranged following her death, I wanted to experience something completely different. In that I was successful.

Recognising the potential for cold weather I had purchased a lightweight, three-quarter-length airbed to lift me off the cold earth (this came with a free repair kit which did not inspire confidence), a synthetic, insulated padded jacket, lightweight merino 'long johns' and lined, winter hiking trousers. In addition to my winter gloves, I added a pair of thin liner gloves (which you wear underneath your other gloves) for extra warmth, they also proved useful for fiddly operations in the cold. Otherwise, it was my normal kit for cooler weather, including gaiters, waterproof trousers (that I also used as an extra layer to keep my legs warm) and a cosy, synthetic sleeping bag with a comfort level of zero degrees Centigrade.

When I arrived at Belgrade, there was plenty of snow on roofs and in parks, highlighting the tops of tree branches, hedges and walls, but the roads and pavements were largely clear that evening as I walked through busy evening streets to a quiet restaurant. The restaurant was suffering from the lack of tourists at this time of year; I felt sorry for the girl outside trying to drum up custom, the snowflakes gathering on her hat and coat glinting in the streetlights. Catching the bus the next day, I returned to Veliko Gradište, driving through a countryside under a coat of white,

163

snow ploughs keeping the road clear. I walked through the town to a promenade beside the Danube as flakes of snow were falling. Visibility was so poor the far side of the river was invisible, but it was ice free. Following farm tracks and small roads I walked beside the Danube on its floodplain, by snow-covered fields with clusters of bare trees. A flock of storks were preening themselves in the distance. I joined the Eurovelo 6 and 13 cycle trails briefly (the Iron Curtain route again). Reading the small print on the sign, which encouraged you to "please lower your expectations", I felt a frisson of momentary deflation. However, I reached the town of Golubac and my hotel for the night without discomfort, and even with some enjoyment. My pork escalope, wrapped around some cheese at dinner that evening was enormous (although I managed to finish it). I would need the energy for the next day. Checking the forecast again I noted that two days of snowfall were again expected.

The next morning, I continued down the Danube as the mountains each side closed in, the road digging into the side of the cliff beneath overhanging rock. Arriving at the fortress of Golubac, built in the 14th century at a dramatic location beside the Danube, I found it partially encased in scaffolding and closed for restoration, although the café was open. While I enjoyed a morning coffee, the barista, having no one else to serve, told me that the first cruise ship would arrive soon, full of Americans, and recommended the 360-degree view from a summit I would soon be passing. It was a steep climb up through trees to that point, a little off my route, but the views while climbing, looking down to the castle on its rocky promontory by the river, in a landscape of white snow and bare grey trees, were impressive; the large fortress small compared with the size of the Danube and the surrounding mountains. Ahead of me stretched many more tree and snow-covered mountains belonging to the Homolje range, through which the E4 would make a large "U", taking me several days of walking. Initially, the five or six inches of snow did not cause too much of an issue. I had the hills to myself; only once did I see human footprints, although there were many animal prints. I passed a few buildings, some in a state of decay, their mud walls partially washed away to the wooden laths within the timber frame.

As the day progressed, snowfall resumed and the snow became progressively deeper as I crossed woodland and fields. One of the problems with snow is that you cannot see what is beneath it, so I stumbled several times on hidden branches and ruts, and once put my foot into a deep puddle, wetting my sock. At one point I fell into a deep snowdrift and struggled to push myself up against its softness.

As I approached my final summit, Golo Brdo, a four-wheel-drive came along the track, beeping his horn at me, for reasons best known to himself, as he did not stop. While enjoying the achievement of reaching this final high point, I noticed the water I carried was starting to freeze, threatening the integrity of my precious water bottle. It was time to lose height and find somewhere to sleep for the night. After steeply dropping into the valley, following car tracks in the snow, I hit the road which took me to Tumane. On reaching this Serbian Orthodox monastery, I was called over to a building nearby, flooded with warm light in the gathering dusk. I was offered a glass of local plum brandy by a friendly bunch sitting at a long wooden table, which certainly provided inner warmth, while the stove beside me toasted my outside. One of the men, called Dragon, showed me around the church and its relics: an icon brought from Russia by monks fleeing communism, and the remains of two saints. The monastery was founded back in the 13th century but the church had been rebuilt many times and the frescoes repainted. They showed scenes from the Bible and paintings of saints, all looking very solemn. My hosts then kindly gave me dinner: vegetable stew with pickled vegetables, and bread, but no meat as it was Lent. For this they asked only a donation. The monastery guest house was full so I asked if I could pitch my tent in the monastery compound, which they agreed to. I was immensely grateful to these hospitable folk, for making me welcome by their stove on such a wintery night.

I woke the next day to curious sliding noises that I had not heard before. It was the snow gathering on the sides of my tent, periodically slipping to the ground in miniature avalanches. After decamping and admiring the various animals (turkeys, ostriches and a donkey) kept by the monastery in the pens next to where I camped, I was kindly offered coffee while the animals were fed and then started on my way. As I found on a number of occasions, the track out of one settlement and into the next settlement were often pretty good, but between the two, usually at some high point, the trail would be overgrown, no longer used by people walking between valleys. I battled my way through to the next village, where the unbroken snow covering made it difficult to see where the road went. Inadvertently I walked into a family's backyard. I then had trouble convincing the owner of the yard (and then his wife, daughter and a passing friend of his) that I actually knew where I was going. After shaking off my helpers, who could have been forgiven for thinking me a little unhinged and were encouraging me to take a road route to Kučevo, the next town on my itinerary, I found my planned track out of town into the surrounding hills. Two days of snow continued to be forecast.

A long climb followed as I pushed through snow to the next summit (Rakobarski Vis). The snow become thicker the higher I climbed. Looking back, I could see lots of mountains, blanketed in white, extending far into the distance surrounded by white fields, grey clouds, pregnant with snow, and black, bare trees. I was struggling to break trail through areas of deep snow. Eventually I reached the summit. There was an aerial and a building associated with it and although the building was closed, the steps made a convenient and sheltered place to sit and eat some lunch: a roll, cheese and oranges. Unfortunately, I had already dealt with the chocolate, which I struggle to avoid eating (very soon after buying it). While munching, I pondered on the many snowy mountains I could see, a number of which I would have to climb over. Continuing laboriously on, up and down trails, I was very pleased by the eventual sight of the snow-covered roofs of Kučevo. Just as I entered the edge of town the street lights came on, looking like brilliant jewels in the valley below among the winter gloom. The hotel where I stayed had some bad reviews online. They were justified, although to be fair the waiter-cum-general troubleshooter was very helpful; without him pushing from the outside, shutting my bedroom door from the inside for the night might well have been impossible.

The next morning, I stocked up with food at the local bakery and at an open-air market. Some of the stalls were just tables with people's own produce for sale: dried chillies, honey and some onions. For the next four days, I continued through the snowy hills and mountains, each night stamping out a flat platform on the snow for my tent. With my airbed beneath my torso and my rucksack under my legs I was surprisingly warm and comfortable at night, even my feet, although ice would gather on top of my groundsheet. Putting on stiff, frozen boots in the morning was not so pleasant but after an hour or so the ice had melted. I kept my water bottles in my sleeping bag to avoid them freezing.

Various landmarks come and went, such as: the caves at Ravništarka (closed for the season); Mount Vrh Štubej (940 metres); Gornjak Monastery, and the Krupajsko Spring. The snow slowed me down, and pushing through the deep drifts tired me. Beneath the snow the track could be rutted which made me slither around. I saw few footprints other than my own, although one group of people had clearly recently climbed the Vulcan Mountains. I perhaps should have followed their footsteps, but not knowing where they were going, I kept to my planned route towards the summit of Mali Vulcan. This was a path through the trees, much of which was waymarked, but, as the path was invisible beneath the snow, I stumbled and slipped on hidden branches. I was glad of my trekking pole which stopped me falling several times, although the basket on the bottom of the pole sheared off, with no great loss as it tended to grow into a ball of frozen snow. Eventually I joined another path, rejoining the footprints I had seen early. This made the walk down the mountain much easier.

An older lady answered my call at Gornjak Monastery where I thought I might be able to stay, or at least visit the church, but the language barrier proved too much and she clearly indicated I should take myself off, so I camped a little way up the valley at a picnic site. I had more success at Krupajsko Spring. This is a spot where a whole river rises out the limestone rock, just like that! The nearby café was probably closed but a man in a white van was visiting and he arranged for both of us to buy a coffee there, which a lady in black was happy to serve. Somehow, I communicated in answer to some question that I was heading up into the Beljanica range; their expressions suggested they thought this an odd and possibly foolhardy thing to do.

While the snow was now slowly melting in the valley, on the higher ground there was plenty around. I pushed on through the mist and falling snow the next day trudging by ghostly trees through snowdrifts, slipping into unseen ruts left by forestry vehicles. It drained my energy despite frequent rests to slow my breathing and limit the stress on my knees. During such rests my body, heated by the exertion, rapidly cooled as I quickly put on my padded jacket, before removing it as I started off again a few minutes later to avoid overheating. Progress was extremely slow. I thought of turning back; the lack of footprints, tyre tracks or noise to break the silence showed that nobody was around and I began thinking of someone who had recently had a heart attack as I listened to the rapid thumping of my own organ. Then I came across a single-lane road I had long been expecting from maps and, joy to behold, the snow had been cleared (or a least compacted) by a bulldozer a day or so ago. There were even car tracks! Walking on the tracks of the bulldozer was comparatively easy now. This was my salvation and, as I reached the highest point on the road, I was moved to start thanking God. Then I saw the abandoned bulldozer. The cleared road ended shortly after. To continue I had to break a trail through snow about 50 cm deep and thicker in drifts, hard to get through. I contemplated following the bulldozer tracks in the other direction, taking me south, but that was completely the wrong direction. Reasoning that as the road now dropped in height from its highest point of 1,260 metres to 800 metres the snow covering should become thinner and easier to walk through, I decided to push on and so it proved. By 800 metres the snow was a more reasonable 6 cm in thickness, wet and slushy. My feet were not enjoying the constant soaking and there were areas of snowdrifts making for particularly hard going, but I was progressing. Visibility improved as I descended and there was even a period when a weak sun came out, making the mountain landscape look a lot more appealing. I passed rocky peaks and deep valleys mainly wooded with firs and deciduous trees, a moss-covered waterfall, and some mountain farms on flatter sections, although none seemed inhabited, or so I thought. Towards the end of my walk that day I heard voices, the first since the previous afternoon, then joined car tracks and eventually a four-wheel-drive passed and offered a lift. Tempting, as it would have been to accept, I had almost finished crossing the Beljanica range in difficult conditions and it seemed a shame not to complete this possibly foolhardy achievement. Instead, I camped in some trees by the roadside. I could have accepted a lift to the next village of Zagubica, or walked there arriving late, but I had not been able to confirm that any accommodation existed in the town or whether transport to somewhere else was available. If there was not, I could be stuck in a town with nowhere suitable to camp.

It turned out that Zagubica did have accommodation at a restaurant beside where another river, the River Mlava, just appears out of the ground. I arrived in time for a breakfast of omelette and bread so fresh it was hot to handle. However, it was not as early as I thought as, unbeknown to me, the clocks had gone forward the previous weekend. Seeing a sign saying *'sobe'* (rooms) I asked for one, having decided to call this a rest day after the exertions of the past few days and a strong desire for dry socks. After some interpreting by the cook, I was safely in my room. I washed the clothes I had been living and sleeping in for the last four days and, joy of joys, the sun was shining. Exploring the town later I found a well-kept pedestrianised main street (although the other streets had potholes). I bought some provisions and a coffee, yoghurt and strudel confection from a bakery for lunch, and ate them outside in the sun. More my idea of a long-distance walk!

From there I crossed a rural, flat, farmed valley from which the snow had thawed. Chickens skittered along before me as I walked past the typical hayricks of the area where the hay is stacked around a central pole. People were out in the sun trimming hedges, pruning and pollarding. Women were heavily dressed, wearing thick black stockings, grey or black skirts, jumpers, headscarves, often a 'gilet' and sometimes an apron, all in sombre colours.

After gaining some height as I climbed up the next range of mountains I was called over by a farmer and offered coffee, always an attraction. He and his wife took me to their two-room house and prepared me Turkish, or rather Serbian coffee, on a wood-fired stove. As he spoke no English and I no Serbian, conversation was somewhat stilted. He showed me photos of his animals and a wild boar he had shot, and I showed him pictures of my trip so far, whilst he enthusiastically named all the sights I had visited. He particularly liked a photo of a gravestone I had taken. Gravestones in Serbia are more imaginative than British ones; this showed a husband and wife sitting at a table sharing a bottle of beer, all etched into the stone. I had seen another gravestone where someone had scratched out the engraving of the wife, suggesting a bit of jealousy on someone's part. My host's wife was busy with some stinging nettles she had picked. Nettles are a popular ingredient which I saw a number of women picking. Later in my trip I enjoyed a nettle pie, much better than it sounds. As I left, my new friend pressed a bottle of lemonade on me.

I climbed up above the snow line to sleep on a ridge that night, among patches of snow. The country spread before me, as I contemplated distant mountains which I would encounter later on my walk.

The following day, I walked downhill on forest tracks, then followed a road up into a tunnel, above which there was a rotating sign with crossed hammers superimposed on the letter "M". On the other side of the dark tunnel, I walked into the vast open-cast mine at Majdenpek, a massive, terraced hole in the ground, opened up to extract copper, with lesser amounts of gold and silver. Huge dumper trucks were going up and down to collect the ore. The town starts where the pit ends, without any transition. I enjoyed a night in a large suite in the Golden Hotel, the deep pile carpets and fluffy towels a contrast to recent nights' camping. In the morning I bought some 'burek' for my lunch before leaving town. Burek was a sort of filling, fatty, flaky pastry filled with feta type cheese or minced meat and was commonly sold from stalls and bakeries across Serbia. I walked up a track past some tourist caves, closed for the season, and a spot where a brook disappears into the limestone. My route through the beech woods, guided by the booklet *Rambling through Serbia*, was based in detail on Google Earth. Unfortunately, what I thought was a forest track on the satellite images proved to be a stream, and I had to push through the forest undergrowth for a few kilometres among the localised areas of snow.

That night I stayed at a huge and empty hotel at Donji Milanovac. It looked so dark and closed that the only other guests, just arrived, asked me if it was open. I am glad I went down to a more convivial fish restaurant nearer the centre of town for diner. Donji Milanovac marked a return to the Danube and an end of the snow as the days now became warmer and spring flowers began to bloom. As I climbed towards my next destination, the mountain of Veliki Strbac, primroses, scilla and wild yellow crocuses beautified my path through oak and beech, by grassland, orchards and small fields of maize. There were some curious, dome-shaped, brick buildings two or three metres high, with a small entrance at the front, and a ramp to reach the top. I realised they were for making charcoal, as some had wood stacked in them ready to be fired. I saw several over the next week. As I approached the mountain that evening, a man from one of the many farmhouses offered me a schnapps. I accepted a small glass from a bottle with some kind of wild plant in it. Although it was good and smooth, I prudently declined a second glass, and soon after pitched my tent for the night. Next morning, I had a glorious view of the Iron Gates of the Danube from the top of Veliki Strbac.

The Iron Gates are where the steep sides of the valley force the Danube into a narrow gap. Prior to building a dam downstream there used to be rapids, but now the tranquil water is home to barges and, later in the season, cruise boats, travelling up and down the river. However, holidaymakers on cruise boats down on the water were not going to see the glorious morning view spread before me, across the Iron Gates to the mountains of Romania beyond.

I followed the Danube for the next three days, up and down into the mountains beside it. One night I stayed in a village house. I knew there should be accommodation but it was either closed or no one was answering the telephone. While I stood looking helpless in the village centre, a man who spoke English offered a bed in his house. An old injury had disabled his arm to a significant degree. So, first, we visited a friend of his who gave him an arm and upper body massage, while giving me fish soup and beer. The soup had a lot of bones, which the cat seemed to enjoy. I gave his friend a postcard of my home town, having brought a few as gifts for anyone who had offered me some kindness. Then it was off to his house for the night, a slow process, as he chatted with other friends on the way; it seemed a close-knit community. His house was like many in that it had three rooms comprising a bathroom, a combined kitchen and dining area, and a sleeping area. A wood-fired range heated the house and was used for cooking. He offered me his bed but I chose to sleep on the floor in the dining area in my sleeping bag, so I did not disturb him.

Later I walked along the flat area close to the Danube by the large Djerdap hydroelectric dam; Roman and Turkish forts a sign of the historic hostilities along the river. It is still a sensitive area and I was shooed off as I walked too close to the dam for a photo. After the village of Brza Palanka, where I enjoyed a breakfast of omelette, bread and coffee after a night camping beside the river, the E4 heads inland for another loop, in part to reach the Vratna Monastery. It began well, reaching the Belederija waterfall with little difficulty, but the route I had plotted from Google Earth reached a river (at four p.m.) that was going to be difficult to cross, and the route up the other side of the valley again appeared to be a stream rather than a track. All the maps I had been able to obtain showed a blank in this area and the route on my GPS had been my best guess from Google Earth. Not having much choice, I made a long detour via a nearby village and followed tarmac roads to Vratna Monastery which meant walking much further than I expected. After forty-seven kilometres, tired and with darkness falling, I finally reached the monastery and quietly camped in nearby oak trees.

But it was all worth it. Although rain was falling on my tent the next day, it could not hide the splendour of a series of monumental, grey natural arches in the limestone rocks behind the monastery. The season proved to my advantage as the leafless trees gave a better view of the arches as they rose above the treetops. On my return from exploring the arches, the monastery was open and I went into its church. A black-robed nun was reading at a lectern. She spoke English and made me welcome. A sister later arrived and asked if I was hungry. She said I could stay for the two-hour long service at eight a.m. and I confirmed that it would not offend anyone if I just attended part of it as I had a long way to walk today. While waiting for the service, I admired the paintings which, typical of Orthodox churches, covered all the walls and ceiling. There were pictures of Jesus in various scenes from the Bible such as his baptism and the last supper, and of course the Virgin Mary, plus numerous saints all with gold halos, all looking solemn, even when welcoming Jesus into Jerusalem on Palm Sunday. Today was the Orthodox Good Friday, later than the date of Easter in Britain, and the service was led by a bishop. A priest and three nuns participated and I was the audience. Feeling privileged to be there, I did not understand the service (in Serbian) yet gained some serenity from the twenty minutes of listening to the liturgy.

After retracing my steps of the previous night to Vratna village, I took a track over the hill to the village of Jabukovac. A café *('kafana')*, with those silvery windows that you cannot see through, looked closed but an all-terrain vehicle outside and a desire for coffee made me try the doors. It proved to be in business and I enjoyed a Turkish style coffee, small, strong and black, served with a piece of Turkish delight (more flavoursome than the British version) and a small glass of sparkling water. The other customers then quizzed me in a mixture of languages (none of which was English) about what I was doing. As I walked by fences made of intertwined branches, I had the sense that I was walking through an earlier age. The next day I passed the ruins of an important Roman palace, on a remote gravel road, which definitely was from an earlier age.

Reaching the town of Negotin, I enjoyed a rest day on Easter Sunday at a Bed & Breakfast hosted by a very friendly, helpful and English-speaking man called Bojan. At breakfast he presented me with a painted egg, an Easter tradition and, with other families, I visited the Bukovo Monastery. I was glad to have a shower after a few nights camping, but was horrified to find a tick on my stomach. As I was not wearing my glasses in the shower, I did not realise at first what it was, and so did not remove it cleanly. Prior to a previous trip I had all the vaccinations needed to prevent tick-borne encephalitis, but Lyme disease was a worry, especially after I Googled it. The tick must have been attached since the previous night's camping and as I said, it was not cleanly removed which, according to some sources, can encourage transmission. I was feeling very fit for a few weeks after I returned from my trip, but became inexplicably tired after that. Although I had not developed the classic 'bull's eye' rash I was worried I had caught the disease. Fortunately, a blood test showed I was wrong.

The next day, the embankments of drainage canals and minor rivers took me back to the Danube for a final time to the point where Serbia, Romania and Bulgaria meet. Flooding stopped me reaching the actual point. Then it was inland to where I camped on fallen leaves among small oak trees by the Mokranje waterfall. It was in impressive sight, the spring meltwaters foaming white across limestone rocks. In summer, apparently, it is often dry. From there Bojan's friend in the local

Mountain Society said that no one could miss the footpaths signs and red-and-white waymarks to Rajac. Near Rajac and in the villages before them, I saw my first wine cellars or *'pimnice'*. These old, stone buildings with characteristic round, masonry arches over double doors, were all closed when I passed, although in the tourist season, which starts in May, a small number of places would be open to passing visitors, or organised tours.

At my Bed & Breakfast in Rajac, which was decorated with traditional items, my hosts were friendly and helpful. He had been a television presenter and, like others I had spoken to, he lost his position with the disintegration of Yugoslavia and had to find other employment. The couple spoke fluent English and showed me around the village. Like so many other villages I came across in southern Serbia, people had moved away to find jobs elsewhere in larger towns or other countries such as Austria, leaving many empty houses. Some were very old and in need of restoration; some seemed abandoned altogether and others were smartly renovated waiting for their owners to return from working in faraway places. The football pitch had been left to the sheep, as the village could no longer muster a team. Everyone seemed to know everyone. Some Hungarian police were sitting in a matt green Czech-registered van, on the lookout for refugees crossing the border, Serbia being on the refugee route to their own country. Rajac is Serbian but my hosts pointed out the nearby Vlach village. Vlachs are an ethnic minority in Serbia and other countries. They speak a version of Romanian or maybe Latin. Their music was on the television that evening while my hosts fed me some lovely, local food: stuffed cabbage, a sort of corn porridge, battered peppers, white wine, rakia and coffee.

I followed a track to the next village. As I was to find on several occasions, fields close to villages were cultivated with vineyards or maybe as goat pasture; between them, on higher ground, more distant from the settlements, the land was abandoned. Remains of orchards and vineyards were now overgrown with thorny bushes. The track itself, although marked by lines of small trees, became impassable, as hawthorn, rose briars and similar thorny bushes tried to damage my clothing and penetrate my skin with some success. Eventually I managed to bypass the most overgrown section of track. After I had negotiated some fallen trees, the track began to improve and I approached the fields around the village of Tamnič, where elderly women were busy planting potatoes while men did things with tractors.

For the next two weeks I continued through Serbia, sometimes on roads, more often on farm and forest tracks, usually on hilly ground. Most of the roads were gratifyingly quiet. The busier roads could be a problem in that people would stop and offer me a ride and it could be difficult (and no doubt to them incomprehensible) to explain that I wished to walk. One of my disappointments centred on the mountain of Veliki Krs. This had a popular, waymarked route up, but despite much effort I could find no evidence of the route down the other side. Satellite photos suggested impenetrable bushes. I asked at a mountain hut maintained by the local Mountain Society which, to my surprise, was open. The caretaker kindly found someone who spoke English after we failed in using Google Translate on my mobile phone. When he arrived five minutes later, he advised going around the mountain instead of over it. This was a disappointment as the rocky ridge of Veliki Krs looked really good from a distance, as well as on pictures I found on the internet and YouTube videos. A bed in the hut was offered but it was still before midday and as I had not done any planning on the revised route it seemed prudent to carry on. First my name was entered in the visitor's book and I was told the story of a Belgian who walked the E4 through Serbia with the help of local Mountain Societies. Rather than continuing on the E4 after Serbia he headed for Istanbul but was stopped at the Turkish border because of his dog.

Following small roads around Veliki Krs, I lacked a good place to camp. I eventually chose a patch of nettles between the road and a stream. The sound of some dogs barking woke me in the morning. Not being sure if I was dealing with vicious biting animals, I decided to stay still until they lost interest and wandered off. Forty-five minutes later all was quiet, and I thought it safe to start decamping. I had finished packing and was just checking I had left nothing behind when I saw two dogs sitting down, quietly looking at me, one a dirty yellow and the other larger one with a bit of husky in him somewhere. Fortunately, they were not the biting kind, just curious, and I cautiously headed on my way.

The following evening, I stayed at a house with rooms rented by an older couple at Borsko Jerezo. They spoke no English. Bojan at Negotin had arranged it for me so they rang him and he translated messages about diner and breakfast. All went well although my host seemed perplexed that I did not want a rakia with my breakfast; I will evidently not make a real Serbian man without a shot of this highly alcoholic spirit to start the day! Borsko Jerezo is a large, artificial lake with many headlands and inlets, popular with tourists who filled the main hotel that weekend. There was a path around part of the lake, with neatly cropped grass, benches, picnic tables, a café and weeping willows, resplendent in new green leaves after a hard winter. Other trees were still devoid of leaves or just coming into bud.

A series of mountains followed as I progressed south, one of these being Malinik. I climbed it on a steep path floored with limestone through stunted trees. The sweat rolled into my eyes making them sting and formed droplets which fell off the end of my nose. The warmer weather, and the new green growth it was bringing, was in sharp contrast to the snow, and its landscape of white and grey of just a few weeks earlier. At 700 metres, the path levelled off for a while and in a meadow sprinkled with cowslips, I met a hiking group from an organisation called Serbia4Youth. Together we walked to the edge of the Lazarev canyon. This ragged incision in the landscape ran for several kilometres, with branches meandering off. One or two trees were somehow able to grow out of the cliffs that formed the sides of this deep gorge. Settling down with their picnics, the group sat on huge buttresses, rather too close to the edge for my liking, while the guide gave some background (in Serbian of course). All the young people made me feel old and clumsy as I set off alone again and, while pondering on the matter, head down, I walked into a tree!

Rtanj was a mystical mountain that I also climbed. Rtanj village is just beneath it and I was expecting a typical Serbian mountain hamlet, but instead it was a ghost town left by an old mining operation with many abandoned buildings. The ruins were not picturesque. There were some occupied houses, a few quite smart, several advertising Rtanj tea, made from a herb that only grows on the nearby mountains. My Bed & Breakfast was not where it was shown on Booking.com and its only sign said 'apartments' (in Cyrillic script). I only went in because on asking a local (by showing him the name on my phone) he made swimming actions, referring to the pool beside the B&B. There was a party drinking inside, who had just walked down from the summit of Rtanj Mountain. I eventually determined it was the right place thanks to a friendly man who spoke English. He enthusiastically told me a great deal about Rtanj. If I understood correctly, he had an organisation called "the spirit of Rtanj pyramid". It seems the pyramid shape of the mountain has great significance; strange balls of light have been seen and there was something about frequencies, other emissions, and intersecting energy lines.

I climbed the mountain itself the next day; at 1,570 metres, the highest so far on my walk through Serbia. Although I sensed no strange vibrations, as I climbed above the clouds, I admired the changing flora; from cowslips to flowers like miniature hyacinths that formed pools of blue on the higher slopes, to what looked like purple anemones near the top. As I neared the summit, the wind became stronger, cold and gusting, with a good gale blowing at the top where I sheltered in the ruins of St George's chapel, only visible when I actually reached them. Various oddments had been left there in a steel box by previous visitors. Despite it being somewhat misty I could see many distant mountains and valleys filled with cloud.

That evening I stayed in the town of Sokobanya, enjoying a rest day after three long days, each of over thirty kilometres, with lots of climbing. A tourist town and spa, there was a clean and tidy pedestrian street in the centre, lined with trees, numerous pavement cafés, stalls selling souvenirs (but curiously no postcards) and areas of park with sculptures and borders of pansies, the purple and white displays looking most fetching. Lines of young school children were being led around by teachers, from the old Turkish hammam or bathhouse to the church to a Tito era hotel. For my last evening meal, I enjoyed grilled chicken with some kind of pepper dressing and a baklava dessert that had a lemon offsetting the excessive sweetness of this dessert. Paul Hollywood, an icon of British cuisine, was baking on one of the café's large television screens.

Nearby, hidden deep in the forest, on a rocky promontory in a steep-sided valley, was the ruined castle of Sokograd. I climbed through the trees above it, now covered with fresh green leaves, wet from the morning rain, following waymarked paths to the Devica range. This long, grass-covered ridge had multiple summits. I followed it east and as the skies darkened with the approach of evening, the track I followed was covered with blue flowers, contrasting with the yellow cowslips each side. After a final summit where the limestone rocks pushed through the rough grass, I found a campsite among some bushes. Civilisation seemed a long, long way away, as I listened to the birdsong and looked down on cloud-filled valleys the following morning. Thirty-four kilometres later, after flower-filled meadows, trees and abandoned fields, I reached the busy town of Knjaževac, something of a contrast.

After a later night camping in magnificent isolation in the mountains I ran into navigation issues. I was headed for the Stara Planina (or Old Mountains) which I could see from my campsite in the distance, streaked with snow, below a pink and orange sunrise. Walking across forested hills, by apparently abandoned farm buildings, I had some modest difficulties finding the route through old pastureland overgrown with thorny bushes. I reached a waterfall by a road, a local tourist attraction. A couple were selling homemade produce on a picnic table. Some Bulgarians on a day out from Sofia were buying some smoked meat. I attempted to cross the next range of mountains, but my reading of Google Earth had failed me, again confusing a stream through woodland for a path. Beneath the trees the undergrowth was too dense for me to force a way through the remaining four kilometres to the next road. Disappointed, and subsequently very tired, it was a long walk along roads around the mountains to reach my planned accommodation. However, I soon recovered on my arrival, with a cold beer and a shower. Some American visitors at the guesthouse commented on the rather large amount of food for dinner but I had little problem cleaning my plate after a long day… helped by a glass of red wine and a walnut rakia with my coffee (the walnut rakia was a little on the sweet side; the plum rakia I had tried previously was great).

The Stara Planina is a tourist area. After breakfast consisting of some interesting pastry things wrapped around in a spiral with yoghurt and cherry jam, I was off down the road to where the track to the rocks of Babin Zub started. After fording a river, removing my socks so that they did not get as wet as my boots, the climb started. It was up through trees for the next few hours: first oaks, their leaves bright green and freshly unfurled. There followed some beech and, higher up, silver birch with vivid leaves. Above them, the buds on the trees had yet to burst, and there were many broken branches, maybe snapped by the weight of snow during the recent winter. By Babin Zub itself there were no trees but instead creeping juniper and the paraphernalia of a ski resort. The chair lifts were silent but beneath them was a wonderful display of purple crocuses. 'Babin Zub' means Grandma's Tooth, although the mountain has a row of several large rock formations like a row of teeth.

I descended from Babin Zub the next day into the valley of the Rekitsa River, passing streams tumbling down the hillside in miniature waterfalls. The Rekitsa valley took me to the village of Topli Do which mainly consisted of empty houses and notices concerning people who had died, outlined in black and pasted onto telegraph poles. For once there were no barking dogs, just the occasional clink of distant cow bells. The dusty shop still had bags of crisps, packets of biscuits and bottles of pop, but it looked a long time since anything had been weighed on its old-fashioned scales. I headed down the valley of the Toplodolska, eventually crossing the river at a ford, where the melting snow had made the water rather deep. I removed my socks and replaced my boots, rolled up my trousers and prudently packed away my socks, camera, wallet and GPS in one of the dry bags I had for all my other belongings. Prudently because, as I splashed across slippery boulders in knee-deep water, I lost my balance. Catching myself with my hands I made my trousers and the front of my tee shirt wet. As I walked up the road to the lake of Zavojsko Jezero, water squirted out a hole in one of my boots. I was disappointed with them. A previous pair of boots of the same type had covered over a thousand miles, but the company had been taken over and the boots were now made in the Far East. My experience suggested that quality had declined.

The lake of Zavojsko Jezero was originally created by a landslip in 1963, displacing the local population. It was later drained and a dam built for hydroelectricity. I walked for many miles around the shore, by holiday houses, floating cabins, boats and fishermen. After the lake, I hiked by the meandering Visocica gorge, through trees, farmland and several villages. I was hoping for a shop in the village of Rsovci to stock up a little, and indeed there was one, but it was closed with no opening times marked. A helpful man fetched the owner and I bought some snacks and an ice cream for myself and the helpful man. Unfortunately, there was some confusion about money. I should have got the shopkeeper to write down the amount I owed, as I gave more than enough notes and he returned some of them. Then they confused me with a mixture of Serbian and German. There was a discussion about two euro, two hundred dinar and twenty something. I could not understand so after a while the shopkeeper just said 'OK'. Maybe they were trying to change money? All very embarrassing. The helpful man then showed me a chapel cut into the cliff on the other side of the river to the village. It included a fresco painted onto the side of the cave as well as numerous icons. It must be an important, local site of interest as a Bulgarian man on his motorcycle was also visiting. Returning to the village and saying goodbye to my guide, I headed onwards, eventually climbing out of the valley on a track that zigzagged its way to its highest point, where I turned off to walk up a grassy ridge to a nearby summit with a panoramic view to the north and south. Finding a flat spot, free of many rocks and with a few trees to break the wind, I set up camp for the night. As I finished my tea, waiting for the sunset, the sun, which had been shining for most of the last few days, disappeared, driven away by towering cumulus clouds followed by lower, black, rain-heavy clouds (a classic cold front). As I retreated to my tent after checking my pegs and guylines, the wind started blowing and the first shower of rain began. I remember thinking I would never get to sleep due to worrying that the wind would collapse my flapping tent. That was the last thought I remembered before slipping into the land of Nod.

My final night in Serbia was in the Happy Hotel, where I merrily celebrated with a glass of wine on a pleasant terrace overlooking the town. As I walked towards the Bulgarian border the next day, passing a small refugee holding centre, a border policeman stopped me. He asked where I had been staying. Hotels and other accommodation should give you a piece of paper confirming that your presence has been reported to the police, but the Happy Hotel had not done so, consequently, I just showed the hotel's receipt. The policeman gave me a ticking-off about not having the right documents, but I was glad he had not asked me about earlier nights when I had been wild camping. In theory, if not staying in official accommodation in Serbia, you should report to the police where you are sleeping within twenty-four hours. This is not practical if you are walking and wild camping, you would spend all day just walking back and forth to the nearest police station.

As the border was really designed for cars, buses and lorries I had a little trouble finding where to go. A helpful lady at completely the wrong barrier told me to follow the cars on the main road, a dual carriageway, then when a border guard saw me queuing behind a German motor-home he told me to go to the front of the queue. A quick processing of my passport followed and I was welcomed to no-man's land by a barking dog. Then the Bulgarian border guard checked my passport after I had waited in a second queue of cars and finally, I was in the ninth country of my walk across Europe.

From Serbia to Sofia

No route has been proposed for the E4 between the Serbian border and Sofia, the capital of Bulgaria, so instead I followed the Sultan's Trail for this section. I had been periodically crossing this international trail since Vienna. It follows the route taken by Suleiman the Magnificent in the 16th century as he conquered a large section of Eastern Europe, reaching the gates of Vienna. In contrast the trail now aims to be "a path of peace, a meeting place for people of all faiths and cultures". There was a dense collection of Sultan's Trail waymarks in one village, but otherwise I relied on a GPS 'track' I had downloaded from the Sultan's Trail website.

The GPS 'track' was not immediately useful as it led from the border to a locked gate. Working my way around it, I encountered border guards who asked for my passport. A hundred or so metres further on, I was asked again for my passport. After a little difficulty persuading the guard that the "autobahn" was not where I wanted to go, I followed a very quiet road through woodland, green with new leaves, for many kilometres. With no vehicles passing me, I became nervous. Would the road lead me inadvertently to a secret military base and result in my imprisonment? Luckily my fears were unfounded and the road climbed uneventfully through trees to more open grassland from which distant mountains could be seen. The route then took a shortcut across grassland and scrub to reach the village of Dragoil, a collection of houses and dogs, where I gained a wave from an elderly lady with a headscarf. Quiet, tarmac roads led me to the town of Dragoman. Not a pretty town, it had seen better days before the grass started growing through the pavements. Yet the hotel was fine, and the English-speaking receptionist helpful, explaining where the Bankomat (i.e., cash machine) was located. There I duly used my debit card to collect a stack of lev, the local currency, thinking what wonderful things a small piece of plastic can do despite being in a strange place. Next to the hotel was a restaurant which filled my belly well, although the resident dog was disappointed he got no scraps from me, despite patiently sitting next to my table trying to look into my eyes...

The remaining distance to the outskirts of Bulgaria's capital Sofia I walked in one long day, starting early before the sun started to cook me. As I walked across fields on a quiet farm track, skylarks were singing their hearts out above the fields. An occasional cuckoo could be heard and the mountain of Vitosha, which lies immediately south of Sofia, was visible in the grey distance. Following quiet roads and farm tracks across agricultural land, through villages and a small town, passing stork nests, lilac bushes and a pack of threatening, barking dogs, I eventually reached the suburb of Bankya. A celebratory whisky at the hotel turned out to be a bad idea, despite the label on the bottle behind the bar—I suspected industrial alcohol mixed with liquorice. The next day I entered Sofia and my destination for this section. While in the city I enjoyed some sightseeing, there being many things to see and do, but most memorable was the "Communist Tour", which included a ride in a Socialist-era Trabant car with an introduction to some of its mysteries, such as whether it really was made of cardboard.

Chapter 12: Sofia to Kalampaka — summits and sore ankles

Across the Bulgarian Mountain Ranges

Although the European Ramblers Association coordinates the E-paths, surveying and management of the route is completed by the member associations in each country. Consequently, the style, waymarking and difficulty of trail varies greatly between countries. In Bulgaria, the E4 is on the more exciting side, travelling south through the main ridge of mountains between Sofia and the Greek border. It includes the Rila and Pirin mountains, alpine environments, where much of the path is over 2,000 metres. It is an incredibly scenic route, much of it well served by mountain refuges providing dormitory accommodation and meals, which is just as well as most of the trail is remote from any villages for resupply or accommodation. My research found many warnings of exposed sections of trail, with scary drops off the edge of steep-sided, rocky ridges, and some light scrambling. I knew that on occasions I could suddenly become afraid when walking on a path with a steep drop on one, or even worse, both sides, a fear in my stomach that could come on quite suddenly. Such fear made it difficult for me to take the next step, forward or back, and this lack of confidence made me feel more wobbly and so even more scared. I knew it was psychological as I do not normally wobble, much less fall off a path, and could sometimes walk quite confidently beside a big drop. On previous sections of the E4 I had avoided the more extreme trails for this reason, but on the Bulgarian section detours, if available were lengthy, and would mean missing the best parts of the trail.

To tackle the issue and develop some skills for climbing over rock, I joined a week-long scrambling course at Britain's National Outdoor Centre at Plas-y-Brenin in Snowdonia. It was a hands (and feet) on, very practical course and overall, I thought I acquitted myself quite well. Only on one day, climbing Crib Lem, did my mind wobble, as I started to think of falling and the drop beside me rather than where my next foot- or handhold was; my temptation at that point being to try and rush on out of the "danger zone". Immediate crisis averted, the instructor sat the group down on the next available small area of flat rock and discussed the issue together with more useful strategies to tackle it. The confidence gained from the course, and a subsequent week by myself climbing some of the easier scrambling routes in the area, meant that I handled everything in Bulgaria without any problems. Although certainly dramatic, I found the rocky, steep-sided mountains and ridges not particularly challenging from a technical point of view, there being plenty of footholds and handholds. Cables and chains had been installed to help on difficult sections, but, in reality, they just got in the way when, like me, you were carrying a large rucksack. Fortunately, the weather was kind to me, as in wet, windy or icy weather the route would have been considerably more challenging.

As I was starting in August, a busy time of year, I paid a guiding company to book the mountain huts for me, and provide some general assistance. Mid-August was a good choice as all but the smallest patches of snow had melted, the weather was good, and not too cold. I also wanted to reach Mount Olympus in Greece on this trip before any early snows.

On arriving in Sofia, I followed the Sultan's Trail through a string of parks to the southern suburb of Dragalevtsi where the E4 begins again, marked in Bulgaria by red-and-white waymarks. The next day, the climbing began, a total ascent of 1,600 metres to reach the summit of the Vitosha range at 2,290 metres. As I climbed, I passed through beech and sycamore trees lower down, then fir trees and finally no trees at all, just creeping juniper at ankle height and protruding rocks. The temperature changed from warm and sweaty in the trees, to cold and windy higher up. I was reminded that the temperature drops about one degree Centigrade in dry weather for every hundred metres you climb. As I looked back, the white buildings of Sofia were spread out beneath the haze. For lunch I had bean soup at an unmarked building at the top, before a steep descent to where I camped, together with a Dutch father and son. As I lost height, in front of me was the next range, the Rila

Mountains, which I reached a day later after walking through flower-coated, summer meadows.

Booking my first mountain hut was problematic as my first and second choice were full, so it was a short day's walk to Lovna hut. It was full but as I was early, I was able to pick a good spot at the end of the long sleeping platform, so that I only had someone on my left side. As in many of these huts the toilet facilities were pretty basic. The shower shared a small room with a WC and wash basin, and the floor was soon awash with water as I washed away the sweat of my last three days. The walls were partly papered with pages from climbing magazines which included some artistic photos of naked ladies climbing vertical rock faces. I spent the afternoon listening to classic hits being pumped out by the music system, Tom Jones singing to the Bulgarian mountains.

The following day was memorable for two reasons; the sight of the White Brotherhood and (quite unconnected) repeated diarrhoea. I had known of the White Brotherhood from Michael Palin's television series on 'New Europe', but it was a coincidence that I happened to be in the Seven Lakes region of the Rila Mountains precisely when they were having a large gathering. This explained the difficulty I had experienced obtaining a bed last night. The White Brotherhood is a New Age religious movement founded in the early 20th century in Bulgaria. Dressed all in white, members dance in large concentric circles to harmonise with the rhythms of the universe high in the mountains. After climbing through trees, I reached the next hut, by a lake and surrounded by tents of many different colours. I then joined throngs of people of all ages dressed in white climbing up the mountain. After they deviated onto a plateau, I continued higher past the last of the seven lakes that gives the area its name, *'Sedemte ezera'*, each lake at a progressively greater height, their calm surfaces reflecting the mountains behind. As I ascended higher, I was able to look down on the circles formed by the White Brotherhood, each concentric circle slowly moving round, with an outer circle of discarded coloured bags. The weather was fine and many people were out enjoying the mountain scenery. This proved a problem. Not long after leaving Lovna hut, I had one of the attacks of diarrhoea which have affected me on my travels throughout my life. Fortunately, on this occasion, I was spared the unpleasant stomach cramps and it only lasted one day, but it meant an urgent desire to empty my bowels every few hours. Being well above the tree line, with little shelter and so many people about, I experienced some narrow escapes from being spotted, exposed in an ungentlemanly position while answering urgent calls of nature. I was glad I was camping in a remote spot that evening, by a small unmanned hut, with no one to see me, tired after a long day and having climbed a total of 2,000 metres.

The walk through the Rila Mountains was superb. On television it would have been accompanied by soaring violins with the horns coming in as the camera zoomed in on a particularly attractive lake. As I crossed boulders and steep outcrops of rock, I found them fun rather than scary. Much of the path was beside or on top of a ridge with long views over mountains progressively more distant, and blue. My next night was spent in a Communist-era mountain hut. Ablutions were served by cold-water showers in a room with concrete walls and floor and squat toilets. Beds were provided in either a dormitory or, what I assumed were more expensive, bungalows. I opted for the latter and enjoyed privacy, a naked light bulb and unpainted chipboard walls. Arriving at another hut the following night, those already there made fun of my inability to speak Bulgarian and, since the warden spoke no English, I was unsure how to secure my bed and some food. Fortunately, a man and his young nephew turned up later. The nephew was on holiday from Britain where he had moved with his family. Despite having been at school in the UK for only few years, he spoke perfect English, putting my language efforts to shame.

My last day in the Rila Mountains was across rounded and greener peaks. Kestrels rose and fell on fluctuations of the wind as they tried to keep position. Grasshoppers jumped out of my way. A few grazing horses looked at me. I dropped through woodland and lost the path but eventually reached my first road for a few days and Predel hut. This was gratifyingly a grade up on the previous huts with separate bedrooms with en-suite bathrooms and a barbecue for dinner.

Following a climb up through trees the next day, into the Pirin Mountains and across a saddle, I reached Yavorov hut. Here again I was back to the more traditional, dormitory style, hut, but this one had been modernised to the best European standards with new sleeping and toilet facilities. While waiting in line for some attention, I was surprised to hear English voices behind me commenting on the rather raunchy pop video showing on the TV. They were a friendly family from Britain on holiday; the first British people I had met since arriving in Sofia a week ago. I bought some chips with cheese and joined them for a while. Later, other English-speaking groups arrived. The hut was bursting with people, my dormitory was full, the area evidently very popular.

The Koncheto saddle (also called the Marble or Koncheto ridge) looks pretty scary on YouTube, with steep, rocky sides dropping away each side for thousands of feet. Looked at with the benefit of my recent training I could see huge numbers of foot- and handholds and by walking a little to the right of the crest it was actually not very difficult. After the saddle I climbed to the top of Mount Vihren, at 2,914 metres the highest peak to date on my E4 walk. This was a fun climb; first up the northern ridge line, then a leftward traverse up a long cleft in the rock and finally straight up to the summit, all climbing over bare rock on a steep-sided mountain. Chains were attached to help you up but I did not need them as the weather was dry, making for good grip. At the summit, in every direction there were rocky mountains and ridges receding into the distance, beneath a layer of fluffy white clouds under blue skies. People were taking pictures of themselves, including a lady and some gentlemen who looked the far side of 70. I hope I am climbing mountains at their age.

After the climb to the top of Mount Vihren it was a very long, steep descent, tiring and painful on the knees. It was a relief to arrive at the Vihren hut where I found myself surrounded by people and cars. I bought a beer from a stall outside and watched while a shepherd drove his sheep into the meadow above me. His brown-and-white dogs looked a bit like the sheep! Inside, a large orange cat reclined in pride of place on a chair in the canteen, benefitting from a sign on the door which advised that dogs were forbidden!

I started my climb up the valley out from Vihren hut early in the morning as there was a risk of rain or thunder. Cowherds were also on the move, shouting "Hi" at their cows to move them to a different pasture. Some of the cows had fluffy ears which looked rather humorous. Chicken soup was on the menu for lunch at the small Tevno Ezera hut, which sits in a particularly scenic spot beside a lake. Then it was downhill to Pirin hut, catching a short but heavy shower of rain after I was safely away from exposed high points. By the look of it this was another Communist-era hut although 'hut' is maybe the wrong word for the stone-built turret-shaped structure. Green and blue coloured paint had been used to brighten things up. As the sheets and mattresses were a bit stained, I was glad I had my sleeping bag. At dinner a group of four Czech students from North Bohemia invited me to join their table. We had been passing each other on the same route for the last few days and I had particularly noticed their happy laughter. Although camping is not allowed in the Rila and Pirin Mountains, like others they were camping discreetly, pitching after dinner and leaving early in the morning. I asked about language difficulties but they said as Czech was a Slavic language, like Bulgarian, they just spoke slowly and were understood.

The Czech students were leaving the trail the next day as did everyone else and I had a quiet walk for the next two days among lower mountains and mainly through trees of beech and pine. Much of it followed the contours along one side of a ridge or another, with occasional clearings often with a herd of cows. Passing four cowherds and one woman, possibly a cowherd's wife, I had what almost amounted to a conversation with two of them. It helps being able to guess the questions, typically being: where are you going? (Popovi Livadi hut); where are you from? ('Anglia' meaning England, better known than Wales), and finally *"Sam?"*, meaning 'Alone?'. Any such conversation happens after they have persuaded their large brown-and-white dogs that I am not to be eaten.

My final day in the mountains took me through the mist to the Greek border. This was marked by white concrete posts and an occasional torn Bulgarian flag, and passes through the crests of the southern summits of the Slavyanka Mountains, with the land dropping more steeply on the Greek side. I imagined people escaping from Bulgaria across this border to reach the "freedom" of the West in communist times. After coming down from Mount Malak Tsarev Vrah I stopped to eat the open sandwiches prepared by the hut keeper that morning, admiring the grass-covered mountains and picking out where the border went with my map. Then it was up the final summit of Mount Gotsev. As the wind had become very strong, I omitted the optional summit of Shabran and headed downhill, back into Bulgaria, as I was planning to cross into Greece at an official border crossing. That night I stayed at Izora hut. Like the Slavyanka hut where I stayed the night before, Izvora hut had been a barracks for the border guards in communist times. There were some interesting, cartoon style, posters on the walls from that period, showing the guards how to stop people escaping from Socialist Bulgaria (although many of those who attempted the crossing came from East Germany or other Warsaw Pact countries). If the guards spotted footprints in the raked sand by the fence that marked the beginning of the border zone, they first had to telephone in the information. Those unfortunate would-be escapees who were spotted were depicted putting their hands up as guards approached with rifles at the ready. For myself, I had trouble finding the hut keeper, so resorted to phoning Margarita, who had booked the accommodation, and now stepped in again to alert my host to my presence and pass on timings for dinner (at 8:30 p.m., after he dealt with his animals). At dinner, as I ate the cheese the hut keeper had made himself with kebabs, tomatoes and cucumbers, rakiya and beer, it transpired that his son had spent a few years in Wales, in Merthyr Tydfil, near where I live. A small world!

To reach the Greek border there was no official route for the E4, so I had created one myself and loaded it onto my GPS. After a breakfast again featuring cheese and tomatoes, the hut keeper left me to lock up. As I set off, he was already herding his goats. I began along an asphalt road down a narrow, wooded valley with plane trees next to the stream and conifers higher up. The village of Petrovo was at the end of the valley. Vines trailed on wooden supports across the pavements, heavy with red and white grapes ready to be picked. Fig trees were dropping their ripe fruits. Leaving the road in preference for quieter farm tracks, my path took in vineyards, grassland and scrubby trees. Apart from one overgrown section my route generally worked well until I reached the village of Novo Hodzhovo. Here I spotted a shop and, since I was hot and sweaty, having left the cool of the high mountains, I bought a Coke and ice cream and sat outside with some villagers to enjoy it. Unfortunately, the lady running the shop seemed suspicious of me. I guess we were near the border and my being alone seemed to worry them.

Maybe they thought I was a people smuggler? They spoke only one or two words of English but they wanted to see my passport and asked where I was going. They were speaking about the police among themselves and when I got up to leave, they made it clear they wanted me to wait, for what I understood to be a police jeep. So I phoned Margarita again and she spoke to them explaining what I was doing. Then I was allowed to leave. Not wanting to look suspicious near the border and require Margarita's help yet again I stuck to the roads for the rest of the way to a hotel at Chuchuligovo. Despite some bad reviews the hotel seemed fine, apart from needing some new, clean carpets and a few new light bulbs. I had to use my head torch in the bathroom, but compared with some of the mountain huts, it was luxury!

Across Northern Greece

I crossed into Greece without anyone bothering me for my passport. For the first twenty kilometres, to where the E4 joined the E6 European Long-Distance trail, I had been unable to find where exactly the E4 was meant to go. The road down the valley from the border crossing was a busy dual carriageway, so I had picked out some nearby tracks to follow. These allowed a deviation into the hills to Fort Rupel, a fortification which saw significant action in World War II. The route I had picked from my maps was a bit overgrown in one part and I was sweating profusely from climbing in the heat, but I managed to reach the War Memorial at the top. In doing so I surprised a group of soldiers who wanted to know where I had come from. No doubt they were expecting any visitors to come in cars up the road. However, they let me admire the view from the War Memorial at the top and one kind chap took me into the tunnels. These extended several kilometres into the hills, with white painted walls and medical facilities, offices and other facilities designed to help stop an invading army. The Greek army held out for five days against the well-equipped Germans, but the Germans eventually outflanked them using a different pass.

Joining the combined E4 and E6 trail, I changed from heading south to heading west. After four kilometres, the route took me into the lively village of Neo Petritsi. At its centre was a group of cafés and tavernas where I had a Coke and Baba cake (a sort of sponge smothered in syrup with some cream). As I sipped my Coke, I watched a typical Greek scene; people sitting outside at tavernas, saying hello to each other or driving by on motor scooters with no helmets and a child between their legs. It was a scene I observed in many a Greek village, typically around a central square sheltered from the sun by old plane trees, with a church nearby.

Coming out of Neo Pretitsi, there was an abundance of yellow and black E4 / E6 signs, some admittedly used for shotgun practice, but these soon disappeared. The European Long-Distance paths were surveyed and waymarked around 1990 in Northern Greece, but there seems to have been little maintenance in the thirty years since then.

As I walked along, to my right was a range of mountains marking the border with Bulgaria. A faded "No Photographs" sign alluded to the historic importance of this boundary as part of the Iron Curtain. To my left, the plains spread out below the low foothills I was crossing. There were occasional olive groves, a sign that in crossing the mountains from Bulgaria to Greece, I had returned to the Mediterranean region. My hotel that first night looked over the great expanse of Lake Kerkini, where all kinds of birds can be spotted. I enjoyed looking for them from the terrace with a pair of binoculars and a guidebook I was lent. The birds on the lake were too far away to distinguish but was it a Lesser Spotted Eagle that I saw soaring above the grassland? As the sky turned pinky grey I enjoyed a celebratory glass (or two) of red wine for reaching Greece. Unfortunately, insects were around as well, and I had to fish a wasp out of my wine. It then walked unsteadily across the tablecloth leaving reddish trail.

For the next ten days, the E4 took me in a westerly direction across Northern Greece. Days walking across plains or low hills, alternated with climbs over higher ground and mountains. I was following a GPS 'track' downloaded from the internet which led me along farm and woodland tracks, quiet roads, and smaller, and sometimes invisible, paths in the high mountain forests and pastures.

In the plains and on lower ground, I was blessed with hotels and guesthouses, cafés and restaurants, mini-markets and street markets in villages and small towns, and I enjoyed sitting out at the cafés and tavernas, under the plane trees in the summer heat, watching the world go by, the local grey-haired men playing cards or backgammon, watched by their fellows. Bakeries were also a joy to me, where I could buy phyllo pastries, maybe wrapped in a spiral, filled with spinach, feta cheese or some creamy stuff, and perhaps a double espresso to give me a boost in the morning. Herds of goats and flocks of sheep were led by shepherds and their barking dogs among scrubby vegetation and low trees. On the dusty tracks that crossed low hills I found wild tortoises, lumbering about their business. House martins on telegraph wires preened themselves. Pomegranate trees by the track bore over-ripe fruit, splitting in macabre "grins", to reveal the seeds inside. There were cherry orchards, fields of sunflowers and maize, ploughed areas, grassland of dry straw and fields of solar panels (the latest crop). Tobacco leaves dried golden on racks below sheets of plastic.

In the mountains, I would climb through woodland; small oak trees lower down, then tall beech, pines and, at the highest elevations, grass-covered slopes, with creeping juniper, blueberries and a few stunted pines. The rocks on the track, silvery mica schists, glittered in the sun, with green chlorite starting to appear. Protruding, reddish crystals suggested a garnet schist in places. I had naively thought the high grassland would be empty, but instead there were little shacks tucked in small valleys, herds of cows bellowing their disapproval of me and, from the woodland below, the sound of chainsaws. Camping one night in those high mountains I enjoyed the early morning, cool and fresh, looking down on streetlights, like orange jewels, in a village far below as pink and grey preceded the sun in the eastern sky. Streams splashed over rocks on those higher slopes. Lower down, small rivers cut narrow, rock-lined valleys into the hillside with little, white foaming falls before spreading out onto the plains as broad rivers with banks and islands of rounded pebbles.

Being early September, the temperature reached the low 30s (degrees Centigrade) and sweat dripped off my face. However, I had come a long way since I started in Tarifa and I had learnt how to cope better, starting early in the morning, with plenty of water, a broad-brimmed hat, sunglasses and suntan lotion. Nevertheless, one day was particularly unpleasant for its combination of heat and insects. For many hours I walked over hills on a vehicle track through low oaks, surrounded by a dense cloud of small flies or gnats. Unlike some other insects, they did not seem to be biting but it was, nonetheless, highly irritating to be at the centre of this buzzing, black, fast-moving cloud. I killed more than a few individuals by clapping my hands on them until my palms stung, only for others to replace them. Stopping was out of the question as it simply rendered me more vulnerable as a sitting target, so I just kept walking, mile after mile of sweaty irritation. Finally leaving the hills, I entered a village where I purchased a most welcome Coke and a creamy sort of snack. My reward was short-lived, however, as a wasp quickly spotted me, soon joined by five others. I resorted to covering my Coke can with my hat to stop them getting in. Next stop was the village pharmacy where I acquired an insect repellent made of eucalyptus and lemon oil. This had no deterrent effect on the local insect population, but it made me smell pleasantly fresh.

That evening I settled in for a rest day beside Lake Doirani, where birds collected in its reedy margins. The "Former Yugoslav Republic of Macedonia" was on the opposite shore of the still waters. On a hillside nearby I visited a British Military Cemetery with the graves of soldiers killed in the First World War. I knew nothing of the Salonika front, which appears to have ended the lives of a great many. Almost half died of malaria, the rest in attacks which appear to have put little value on the lives of the soldiers. Many of the dead were from the Welsh and South Wales Borders battalions with names like Jones and Thomas. They may once have lived close to where my own home is. The cemetery looked immaculate as such places always are thanks to the War Graves Commission, although I doubt many visit its neatly cut grass and red roses, like splashes of blood among the white gravestones. On top of the hill was a monument to those British soldiers who have no graves. It had sculptures of lions. I would like to think they looked sad due to the loss of all those lives.

The village of Loutraki was a happier place, popular with tourists enjoying themselves, the main attraction being the spa. A small river flowed down a steep-sided valley and there were a number of artificial waterfalls, below which little bathing pools had been constructed. There was also a bathing area the size of a swimming pool. The facilities seemed popular with older people; grey-haired men arguing with each other as the Greeks seem to, despite it all being friendly, and full-bodied ladies in their bursting swimming costumes. The water did not seem especially hot, but at least it did not smell sulphurous as in so many spas.

Churches and monasteries provided a religious element to my trip. On my second day in Greece, I reached a monastery, and, as the sign on the door said I was within the opening hours, I proceeded cautiously inside. On entering the main church, I met a nun who spoke English. Although everything looked ancient, the Monastery of St John the Baptist was actually only six years old, and additional building work was still in progress. As the friendly nun explained, everything had been built and decorated in the old style, with lots of handmade 'gold' artefacts and traditional icons. While in Britain the established church seems in decline, it was good to hear that in Greece they were still raising buildings dedicated to God. The nuns kindly gave me a coffee and a type of shortbread biscuit in the visitors' room and I bought a fridge magnet of St George and the Dragon in their gift shop as a small way of repaying their kindness. (It was either that or hand knitted babies' booties for which I would have little use.)

There were little shrines like miniature churches in many of the gardens of village houses and often by the roadside as well. Each village also had a normal-sized church with white walls and red-tiled roofs. In fact, most houses had white walls and red-tiled roofs but the churches also had rounded domes and a tower for the bell. One Sunday, I stopped at a village for a Coke. While drinking it at a table outside the bar, people were coming out of the church. They were picking up packages of food as they left. I was surprised and pleased when a young girl of five or six brought over a package for me. It contained cake, almond and cinnamon flavoured shortbread, and what looked like maize soaked in something sweet that you ate with a plastic spoon. I tried to ask at the bar what the food was celebrating. As I understood it, they said St Athanasios, the saint to whom the church was dedicated. I was touched by the gift which I greatly enjoyed whatever the celebration.

Enough people spoke English (or in one case French) for me to get by, or else a passer-by or neighbour would help me order a souvlaki and a cold drink. Although generally friendly, in one case on a lonely road, a pick-up stopped beside me. I had the impression the driver thought me Albanian, and maybe suspected me of some skulduggery.

Shortly after the busy town of Florina, the E4 parts from the E6 and heads in a more south-easterly direction for the next eight days, crossing the Verno, Vermio and Pieria mountains. Climbing out of Florina through the beech woods, I passed two small churches. The Church of St. George was open and I admired the wall paintings of solemn saints on its walls and icons on the iconostasis (a screen which separates the congregation from the altar). Many such small churches dotted my route, often located in the hills, away from villages. Like the Church of St. George, they exuded a quiet, timeless serenity (although the green plastic chairs were somewhat anachronistic). That evening I slept in the mountains, among the trees. The track I walked along next morning had a sandy surface which retained the tracks of tyres and animals. Superimposed on older tracks were some recent, large paw prints. Of a similar size to my boots but a little wider, it took me a few moments to work out that they must be bear prints. This inference was further supported by the fact that the hind foot print was longer than the front paw print (an anatomical feature that allows bears to stand on their hind legs and threaten you with their front paws and jaws). The prints also had five toes or claws. I had known there were a few bears in the Bulgarian mountains, not that I saw any sign of them, but did not realise they extended into Greece. I also saw what looked like bear droppings. That evening I reached Nymfeo, a village with a bear sanctuary. I confirmed with the man in charge, that I had indeed being looking a bear prints. I bought a ticket for the tour during which there was a talk in which I was told that although you could find numerous bear prints, because the animals travelled considerable distances, these prints were made by only about five hundred Greek bears (based on genetic analysis of hairs left when they scratch trees). The sanctuary is for rescued dancing and circus bears, unsuitable for release in the wild, and orphaned bears, kept until they could be released. A few of the residents could be observed, wandering about, scratching beneath the trees for beech nuts, which they were eating. Although many of the bears were too domesticated to be released into the wild it was good that they were being cared for in a setting as close to their natural wild habitat as possible and a vast improvement on their previous lives.

Nymfeo (which like many places in Greece is written in various different ways depending on how you transliterate the Greek letters) was a charming village of grey stone buildings and streets of slabbed stone, a popular tourist destination. Leaving the village, I met foresters busy at work thinning the trees. Unlike the modern machines with many arms, I had seen in Switzerland and Bavaria, here a team of small, docile horses was being used to bring the cut logs down to the forest track on their backs which saves creating lots of extra vehicle tracks. Leaving the mountains, I crossed a plain of grassland, vineyards — some heavy with grapes — abandoned farmland, and industrial-scale orchards of peach and apples. Apple picking was in progress with lorries and tractors coming and going on the dirt track. The harvesting was timely as ripe apples were collecting on the ground. A great deal of effort was being put into these orchards including irrigation and netting installed to keep away the birds. Pirgi was a village in the midst of the apple orchards. Walking into the open area in front of what appeared to be a taverna (signage was often lacking in this area) looking for lunch, I was addressed by a kind Greek gentleman with grey hair who spoke English. He ordered some food for me and insisted on paying. He had his son with him who was visiting from Miami where he worked. Although they were familiar with the E4 (or "Epsilon Tessera") they seemed to think it a bit odd that I wanted to walk it (although they said it was very beautiful in the mountains I was about to climb). In particular they were concerned that the path up was overgrown and that I might get attacked by unspecified animals while camping in the mountains. To avoid the overgrown section of path they described a different route. I had difficulty following their instructions; there were so many roads leading out of the village to various orchards, so I stuck with my pre-planned route, overgrown in places, but I managed to push the pine saplings and tree branches aside without too much trouble. This was not always the case on my trek across Greece, and on occasions I had to find an alternate route, following tracks marked on my maps rather than paths through the trees that had long since disappeared under the undergrowth.

While camping in the high, grass covered mountains no wild animals attacked me (although I was suspicious of the intentions of some sheep dogs). Some men who stopped their pick-up by my tent one evening thought I was very odd wanting to sleep out in the cold, rather than at a nearby ski resort where there may, or may not, have been accommodation. It was a little on the cool side at 1,900 metres, with a light frost one night, but nothing I was unprepared for. Among the mountains I was crossing I enjoyed pleasant walks beneath blue skies on grass-covered ridges passing flocks of sheep and buildings where the shepherds slept beside pens where the sheep were kept overnight. There were trips down into tree-filled valleys followed by a struggle up the other side. Of note was a large wind farm, after which I walked down to the Panagia Soumela Monastery. I am glad I did as in addition to a church full of frescoes and icons, candles and golden finishes, there was a selection of restaurants. I thought a late lunch was much deserved and it was certainly much enjoyed. The grey bearded owner said "meat?" and "salad?", and I just replied yes. Yes in Greek is 'ne', which sounds vaguely like the English "no" so I generally stuck to an English "yes" to make sure I did not turn down any food. The monastery replaces one in Pontus in Turkey from where the monks were forced to flee in 1923 and is associated with the Pontic Greeks who came from that area.

During this period my right ankle started giving me pain, something that would affect future trips, and was later diagnosed as Achilles tendinopathy. Possibly the result of the long distances I was covering each day, it would give me a stiff ankle after resting for a while. For my remaining trips across Europe on the E4, I just lived with the problem. Inevitably, on my long-distance hikes there are pains in my hips, knees, back or some other part of my body. I was fortunate that on this particular trip I had no problems with blisters for the first time, as they usually developed on the sides of my heels. Whether that lack of blisters was because I was using a stiffer boot with a higher ankle, or because I avoided long daily distances in my first two weeks, I am not sure.

From Florina I was using GPS 'tracks' I had downloaded for the E4, but these did not cover all the route. To cover the gaps, I constructed my own routes based on my GPS map, hiking maps I had bought from a specialist Greek company called Anavasi, and the tracks I could see on

Google Earth. A small but important gap was at the Sfikia dam, which lies in a deep valley separating the Vermio and Pieria Mountains and is one of four dams used to generate hydroelectricity in this valley. I had downloaded a GPS 'track' that took me down to the dam, another started on the other side of the dam. Naturally I assumed I could simply walk across the top of the dam on the road I could see on the satellite imaginary. To reach the dam, the downloaded GPS 'track' took me down the steep side of the valley on a zigzag track. Possibly created to install some electricity pylons, it was now grossly overgrown. At one point I met a hunter (in camouflage with his rifle in his hands). He was no doubt displeased with the noise I was making slithering over loose rocks. The most difficult bit was the last section, straight down a narrow chute of loose scree, the rocks slipping beneath my boots creating minor avalanches. I can see why this route was chosen; the surrounding, very steep slopes were covered with impenetrable vegetation, stunted trees and bushes with thorns, or else there were vertical rock faces.

On my approach to the reservoir, there was a terrace which I followed towards the dam through an area of rusting oil drums. I stuck to the GPS route as it followed the side of the valley up to where electric transmission lines rose out of a securely fenced area. I was prevented from going around one side of this high-voltage enclosure as it abutted the near vertical, concrete-coated side of the valley so I had to go around the other side. Here I followed a narrow ledge between the fence and a significant drop to my left, but at least I could grip the wire netting of the fence for support. This led me to the roadway across the dam which continued around the side of the valley to where closed, electronic metal gates, fencing and a security guard prevented me from leaving the site. Thankfully the security guard was both professional and considerate, giving me a coffee and biscuits while he made and received various phone calls and I showed him my Anavasi map with the E4 marked. After some discussion with colleagues, he handed me the phone so I could be questioned by someone who spoke English. I explained I was walking the E4, which was marked as crossing the dam. He seemed surprised I had managed to get down to the dam from the other side and wanted to confirm where I was going next. In the end it was agreed that I would show my passport to the security guard so that my details could be recorded in what I took to be the visitors' log. The gates were opened and I left the guard dealing with a group of leather clad motor bikers who had just arrived. Due to the hazardous descent and because there is no provision for hikers to cross the dam, I do not recommend anyone take this route in the future.

After another two nights in the mountains to the south of the dam, I was heading downhill through trees on a forest track. My objective that evening was the village of Dion in the middle of a large coastal plain. After five days and nights of wild camping in hot and sweaty weather, I was needing a hotel to shower and recharge my phone. As I had a long, 36 kilometre walk I started while it was still dark, causing a pick-up to stop (the first I had seen for over 24 hours) and ask what I was doing. People demanding something that sounds like *'qui passe?'* was a frequent challenge. Walkers are rare in these parts, and they may well have thought me suspicious. I usually said, "Anglica," which is meant to mean English (and by implication I don't understand a word you are saying).

In walking to Dion, I followed a mixture of quiet, tarmac roads, gravel tracks and the occasional rough path. I was on the correct E4 route at least occasionally as I spotted some waymarks. I walked through the village of Ano Milia just as the sun was rising and was excited to see the top of Mount Olympus before it was later lost in cloud. It is the highest mountain in Greece, home of the Gods, and one I would soon be climbing. By the time I reached the village of Kato Milia, its cafés and shops were open. After a coffee from the first café, a bar of chocolate from the shop next door and a flaky pastry affair from a bakery shop, I was feeling ready for anything.

I continued by olive groves, fields of vines, drying tobacco leaves and fields of hay. In contrast to the recent mountains, the ground now became very flat. After a final busy road, I reached Dion only to be disappointed when the first hotel I encountered was long closed, its front yard overgrown. But a sign pointed to a second one, opposite the museum. An elderly lady in black with a walking frame was on reception. After struggling to get up, she pressed a bell and another lady took me to a room; in fact, it was an apartment, comprising a few rooms. I was very thankful as I was very dirty, smelly and unshaven after five nights of wild camping. I gave her the money quickly before she changed her mind and then headed for the shower, tasting the salty sweat as I washed it off my head. When I had finished the soapy foam that had not drained away had formed a dirty brown scum, which I spent some time cleaning up before I left. I now smelt faintly of soap, rather than the smell of freshly baked bread that seemed to emanate from me after a few days of unwashed wild camping.

Dion was an important town from 5th century BC to the 4th AD. The museum had some impressive exhibits (what was Leda doing with the swan, or vice versa?) including an early organ (the kind with organ pipes) from the 1st century BC. At the archaeological park, however, the remains of streets and temples were less impressive than many around the Mediterranean. They were also spread out and after a long day walking perhaps that made me less enthusiastic.

On reaching the town of Litochoro, I took a rest day before my climb up Mount Olympus, a major milestone of the trip I was looking forward to. This began with a walk up the tree lined Enipeas gorge. Unlike the E4 in the rest of Northern Greece there was a good footpath, clearly marked. Crude steps had been created in places and there were even some handrails made of tree branches. Although there were some rocky bits to clamber over, the path was not difficult apart from the unrelenting upward gradient. Owing to the trees, the water running in the base of the valley was rarely visible, but when it was you could see cataracts of clear, blue water running over the rocks. After leaving the environs of Litochoro, I had the gorge to myself, although later, groups of people started coming down the path towards me, especially after reaching the cave where Saint Dionysios lived as a hermit. A tiny blue and white chapel stood on the spot. A little beyond were the ruins of the monastery he founded, destroyed during the Second World War but now partly reconstructed. Priona is where the road ends at a car park and taverna where I enjoyed a goat hotpot and Greek salad. After walking for three weeks across Northern Greece seeing few tourists, no walkers I could recall and only a few shepherds on the mountains, the path up Mount Olympus from Priona was something of a shock. Throngs of people of all nationalities and various states of fitness were climbing the rocky track through the pines. Early on there were many day trippers, whilst higher up, it was only those with backpacks, who, like myself, were heading for Refuge 'A' (officially Refuge Spilios Agapitos but nobody calls it that). Coming down the path was a string of horses, used to carry food and supplies up to the refuge and bring down the rubbish. Fortunately, I had booked a bed as the refuge was full; indeed, somehow two people with my name had booked a bed, which meant that the bunk above me in my dormitory was empty. A large group from Israel occupied the remaining beds.

Breakfast at the well-organised refuge was at six a.m. and a queue of people had already formed by that time. I was not the only one planning an early start. Some of the men looked pretty tough, muscular with sharp haircuts that meant business, blue, mirror sunglasses and no smiles. It made me wonder if I was up to the task of climbing Mytikas, the highest summit of Olympus, which requires some skill on rocks and a head for heights. In fact, I soon overtook the tougher looking guys much to my delight, only being overtaken myself later on by a thin, wiry couple as they moved effortlessly from rock to rock like gazelles. Mount Olympus looked particularly beautiful as the sky brightened and the rising sun coloured the rocky peaks ahead of me, pink against a blue sky with sharp black shadows marking ravines. I climbed out of the trees admiring the grandeur of the place, myself and the people following tiny compared with surrounding summits and the ridge, a huge slab of rock, which I was climbing on a loose gravel path. Reaching the first peak of Skala which some dogs from the refuge had reached ahead of me, I had to decide whether to tackle the much more difficult climb up to Mytikas, the highest peak at 2,918 metres, home of the God Zeus. The God of Thunder (among other things) was being kind today and the weather was perfect with no wind and empty blue skies. The climb up Mytikas was classed as a Grade 1 scramble which was within my capabilities, the rocks were dry and seemed to have plenty of hand- and footholds. Everything suggested I could give it a go. Following the red spots helpfully painted on the rocks, I climbed down from the top of Skala towards Mytikas. Going down is always more difficult than going up and I carefully looked for each foot- and handhold before making a move. I reached the saddle between Skala and Mytikas, averting my eyes from the endless drop to my left, and started to climb the steps of rock. The difficult bit was going down and around a pinnacle that stands to the west of the Mytikas summit. There was a length of wire attached to the rock to help. The final few metres going down is awkward (unless you are brave enough to stand up) but then I was rewarded by a simple climb to the pointed peak of Mytikas. There I found the couple who had passed me earlier and who were now enjoying the view, one standing on the pillar on the peak, oblivious to any fear of heights. At 2,918 metres it was the highest peak on my trip so far, narrowly beating Mount Vihren in Bulgaria by a mere four metres.

Heading back down was not so bad although there were now an increasing number of people on the mountain. As I climbed back up to the Skala summit I needed to move around a large group on a rope, a guide at each end. Others were preparing to follow them. I was glad I had started early to avoid such a crowd. How would they all fit on the small summit of Mytikas? I sat on the broader and slightly lower Skala summit, feeling pleased with myself, a little smug, and enjoyed a few biscuits, working out what all the mountains I could see were. To the north I identified the Pieria and Vermio Mountains I had crossed as well as the large windfarm I had walked through. Looking west, I tried to see the next stages of my trip. In the far distance, a range of mountains marked the horizon which I took to be the Pindus Mountains that I planned to walk along the following year. Lots of people on the now crowded summit of Skala were taking pictures and I worried that someone would step back too far in framing the perfect selfie with Mytikas in the background and fall off the near vertical northwest face of the mountain.

The E4 now took me away from the crowds as it headed for the village of Kokkinopelos. On the trail descending to Refuge 'C', I passed three Balkan chamois with their curious bent-back horns. Having been very careful on Mytikas, I now slipped and landed on my bottom on the easy but gravelly path down! Fortunately, nothing was damaged but my pride. I passed a few walkers coming up, but from the number of cars parked at Refuge C, it seems they were taking an easy route to the summit as Refuge C is at 2,450 metres, whereas most people climb from Priona at 1,100 metres or, like myself, from Litochoro, at around 300 metres.

After the unmanned Refuge C, I saw no one as I followed the E4 on a footpath down a narrow, wooded valley, losing height rapidly. In places the path looked about to disappear among the undergrowth, but after some ruins, it followed a good mule track that climbed out of the valley and around the hillside to Kokkinopelos, giving some long views across the farmland and mountains to the west. The hotel, booked for me by the tourist information office in Litochoro, had seen better days and I was the only person staying there, but it was half the price of places in Litochoro and, after the owner cooked my dinner, I was feeling satisfied with all I had achieved that day.

Kokkinopelos was pretty quiet, but at the next village of Livadi, I found the streets full of people spilling out of the local tavernas. I noticed the old men had shepherds' crocks with ornately carved hooks. Apparently, it was a Vlach village, the same Latin-speaking ethnic group I had come across in Serbia, and there was a conference on their culture taking place in the village. That evening I sat on the hotel terrace with a beer and watched the full moon rise over Mount Olympus. Beautiful!

For the next three days I would be heading in a southwesterly direction to reach Kalampaka, known for the monasteries of Meteora. I had worked out a route from the available maps which led across farmland and over hills, through a few villages. There were a few E4 signs but, not knowing where they were trying to take me, I generally stuck to small roads and tracks I could see on my maps. There were a few notable sights, such as the Holy Monastery of the Assumption of the Virgin Mary, which was last in operation in 1919. Sadly, people had carved graffiti into the obviously old paintings on the front of the church, although all was untouched inside. As usual the paintings on the iconostasis had a lot of gold leaf around the solemn faces of Jesus and the Virgin Mary.

At Livadero, I stopped for a breakfast coffee after spending the night camping on a nearby hillside. Not seeing many British tourists in town, or indeed anyone with a rucksack, I was of great interest to the customers and the lady serving. They were curious as to what I was doing. One of the men paid for my coffee and the lady serving gave me some extra biscuits. They tried to insist on driving me to the next town of Descati but I had to insist on walking, being quite firm! These very kind people must have considered me strange indeed. At the entrance to Livadero I noticed a yellow sign saying: "E4 Descati 5hr 30". The timing was about right, but, as it was pointed in the opposite direction to Descati, I ignored it. Following my planned route out of town, I found an E4 waymark indicating I was going in the right direction, as I followed a small road along a valley. Dry grass fields with Lombardy poplars dotted with farms formed the base of the valley, with woodland on higher ground. It felt a little Italian.

At Descati, the waiter at the restaurant where I had meatballs with yoghurt and tomato for lunch was concerned that it was cold for my trek, and indeed, it seemed summer was ending. It had been overcast with dark clouds since this morning; as yet there was no rain. He felt I should catch the bus. Instead, I camped that night among small oak trees by a track that had fallen into disuse, and started early the next morning. Although I had covered some large distances in the previous two days, I was fit after weeks of walking, and knew I could reach Kalampaka, and the end of this trip, that evening. Soon I was among large sandstone outcrops, which rose out of the landscape, with layers rich in rounded pebbles and streaked with grey where the water had weathered the rock. On my reaching Meteora, these outcrops had become large columns of rock, towering above me and surrounding trees. It looked like a picture from a science fiction, fantasy world, with the famous monasteries sitting on top of these rocks, or built into the side of them. The monks built them here so they could be isolated, difficult to reach, leaving them able to focus their thoughts and prayers on God. Times have changed, and the area is now a UNESCO World Heritage site. After walking through the many kilometres of quiet and empty countryside I felt I had suddenly crossed an invisible line, and was now in a quite different time and world full of coachloads of chattering tourists. As I stood in the church of one of these monasteries, surrounded by selfie-snapping visitors from all corners of the world, I could not help feeling that I was brought closer to God in the empty little churches I had visited in the mountains.

As I left on the bus the next day, beginning my return journey to Britain, I peered through the rain-streaked window at the next range of mountains, over which I would climb on my return. They seemed to be crested, by a faint layer of snow.

Chapter 13: Kalampaka to Zakros — a trinity of terrains

The Pindus Mountains

For the next section of the E4, I planned a somewhat longer trip crossing the Pindus Mountains, Peloponnese and the island of Crete in one eight- or nine-week trek. Starting on the 20th April was a risk; I had been warned that April can be "tricky", with snow covering the higher ground, snow I could indeed see from the coach as it took me back to Kalampaka. I had prepared by bringing my warm winter sleeping bag and warm clothes, but I knew that at the end of my trip in June and further south, the weather would be much warmer, forcing me to pack for a wide range of conditions.

My research on this section of E4 through the Pindus Mountains came up with a number of routes. Anavasi hiking maps show what may have been the original route; however, in places, even in the earliest reports, hikers have taken different trails, maybe to avoid overgrown sections or long stretches of road, where the original mule tracks have now been straightened and tarmacked. Leaving Kalampaka, on reaching the start of the mountains, I had a choice of three routes. None of the previous walkers I had information on had taken the route on the Anavasi map and I suspected that it no longer existed. I chose one supplied by Nikolas Kroupi of a local hotel, Hotel Kroupi. It led up a steep slope through oak trees, their branches eagerly snagging me and my rucksack. Vague paths came and went until I reached one that was more persistent, leading to a dirt track. I diverted along the track to visit the small, simple church of Agios Ioannis, a spot made beautiful by the views of distant Meteora and the bright yellow flowers and purple blossoms in front of the church. The church made it worth the effort of taking this route. Subsequent views into the Pindus Mountains showed snow-capped peaks, the upper slopes streaked with gullies of snow between rocky ridges, above forests of pine, and oak trees lower down. Grand and impressive as they were under the sunny April sky, I did have some misgivings concerning the amount of snow. These proved justified on my second day of walking.

After camping beside a stream, not far from where I saw some bear tracks, I began climbing in the hope of reaching the Koziakas refuge by lunchtime. The track through pines was awash with water from the melting snow higher up, and several trees had fallen across my path. I was surprised to see mistletoe growing on the pine trees. Higher up, above 1,500 metres, I was wading through snowdrifts, picking up the footprints of a bear, who had preceded me. As I neared the refuge, the path traversed a steep slope, covered locally in snow several feet thick and posing a risk of injury if I slipped off it. As the snow on these higher steep slopes was so hard, my boots made little impression even when I kicked into it. With crampons and an ice axe it would have been easy, but I carried neither and, facing a particularly steep and hard area of snow above what appeared to be a cliff I decided that "discretion was the better part of valour", and turned back maybe only 100 metres from the refuge (although my maps where somewhat contradictory as to where the hut was precisely located). I had a back-up route for this eventuality but it did mean several kilometres of road walking to reach the tourist town of Elati. Later in the evening I met George, a local hiker and his friend, in a nearby café. He gave me advice on the condition of the tracks I would be following in the next few days.

The next day started with a pleasant path *('monopati')* through the woods, but later, after a small road and dirt track, I was pushing through trees on an overgrown route, partly on a ridge. Branches, juniper bushes and the rotten remains of old trees made the going slow and tiring. I was glad of my GPS to show me where I should be heading. After a final track along a grassy ridge, followed by a section down a valley pushing through beech saplings, I reached my next hotel at Psarro. My tiring day was rewarded by dinner in front of a log fire.

I woke to hear the forecast rain pattering on the veranda roof outside my bedroom. Clouds obscured the mountain tops. I had originally planned to follow the E4 route on the Anavasi map which climbed up a mountain to a 1,760-metre summit but the experience of the last two days suggested there would be a bit of snow and possibly poor paths.

Mountains in the area all have very steep sides so the risk of sliding and injuring myself seemed very real. In addition, the poor visibility would mean I would not be able to see far enough ahead to ensure I did not enter difficult terrain and the path, if it existed, could be hard to spot. Fortunately, Nikolas had given me an alternative route peaking at around 1,500 metres. After assessing the risks, I headed off along Nikolas' route. Sadly, this involved descending to the bottom of a valley losing some 600 metres in height which I then had to regain climbing up the other side. The valleys in this area are steep sided, V- shaped and very deep, about 1,000 metres from the top of the mountains to the bottom of the major valleys, very much alpine terrain.

The climb up the valley was on a vehicle track, crossing a stream, swollen by meltwater. I worked my way over a few landslides, admired a stream falling over rocks in a long waterfall, and reached the top without too much difficulty. I now had to branch off onto a path going to the village of Argithea. Shrouded as I now was in the clouds, with visibility down to ten metres and banks of snow hiding landscape features, locating the path was challenging and I soon began to doubt whether it really did have any physical manifestation, albeit shown promisingly on various maps. I followed my GPS route through the mist, picking up small animal tracks where the ground was not covered in snow. The slope I was traversing became progressively steeper with ridges of rock alternating with lengths of snow. As I crossed the steep, snow-covered sections, it was perhaps for the best that the mist prevented me from seeing how far I could slide down if I slipped, the white snow blending in with the white cloud. I was thankful that I had brought a trekking pole to dig into the snow and provide support. After a very slow, cautious kilometre or so, and some rusty barbed wire that entangled my boots, the slope became easier and the ground grassy. I was able to pick up a goat track heading in the right direction, and I was ready to face the next obstacle. This soon presented itself in the form of creeping juniper bushes, blocking the path, the branches grabbing at my clothing as I pushed through. Finally, as I dropped below the clouds, I joined a dirt track that wound down to the village of Argithea. Disappointingly, the café and taverna were both closed and most of the houses also looked shuttered up for the season. This would prove typical of many of the villages I passed through in the Pindus Mountains.

I camped in a nearby field and that evening reconsidered my planned route for the following day. It climbed to 1,750 metres and would undoubtedly be under yet more snow. Rather than sticking with the E4 path, I therefore decided to take a vehicle track, hoping that it would at least be better defined. So it proved. I saw no sign of the E4 footpath, but the track I was following was obvious and passable rising up to a pass of grass and stone, before taking me along the mountain side. Whilst there were extensive drifts of snow across the track, there was nothing unsafe that I could not wade through. My reward was a view down onto the top of the clouds covering the plain of Thessaly. I find looking down on clouds from a height especially appealing, making the effort of climbing many hundreds of metres worthwhile. The thought that the population on the plain were having a cloudy day while I had weak sunshine also gave me some satisfaction, while I chewed on some sticky dried cherries and admired the yellow coltsfoots and purple crocuses nestled among the rocks.

As there is little flat ground at the bottom of the valleys, the village of Vlasso, like most others, was built on the side of a hillside among the trees. The café was closed, but, at the next village of Petrilo, it was with much joy that I found a taverna-cum-shop which was open. The smiling couple running the place spoke no English but translation was provided by a workman installing what appeared to be a red LED sign advertising the place and giving the time and a temperature, although the latter was about five degrees too high judging by the traditional thermometer inside. Soon I was tucking into a three-egg omelette, tomato salad, cheese and bread, and my cup of coffee, a repast that set me up nicely for a night camping among the pines at the next pass.

Much of the next two days was spent on rough roads, which moved up and down the sides of the valley among the trees. Periodically I would see a tree with dark pink blossom that brightened the scene. The extensive areas of rocks exposed by the recent road cuttings were a geologist's dream, showing contorted folds and faults. At one point I tried to follow a mule track but it rapidly deteriorated, threatening to slide over a cliff, and I suspected it would disappear altogether in some landslip on the steep slope it was climbing up. My GPS was also giving erratic readings owing to the narrow valley obscuring its satellites, so I had no good guide to where exactly the overgrown path should go. So I retraced my steps and followed a gravel road to Agrafa, and a guesthouse where the two cheerful ladies running it served me baked aubergine stuffed with onion, feta cheese and a dish of local 'mountain greens' called *'horti'*. *Horti* was to be enjoyed at various places in my travels through Greece.

The following night found me camping on a grassy promontory among the pines. There was a small shrine nearby, and as usual oil and matches were left inside. I wondered whether to light the lamp (but didn't). A deer barked nearby; birds twittered; in the far distance, bells rang, and I thought I could just pick out Mass being sung, far away down in the next valley.

In walking down to the town of Karpenesi, I crossed one of the ancient bridges. I had seen a number on my trip, most next to ugly, new road bridges, but this one stood alone, unspoilt by any modern surroundings. These older bridges, built of stone, had thin, graceful arches rising high over the river, and were used in the days when mules, rather than pick-ups, carried the goods. I took a rest day in Karpenesi over the Orthodox Easter. On Saturday evening there was a special meal to mark the end of lent at ten p.m., then at midnight, church bells rang out to celebrate Christ's resurrection. On Easter Sunday I had a traditional roast lamb diner in one of the town's restaurants while a guitar and bouzouki player entertained the customers. Fortunately, I had earlier found a chemist open, as I had been attacked by some biting insect which had left my midriff with lots of itchy red spots.

For the next seven days I continued through the Pindus Mountains. Snow was no longer an issue, at least on the route I took. Reluctantly, I avoided a possible route over the Giona Mountains. Although I had been told it was very beautiful, at 2,000 metres, the steep slopes were covered with snow. Mainly I walked through pine forests or, at lower altitudes, through areas of holm oak. Holm oak, also called the holly oak, has leaves like holly and numerous prickly examples thereof went down my back as I tried to push my way through on some of the smaller paths.

Apart from one notable day the trail was reasonably well marked, a mixture of paths, quiet roads and forest tracks.

There were a few challenges. Two rivers blocked my way, bloated by meltwater into deep and fast-flowing torrents. I removed my socks and trousers to cross them, the water coming up to my knees, but kept my boots on due to the rocky nature of the river bed. My boots, with their thick padding, took days to dry out in the cool weather and, walking with my feet damply cocooned, led to some painful blisters. Another challenge was a section of path which ran along sections of scree slope. A previous hiker, of a similar age to me, had slipped and scraped all the skin off his hand, causing his partner to note that there is no mountain rescue in Greece. So warned, I cautiously and safely passed the difficult sections. A third challenge was a common one: lack of a path. I generally managed by pushing my way through, following the track on my GPS, picking up a faint track then losing it again among the undergrowth and tree branches. GPS tracks are only accurate to maybe thirty metres, due to errors in calculating the position combined with errors in the original track, so when possible, I would move to the left and right of the GPS 'track' in an attempt to find the trail. Some paths were more overgrown than others, and some had plenty of yellow-and-black waymarks to help, whereas others had none. On one occasion, suspecting a path would be impassable, I made a nine-kilometre detour to join a 'track' I knew that others had taken. However, it was not all hard going; there were long periods on tracks and minor roads when I could admire the scenery. One day I came upon an open-cast bauxite mine, its deep, terraced pit beside the road. Another point of interest, was a small monastery I visited, its church carefully tended with lighted lamps in front of the gold-haloed icons on the iconostasis. There were no longer monks in residence but some workmen were undertaking restoration work on the paths. One of the them offered me a cube of loukoumi, the Greek version of Turkish Delight, and poured me a drink from a mineral water bottle to accompany it. I drank, mistakenly thinking it was water, and spluttered. Of course it was some spirit, maybe tsipouro, and he had tried to warn me, but it was all Greek to me. However, it went very well with the loukoumi.

A few of the red-roofed villages were showing signs of life. It was the Easter holidays and many Greeks seem to retain houses in the mountain villages, perhaps owned by their family for generations, while working in cities elsewhere. In the holidays they would return and cafés and tavernas opened to accommodate them. In one village, I hesitated in the empty village square wondering if a place was open, when a man beckoned me in. A helpful customer who spoke good English (having studied in Newcastle) arranged food for me. They were maybe pleased to see me visiting their village as my coffee and Coke were on the house! In some places I found rooms to stay at; other times, I camped in the woods.

Supplies, or lack thereof, had now become a preoccupation. Karpensesi was the last place where I had found shops but most had been closed due to the Easter holidays. Initially I had been able to find a few places to eat but there arrived two days during which no shops, cafés or restaurants were open and my supplies were running low. I was therefore keen to reach Eptalofu, a village with tourist accommodation, before I ran out of provisions altogether. It was a long day pushing through undergrowth, and crossing mountains. The final 'path' to the village, which I initially missed, was down a steep slope. Although I spotted bits of paths in places, and even the occasional E4 waymark, really it was more of a routing that you follow with your GPS as best you can, down the mountainside, pushing through trees, stumbling over rocks and squashing plants and flowers. In the meadows lower down a pleasant, herby smell arose from the wild thyme crushed under my boots. Finally reaching the village, tired and footsore, I stopped at the first accommodation that had signs of life. It proved a good choice, with English-speaking staff, heated rooms and reasonable prices. My dinner of locally produced lamb chops was really tasty and much appreciated.

The Pindus Mountains were beautiful, wild and untamed; unlike the Alps, there were no mountain huts waiting for me each night. However, after sixteen days of walking and 410 kilometres I was ready for a different type of landscape and indeed the change I was anticipating came suddenly. As I stood on a hilltop high above the ancient city of Delphi, behind me were pine trees and rocky mountains; in front of me, dropping away was a more Mediterranean landscape, dryer, with bush size holm oaks, brightly coloured flowers in crevices between stones, and the odd tortoise. For this final descent the E4 was on a well-made path with rough limestone blocks forming the edges and crude steps. The path made long sweeps back and forth across the mountainside as it slowly descended, so slowly I wondered if I would ever reach the town of Delphi that I could see below me. There were tantalising glimpses of the stadium in the famous archaeological site where naked Greeks once raced. Finally, in a profusion of yellow flowers, I reached a road on the edge of Delphi and a little later booked into my hotel. Although I had visited the ruins twice before I felt I could not leave Delphi without a brief walk up the Sacred Way to pay tribute to Apollo and the view from his temple, the tall yellow fennel growing among the ruins adding to the beauty of the scene in the evening light.

From Delphi the E4 follows a truly old path, used by the ancients as they climbed up from their boats to consult the famous oracle. I lost it somewhere in the olive groves of the coastal plain, but managed to reach Itea in time for a lunch of calamari and fries in a café full of rough-looking men with stubbly chins playing cards, eating fried sardines, drinking some clear spirit or just talking. When the E4 was first surveyed, there was a ferry from Itea to the Peloponnese. Now there is a huge white cantilever bridge to the west. This I crossed on a coach which left me for the night at the city of Patras. Although Patras is a little shabby, it was lively in the evening with people meeting and greeting each other in cafés and bars. In the morning I walked by the castle and Roman remains before catching a coach to the town of Diakofto, on the north coast of the Peloponnese.

The Peloponnese

From Diakofto to Kalavryta the E4 follows a 120-year-old railway line. Using a rack and pinion system in the steepest sections, the line follows a gorge into the mountains across numerous bridges over foaming waters and through several tunnels cut into the rock. The walls of the gorge, of conglomerate and limestone, force you to walk on the tracks themselves through the tunnels and across the bridges (despite signs saying "no pedestrians"). I checked at the station before starting, and was informed that no passenger trains were running on the day I walked this scenic route, which was fortunate as the gap between the rails and the river or rock face was not always very large. In retrospect, however, the station staff may have surmised that it was a ride I was seeking, not a walk along the tracks, since a maintenance train did indeed pass me, fortunately when I was sitting down on a pile of sleepers beside the track having a snack. The moratorium on trains that day clearly only applied to would-be passengers, not E4 walkers.

It was an exciting start to my fifteen-day trek on the E4 across the Peloponnese. Here the E4 was far better maintained and waymarked compared with my previous experience in Greece. This was thanks to two volunteers, Rolf Roost, originally from Switzerland, and Giorgos (or George) Kanellopoulos (of whom more later). Having walked through Greece for over two months on this trip and the previous one, without meeting any hikers on the trail other than the multitudes climbing Mount Olympus, it was pleasing to meet a handful of people walking the E4 in the Peloponnese, including two Russians and a two people from Britain. Rolf and George were in a large part responsible for this greater popularity.

I spent two weeks crossing the Peloponnese through a variety of landscapes. The first few days were over low hills, walking on paths through meadows with occasional bushes of prickly holm oak, or areas of holm oak bushes with patches of grass in which I had trouble following the path. When I walked the trail in May, the grassland and meadows were stuffed full of flowers: yellow, pink, blue and white. I thought the flowers looking like pink dandelions were particularly fetching, I later learnt they were called Crepis Rubra. Although the hills were rounded, a fair bit of rock was exposed and the paths could be quite stony. Few people were about until, in one of the valleys, by an overflowing river, shaded by plane trees, I found a restaurant, several stalls selling honey and herbs, two coaches, many cars and crowds of people. Fortunately, the restaurant was not too busy to sell me a lunch of two trout, a pile of 'mountain greens' and a large plate of chips. This set me up for wild camping that evening, at a spot where the path crossed a ridge, where I thought myself miles from anyone. However, as the light was beginning to fade, I became aware of goat bells. Soon I was trapped in my tent surrounded by goats and a few barking dogs. Fortunately, the goatherd called them off and the jingling bells faded away as they were gathered into some pen down in the valley.

I was passing through little villages, which often had an open coffee shop, each of which naturally required my custom and a shot of strong coffee. Among the white-haired men gathered there, with their good Greek moustaches, not much older than myself, I felt quite at home. Sometimes one spoke English and, after the usual questions, where was I from, where was I going, was I alone, they would sadly talk of the decline in the village; younger people moving away to the cities, there being no nearby doctor, empty houses, some abandoned and falling into disrepair. Many seemed to have emigrated, heading for America, even setting up societies of people from their village in the New World. In one village, later in my walk through the Peloponnese, I was offered a plot of land as an encouragement to augment the village population.

In addition to paths through the hills, there was some road walking, some over flat agricultural land by a river. Although I passed fields of barley with scattered trees, one or two plots of potatoes and some small, overgrown vineyards, I was surprised that much of the land was not more intensively farmed given its apparent suitability. Much of it was either fallow, old fields of barley now with drifts of red poppies, or meadows full of flowers, maybe kept as pasture. Vytina was a tourist village with whole shops devoted to selling honey. I walked to the grey, cobbled, village square for my breakfast. The lady at the bakery broke off planting flowers in troughs to serve me a cappuccino and a spiral of flaky pastry with feta cheese inside. It was Sunday. As I sipped my coffee, I could hear the service being sung inside the church opposite. The Orthodox tradition sounds much more holy and religious than the Church of England, although maybe the foreignness of the language helps to increase the sense of mystery and wonder. Older ladies in black periodically crossed the square and entered the church.

After Vytina, I crossed the Menalon Mountains, an excursion back into pine trees, the sun releasing their sharp, refreshing scent. Higher up where the trees thinned, there were patches of snow and the desolate, skeletal structures of idle ski lifts. The following day I was back among the holm oaks and flower meadows as I walked through rain into the city of Tripoli. When, in answer to her question, I told the receptionist at the hotel that I was walking along the E4, she thought I was referring to the motorway! The city had a lively centre with coffee shops and eateries centred on a few squares, with older churches squashed in between more modern buildings. I bought a beer in a café filled with men, where the television was showing a water polo match.

The general advice for those walking the E4 is to take a taxi out of Tripoli, but I walked along the road south, through a neglected farming area to the village of Stadio, with its archaeological park containing ruins of medieval, ancient Greek and Byzantine times, set among avenues of horse chestnut trees, and an attractive café at which I was the sole customer. Later the E4 took me up a stream bed. I stumbled over boulders and small outcrops, trying to avoid getting the inside of my boots wet as I worked my way around pools of water. Stream beds are not my favourite routing. The danger of injury on wet, slippery and loose rocks is high and progress slow. Eventually I gave up and followed a nearby road up to the mountainside village of Ano Doliana. Signs indicated where actions took place when, in 1821, a smaller Greek force defeated a much larger Turkish army in the Greek War of Independence. I enjoyed a late lunch at a small hotel, which included a lovely orange cake for dessert. Climbing out of Ano Doliana on various paths (some overgrown) and tracks, I admired the views back at the village, set among trees, and Tripoli and the Menalon Mountains in the white, hazy distance. After walking past orchards of sweet chestnut trees, I found a place to sleep on a wooded slope, among terraces that I assume were farmed long, long ago, but now made a flat place to pitch my tent among the evening midges.

In the early morning light on cresting a hill, I had my first sight of the ocean to the south of the Peloponnese and a little later the Taygetos Mountains. They rose in the distance, black ridges pointing upwards, highlighted by white snow, set against the morning sky, which looked like watery blue silk. Later they were hidden by cloud. I made fast progress among the trees, stopping for a morning coffee and a croissant out of a sealed plastic bag. Back on the move, the mountains around me were covered with small holm oak, occasional areas with pine trees, some regular oak trees, even the odd Italian cypress, tall and thin. The track was bordered with flowers, especially cistus, white with yellow centres, and also a pink variant. I passed one isolated church, and there was another, looking picturesque, down in the valley. The flowers, the sun, the views, and the easy walking all put me in a cheerful mood. After another coffee, discussing Brexit and the troubles Greece had with the European Union, I realised that if I kept up my pace, I could reach Sparta that evening, a place whose name resonated with memories of childhood tales of the contrast between the tough Spartans and the more intellectual Athenians. Initial progress was good until the E4 decided to follow the inevitable stream bed. To avoid water coming over the top of my boots, I put on my lightweight, canvas shoes I used in hotels and waded through the clear waters, over pebbles, in the dappled shade of plane trees that lined the banks. Progress was slower than I had anticipated and I became impatient; never wise in such circumstances as it contributes to accidents. Finally, to my great relief, the E4 followed a track away from the river. I dried my feet with my hanky and put my socks and boots back on. Progress, along various vehicle tracks, then improved. Gradually the holm oak and pines were replaced by olive trees. The flowers growing thickly between them suggested they were not intensively farmed. I arrived at a hotel at 7:30 p.m. and was soon eating dinner in the garden of a nearby restaurant, members of a German tour group nearby. In the central square that evening it looked like there was a communist party rally, as a small group of people with red KKE flags listened to a man on a platform reading a speech in a monologue. They needed a more rousing speaker to bring in the crowds.

Not far from Sparta the remains of the 13th century Byzantine city of Mystra are spread over a steep hillside. A fortified city with a fortress at the summit dominating the plain below, churches and monasteries were the most intact buildings still standing, one of which appeared still to be in use. Ancient wall paintings, fragmented and much faded, reminded me of modern Greek Orthodox churches where the Byzantine double-headed eagle still features as the emblem on their yellow-and-black flags. The site was very popular, with several coach parties, noisy school children and tourists of various nationalities, wandering around the narrow ancient streets. Blue campanula spotted some walls, ivy covered others and between the ancient remains and cobbled paths, the undergrowth grew in green profusion.

I woke early next morning to the sound of heavy rain pounding my flysheet and grumbling thunder. Fortunately, my tent was watertight and as breakfast was not served at the campsite café until eight a.m., I snuggled deeper into my sleeping bag for a pleasant sensation of warmth and security if not sleep. Fortunately, the rain stopped soon after I set off for the village of Anavryti in the Taygetos range. The E4 seemed to follow a vehicle track (probably, the signage was confusing), however, as advised by various sources, I followed a more interesting route up a gorge. The path was well made and well used, following a metal pipe. Although an easy walk, it was an adventurous route as the path was on the side of a steep slope and, in places, dug into a cliff. Looking ahead it was difficult to see what route the path could take, but its orange triangle markers kept me on track. The gorge itself was impressive, especially looking down it and seeing Sparta in the distance between large grey and orange cliffs. In one place a chapel had been built in a shallow cave, complete with candles, lamps and wall paintings. I stayed at a guesthouse at Anavryti, run by Mary and George. Dating from the 1930s it was a doctor's house, and they had tried to preserve its original features and character. George, together with Rolf, maintains the E4 in the Peloponnese. He gave me an E4 waymark sticker as a memento.

As I was passing by Profitis Ilias, the highest peak in the Taygetos range, and indeed in the Peloponnese, it seemed a shame not to climb it. So, leaving my tent at the (locked) refuge at its base, I climbed through trees, then over rocks, up the steep slope following painted red squares. A dramatic vista opened up to the east. Higher up, there was ground-hugging vegetation among the rocks, some with sharp thorns that caused me some pain when I put my hand on them. This is the altitude where the local mountain tea comes from, of which I had enjoyed a cup yesterday. It is a popular walk and I met several hikers. As I gained height it became necessary to cross areas of snow which filled shallow valleys on the mountainside. George had lent me crampons and an ice axe (which fortunately I knew how to use after a course earlier in the year) but neither was really necessary as the season was late, the snow was soft, and my trekking pole on its own sufficed. Nearer the top, the path avoided the snow, following a ledge of rock which provided a natural pavement. As I crested the ridge two things hit me: the wind and the enormous view across the sea on the other side. From here I could see both sides of the Mani peninsula, the spine of which is formed by the Taygetos Mountains. Picking my way through and over the rocks and scree, avoiding the snow, I laboriously climbed towards the Profitis Ilias summit. The last 200 metres were painful but I was finally rewarded when I reached the little roofless chapel at the top in an area sheltered from the wind. There I enjoyed bread and cheese Mary had given me for a late lunch and took some pictures. However, no photo could capture the scope of what I saw before me. I could see all three prongs of the Peloponnese extending into the Mediterranean Sea. Between myself and the sea, the ground fell away to lower wooded mountains, plains, towns and cities. Definitely worth the long climb on such a clear day.

From Anavryti, the E4 follows paths through pine forests for two days. At one point I disturbed a herd of wild boar, some very big, black and brown ones, others smaller with dappled fur. They were pushing up the pine duff with their snouts, searching for food, their little tails wagging furiously. I also saw what I took to be wild sheep with long fur, or they might have been goats. On the last part of my walk to the village of Arna my progress was very slow as the rocky path, while certainly scenic as it snaked along the side of a steep valley, was making my feet very sore. When a customer at the taverna I stopped at for a late lunch offered to arrange a room for the night, I accepted immediately. His offer of a beer was also accepted with alacrity!

Over the next two days, I walked down to the port of Gythio on quiet roads and old mule tracks. Higher in the hills I passed woodland with low deciduous trees; lower down, olive trees on terraces overgrown with a florist's shop of wildflowers. Among the olives were fig trees and the odd walnut and apple tree. In places the roadside looked like a painting by a very enthusiastic Impressionist artist, with splashes of yellow and white all over the place, clusters of red spots acting as highlights, and drifts of purple and blue, with some giant dandelion clocks for contrast, all set against an olive-green background. Small green lizards scurried away on my approach, as did a snake. I drifted along lost in my thoughts as the road or track went in and out valleys, up and down hills (although as usual I remembered more 'ups'). Over the last few kilometres into Gythio, I was again suffering from problems with my right ankle, so I was glad to reach the edge of town. I walked down to the harbour, with its restaurants grouped around it and booked into a seafront hotel, enjoying an uninterrupted sea view from my bedroom. Downstairs the restaurant served me dinner of a plate of small fish and I finished with coffee and a Metaxa brandy to celebrate completion of the Peloponnese stage of the E4.

Crete

I had timed my arrival at Gythio so I was there on a Wednesday, that being the only day a ferry was running to Kissamos in Western Crete, where the E4 continued. After sailing late in the afternoon, the ferry stopped to drop off and load cars, lorries and people at the island of Kythira shortly before sunset; indeed, connecting Kythira to various places was perhaps the main point of the ferry. I watched the sunset as we left the southern tip of the island behind, the conditions overcast, the dying sun colouring the clouds on the horizon a deep red, shading to deep purple higher up. Alone on the deck, in the cold wind, I watched the last of the colour disappear. Arriving on Crete, I walked along the road in the dark for a few kilometres from the harbour to my hotel. Well after midnight, I was concerned that it would all be shut up. I need not have worried. Reception was expecting me and I received a warm welcome. It was a beach resort, evidently used by tour groups, very different to the little guesthouses and hotels I had been staying at in Greece to date.

Unlike many other parts of Greece crossed by the E4, Crete is very popular with tourists and well-endowed with the infrastructure to cope with them. It also has some of the most popular sections of the E4, with many people walking them, sometimes up to twenty times! This means that, at least in the most travelled sections, hotels, rooms and guesthouses are available. I was glad as I did not find the wild camping options very attractive. Outside olive groves, vineyards and wheat fields, the slopes were steep, and the ground too full of rocks and thistles to make for good campsites. That said, accommodation on the less-travelled eastern section of the E4 in Crete was in distinctly short supply. One of the frustrations in Crete was the number of routes claiming to be the E4, making it difficult to know which the official ones are, which ones should you walk? On the plus side it gives plenty of scope for creating your own route. I tried to combine some of the "must walk" parts of Crete, such as the Samaria gorge and the coast sections in Chania province, while also avoiding too many needlessly circuitous options. The route's popularity also meant that there were GPS 'tracks' to download and a guidebook for the route called 'The Cretan Way'.

For the first day's walking on Crete, the E4 officially followed a tarmac road, but there were better options. I made a deviation via the ancient ruins at Polyrinia and then climbed up the Sirikari gorge, before crossing a saddle to reach a village near the east coast of Crete. Although the remains at Polyrinia were thinly scattered, the view from the hill top and the wild flowers were impressive, particularly the alliums—purple balls of flower. In the village there was a little tourist information house, where a lady exchanged coffee and apricot cake for a donation. In addition to pointing out Venetian arches she told me of the three months of rain and thunderstorms that had devastated the area over the winter, washing away bridges and sections of road. I later saw the damage for myself, including where a complete section of road had collapsed leaving cables and pipes hanging loose. It was yet to be repaired but I managed to cross the collapsed section on the loose dirt and rocks in the landslipped scar. In the Sirikiri gorge a good path wound between the bare, steep, rocky sides of the valley. The river itself, falling over rocks in its bed below plane trees, looked refreshingly cool. I would later walk through more impressive gorges, but this was the first. Leaving the gorge, I climbed a track through trees up to an exposed ridge, populated by wind and wind turbines, before I descending back into woodland.

Here I encountered fencing of a type I was to see frequently on Crete, constructed of rebar posts and the wide steel mesh normally used to reinforce concrete. Gates were made of a section of mesh tied onto the posts with rope or twisted wire that I had to untangle to get through and then make good again to keep the gate up and closed. It's not an ideal arrangement nor is it likely to last, I think. I assumed this effort at fencing is to keep the goats or sheep in a particular area without needing a goatherd or shepherd to follow the flock around, as they do in much of Greece; probably a less expensive way of looking after your animals.

After a night at the little village of Berpathiana, I walked down towards the sea in the Kabou gorge, between towering rocks and by a steam splashing over rounded rocks. It was a pretty path, which was fortunate, because, on reaching the end of the gorge, I realised I was not on my intended route and had to retrace my steps, all seven kilometres of them to be enjoyed again and added to my day! Back on track I eschewed the official E4 route which follows the coast road. Rather than follow such an unimaginative route, I followed a smaller road that went close to the sea, passing empty pebbly beaches with some lone straw umbrellas, a village and a place selling ice creams. My destination for the day was Chrisoskalitisa—a collection of tavernas offering rooms, popular with tourists. After checking into one I visited the 17th century Golden Monastery. Although quite plain now, it is said once to have boasted golden steps, later sold to pay Ottoman taxes, although devout Christians can still see one step of gold. This was one vision which eluded me!

The following day I also deviated from the official route along the road, taking an alternate one marked by two red stripes, the mark of the 'Cretan Way'. For much of the walk, the path was difficult to spot as I pushed through low bushes, some of them thorny, releasing a scent of thyme. In several places I lost the red markings and the mixture of large rocks and bushes made it difficult to find a way forward. After much effort, I reached a bluff. I climbed down, negotiated a typical Cretan rebar fence and reached the start of Elafonisi beach. A naked man discreetly sunbathing under a tree marked the outer perimeter. The beach was a complete contrast to the empty area I had just crossed. Coaches were disgorging people who joined many others sunbathing on the white sand by the turquoise blue sea. Bars offered drinks; there were sunbeds and umbrellas; an air of hedonism prevailed.

Leaving the beach E4 signs and yellow-and-black stripes directed me over rocks a little way, passing a boatload of tourists. Beyond the rocks the E4 went through, according to the sign, a rare ecosystem of sand dunes and juniper trees. Whilst undoubtedly very pretty, the sand made for slow going. I continued on sand or rock past a few small beaches. Unlike Elafonisi beach, only a few people were enjoying them, others possibly discouraged by the longer walk from the nearest car park.

Then there was a section involving climbing up rocks and traversing steep slopes, passing occasional, long-haired goats, and climbing up and over a headland. The E4 left me on Krios Beach, where the taverna at which I had hoped to refresh myself was closed (although I found a café on the road a kilometre or so later). Moving onto the coastal plain I walked past acres of 'greenhouses' made of plastic sheeting. Inside were lines of tomato plants, the fruit in various stages of ripeness. I decided to spend the night camping in Grammeno a few kilometres short of the town of Paleochora. My choice was in part because the site was beside a beach and I fancied a swim in the sea, having seen so many enjoying it as I walked along, hot and sweaty. Full of enthusiasm, I pitched my tent, ignoring as best as possible the cold wind that had suddenly sprung up. It proved more difficult to ignore the cold water and my bathing was extremely brief! Sometimes the idea of something is more pleasant than the actual experience.

My debit card had been rejected on my last three attempts to pay. "Connection errors" were reported. This difficulty was causing me some anxiety and a little embarrassment, as it made it look as if I was trying to make fraudulent transactions. Although my bank assured me the card should work, as it was not working this was not very helpful. I also carried a credit card but the provider decided at this inopportune moment to change the card before its expiry date, so the one I was carrying would soon run out. I relied on cards to avoid carrying a load of cash, so I had less to lose if it was stolen; consequently, without the cards I was a bit stuck. It was therefore with some trepidation that I tried the cash machine in the town of Paleochora, the first town of any size since I had started my Cretan walk. Fortunately, this time the cards worked and I withdrew as much cash as I was allowed. I celebrated with a breakfast of yoghurt and fruit at a café, it came with a free piece of cake, which made me even happier. Then I wandered up to the Venetian fortress which provided a vantage point to look down on the old town, built on a peninsula with red-tiled roofs and white- and cream-coloured walls. That day's walk to the next village of Sougia was along the coast, again very scenic and, as such, contributing to the popularity of the E4 in Crete. After a section of gravel track to the first beach, my path snaked around the dry, rocky slopes overlooking the azure and, in shallower water, turquoise sea. In one place there were ancient ruins, bits of an amphitheatre, the walls of a building with a mosaic floor, and a small Orthodox church of some more recent period with old wall paintings. The day ended with a descent into a short gorge of unexpected beauty, a great slab of rock curving above me, shrubs with red flowers decorating the dry gorge bed.

The next day, I climbed the much longer Agia Irini gorge, up to the Omalos plateau. A fine gorge, narrow in places beneath high cliffs out of which occasional pine trees somehow managed to grow. Rough wooden ladders, steps and railings helped me and my fellow walkers over rocks and large bounders. I was struck by the dragon arum lilies, a somewhat vulgar flower, like normal arum lilies but deep reddish purple in colour with an unpleasant smell. At a fork I branched off up the steeper and rocky Figou gorge, an old mule track at the top left me at the edge of the Omalos plateau, a flat, farmed expanse of mainly grassland, guarded by a ring of mountains. At this higher altitude the grass looked green rather than straw coloured as it did nearer sea level in Crete, although it was only May.

Fresh from sharing the pleasures of Agia Irini with a small number of other walkers, the following morning I joined throngs of tourists piling out of their coaches at the start of the famous Samaria gorge, an extremely popular challenge that features prominently on the 'to-do' list of many visitors to the island. Arriving relatively late, at around 9:30 a.m., I noted that most of my fellow walkers had got a good start on me, with the result that it was pretty crowded on the initial steep descent. As the kilometres progressed, however, people became more strung out, so that at one point I could see no one and began to wonder if I was on the right path! Some of the people had clearly not been hiking for a while and were moving very hesitantly down rocky bits, and I worried that their knees would feel like jelly at the bottom. As you might expect for such a popular walk, a lot of effort had been made to create the path, with wooden railings next to drops and some crude wooden bridges. However, there were still boulders to negotiate and several crossings of the clear, fast-running water in the gorge on carefully placed stepping stones. The first part was through pine trees flanked by large rocky mountains. More spectacular sections came later with huge cliffs each side of the narrow gorge, making people look really small and insignificant, despite their brightly coloured clothing. The layers in the rock, grey and brown, dipping down to the water and folded in places, added to the beauty of the surroundings. These areas were more crowded as the people going down slowed to admire and photograph the scenery and were joined by others coming up from the bottom entrance. Finally, I arrived at Agia Roumeli, at the base of the gorge, where most of my fellow hikers departed on a ferry, thus missing this little village beside the sea, dwarfed by the surrounding mountains. I had opted instead to stay the night and spent a restful evening, enjoying a lugubrious-looking fish for my dinner at one of the many restaurants. Fish had been a prominent feature of my dinners since my arrival in Crete.

The E4 from Agia Roumeli to Hora Sfakion was my final and most exciting section of coastal path in Crete; wrapped around the side of the steep slope above the sea, among rocks, prickly shrubs and small pines. Most people miss it by taking the ferry. As the village of Agia Roumeli shrank into the distance, the path reached a beach with a taverna, where a party of people were relaxing, and St Paul's chapel. This small, roughly built Byzantine church, sitting on the beach, is on the spot where St Paul is said to have baptised people while travelling to Rome. Built in a traditional cruciate shape beneath the central dome, the iconostasis, with its collection of icons, was somewhat crude, but perhaps evoked the era of an early, rougher-edged church. I continued with cliffs present above or below the path, which at two places took a somewhat precarious route across the cliff. The first was just before Likos, where the E4 followed a ledge extending from the middle part of the rock face. I made sure I did not look down. At a miniscule taverna by the beach I lunched on peas and artichokes as I recovered my composure. The villages along the south coast of Crete were all charming, the restaurants and guesthouse clustered on a small area of flat land between the mountains and the sea; however, the village of Loutro caught my attention for rather overdoing the charm. There must have been some kind of regulation as all the buildings had white walls and dark-blue shutters and doors, below flat roofs. Even the beach umbrellas and restaurant chairs and tables were blue and white. Only some yellow plastic canoes took issue with the theme, and a few houses that had dared to use the wrong shade of white or blue.

Continuing on, I came to the curve of Sweet Water Bay with its line of sun loungers and umbrellas beneath a steep and rocky slope. I was not sure how wise it was to relax below such cliffs as at the far end of the beach there had been a recent and massive rock fall. I clambered over the zone of fallen rock at a slow pace, until the E4 followed a recognisable path paved with rough rocks over older landslips. Ahead, the path seemed to be cut into the cliff with a large drop to the sea on one side. For most of the day, as far as Sweet Water Bay, I had frequently met walkers coming the other way, but here I was noticeably alone. It made me a little concerned, as, looking ahead, it seemed that one section of the path on the cliff was missing, and I was not planning on risking any heroic rock climbing if the trail had fallen into the sea. I considered catching the water taxi service rather than completing the walk, but there were no reports that the path was impassable. Provided I was happy to retrace my steps, there seemed no reason why I should not continue to see if it was possible to pass the questionable section safely. As I progressed it was apparent that a good path had been cut into the cliff at some point in the past, with concrete being added in places at a later date. The section I thought was missing was intact; I had been misled by the perspective, although I was careful not to look at the drop beside me. Soon I was at my hotel. The man who showed me to my room joked that it was a thirty-minute walk away; being rather grumpy after seven hours' walking, I was not amused. Once installed, I found my room was worth the walk, as it looked directly over the seafront. Relaxing on my balcony I watched as hundreds of tourists disembarked from the ferry from Agia Roumeli.

The remainder of my eastward walk across Crete on the E4 was along the mountainous spine of the country. To reach the higher ground I climbed up the Imbros gorge, a more intimate experience than the more famous Samaria gorge. It is narrower than its bigger brother and in places I could simultaneously touch the cliffs each side, as they ascended vertically above me, providing some welcome shade. After the gorge, I left the other tourists behind, and continued climbing, sweating profusely. I noticed the sheep were all huddled under trees to find shade from the heat of the sun. That evening I had decided to wild camp, where the E4 (or a version of it) left the road, in an area of rocks and small trees in some hilly terrain, used to graze sheep. Many of these animals had bells around their necks. Periodically in the night the noise of jangling bells came close to my tent before receding. I surmised that at least some sheep grazed at night and slept under a shady tree during the day. Not a bad idea with their woolly coats.

After decamping next day, I walked a few kilometres down into Kallikratis. Shadows cast by the low morning sun picked out in high contrast the fine detail of the trees, houses and plots of land in the village, which was located on a flat area of ground, against a backdrop of stony mountains. From a distance it did not look like there was much in the village, so I was very pleased to find at 7.10 a.m. an open café (or one which opened on seeing me). I ordered a Greek coffee, and the proprietor (an unshaven grey-haired man with a moustache) said "feta?", to which I said yes. So I had a breakfast of feta cheese, dressed with olive oil and some bread. The feta was a fresh, soft and crumbly variety and my host indicated it came from the two goats in the small field opposite, which he proceeded to feed. As I sat eating my cheese the occasional battered pick-up passed by with plastic churns, some white and some brown, containing, I deduced, milk from freshly milked goats or sheep as there were no cows in the area. A flock of sheep gathered on the road nearby, two of which were having a headbutting competition. On a gate being opened mysteriously, by an unseen hand, the well-trained sheep went through it, though I saw no shepherd or sheepdog organising them. Whether headed for milking or feeding, they clearly knew what they were doing.

For the next four days, I crossed hills and mountains, at times on roads and on others on paths. The latter could be overgrown and once, among a tangle of trees in a rocky ravine, I was forced to stop, retrace my steps and follow a road. The rebar fences continued to get in my way. Vegetation varied: in the more mountainous areas there were outcrops of rock, rough grass, low scrub with yellow broom or gorse, and various prickly plants; on lower slopes, there were old olive groves or low oaks. In the valleys, it was predominantly fields of grass and golden grain already harvested. Terraces were cut into the mountainside around some villages to increase the farmed area. At Argiroupoli, there was a natural spring which a string of restaurants had used to good effect to create water features for their customers who sat under trees, cooled by the water, eating trout. Sections of the water features also served as holding stations, in which trout could be observed swimming, a staging post on the way to the dinner plate. Coachloads of tourists were enjoying the food. A quite different scene met me at the abandoned village of Nisi. As I climbed up the hill approaching it, I noticed the old terraces, constructed with big white boulders to trap the meagre, dry earth. Once constructed with much effort, the terraces were now used only by goats, the abandoned olive trees competing with holm oak and other species trying to colonise the old farmland. Aside from a small building roofed with corrugated steel, there were no houses still intact, only walls and piles of masonry. Some of the old entrances had attractive arches, making it appear that their owners were once wealthy. Now the village was occupied by goats who stared at me, and a flock of sheep, heading purposefully along the track to some appointment. As is typical of Greece, I passed a number of small Orthodox churches, some in villages and some standing alone on the hillside. Each had the same design and interior fittings: an iconostasis; a lectern; a place to burn candles; a lamp or two, and some icons and maybe wall paintings. The paintings of Jesus, Mary and the saints always looked so solemn. Some of these frescoes dated back as far as the 13th century. The style in which they are painted seems to have changed little over the centuries; the older ones are just more faded.

On this section, I had periodically met up with an Austrian party of friends, following the same route as myself. Seeing them following me gave some confidence when pushing through undergrowth that I was actually on the correct path. My last sight of the Austrians was when I passed them on the climb up to Timos Stavros, the highest point on Crete at 2,456 metres, in the Psiloritis mountain range. I had started early from my rooms so I could begin the day's enormous climb in the cool of the morning. Being west-facing, the mountainside was also in shade as I set out, so I made a good start on the 2000 metre or so climb up to the summit, before the sun heated things up. Early on I missed a few turnings on the dirt tracks I was following, as I watched the sun colour the mountain of Kedros on the other side of the valley. After passing olive trees, gates and herds of goats on terraced pasture, my route headed up a path which rose steeply through stony ground with scattered thorny oaks. I passed a (locked) mountain refuge, after which it was a steep climb over loose rocks with the usual low thorny bushes, aromas of thyme and sage hanging in the air as I pushed past the straggly herbs. Waymarking on this popular section was very good, which helped me to pick the correct path among the many created by sheep and goats. Patches of snow interrupted my passage, not so easy to negotiate on steep slopes. Most I could walk around. On one large patch, someone had laid out a lengthy fixed rope over the snow, with loops so you had something to hang on to if you slipped. Eventually I arrived at the summit of Timos Stavros, with its small chapel built out of the loose stone covering the mountain. I was fortunate there was no cloud, unlike the day before, so I could see the sea both to the north and south of Crete, the White Mountains to the west, and the remainder of the Psiloritis mountain range to the east, although a haze precluded decent photographs.

Coming down after some lunch and admiring the view, I was following a different path that would take me the length of the mountain range. This path traversed the very steep northern slope of the adjacent mountain, called Angathias, and unfortunately that side of the mountain was completely covered with snow, despite it being June. It would be far too hazardous to cross. Instead, a couple coming from that direction told me they had avoided it by climbing up and down Angathias on snow-free areas. So I headed up towards the summit of Angathias and worked my way around to find a snow-free ridge down. This was not easy as snow often lay out of sight hidden by the convexity of the slope. I continued over higher ground rather than attempt the alternative route down a snow-filled valley. Whilst I could not avoid the snow completely, I was spared having to cross it where the slope was steep. On some patches of snow there were pieces of rock completely covered with lady birds; their presence there was a bit of a mystery to me. I passed a 'mitata', a hut made entirely of loose stone found on the mountain piled up into a dome. Such huts were once used to make cheese by shepherds as it kept longer than milk, so allowing time for it to be transported to market, although the hut seemed rather small for this purpose. My legs were tired and I started thinking of where to camp. This was easier said than done as the ground was covered in rocks, too large and embedded in the ground to move, and thorny bushes that would make short work of my groundsheet and airbed. Instead (after due consideration of avalanche risks) I flattened a suitable piece of snow and camped on that.

An avian choir woke me early. I packed up and decamped while the sun was still below the mountain tops. Overnight, the snow on which I was pitched had changed from soft and crystalline to a hard and icy consistency and rocks I had placed on the pegs to keep them secure had become iced into position, so I used another rock as a hammer to free them. Finally, I set off, carefully picking my way down the valley over yet more rocks and thorny bushes. High above me a shepherd was already herding his sheep, and they were making faster progress down the mountain than me. At the bottom of the valley the Nida plateau spread before me, a flat area of grazing land. It was there I saw a goat grazing on the top of a tree, its stunted shape, trimmed by generations of goats, rendered it more accessible to these intrepid animals.

My way led along a dirt road, out of the Nida plateau and into a series of smaller flat areas. Each of these was surrounded by higher ground, the track climbing out of one and descending into the next. It was a typical limestone landscape and there was no river drainage. On these flat areas there might be a pick-up truck or two, a small building, a fenced area, and sheep being corralled and loaded into the pick-ups. The dirt track ended and the route followed a 'path'. As I was beginning to expect, the path was difficult to spot. The one I wanted headed around the mountain. I followed the route on my GPS, surrounded by the familiar terrain of rocks, trees and thorny bushes. It led me to the top of a steep, rocky drop. I needed to get down but it was difficult to see how. I scrambled down the rocks a little but, due to the convexity of the slope, I was unable to see if there was a sheer drop beneath me or not. Recalling the advice I received on a scrambling course, I followed a route marked by brown staining on the rocks, on the premise that it could have been caused by mud carried on the boots of people before me, or goats' hooves. Relating this theory to my wife later, she noted that it could also have been the bloodstained remains of some hapless hiker who had preceded me, but this did not occur to me at the time. In the event, it led me down to the gentler slope below. It may be that the route I followed was outdated, as some red markings and a sign I later came across suggested an alternative had been developed from the Nida plateau on vehicle tracks, to the north of my route.

I continued on a dirt track and then a gravel road cut into the rock which took me around a great bowl in the mountains. Above was mainly naked limestone, below what passes for a forest in Crete, composed mainly of sparse holm oaks. I could see an eagle circling. Then it was up a path to a pass. Again, the word 'path' was a misnomer and I just had to pick a way through the inhospitable vegetation, up a valley in the general direction indicated by my GPS. In places steep rock outcrops required some thought on how to get around them. As I climbed higher there were occasional waymarks, red stripes or spots, or E4 signs on posts, not on the route but confusingly on a prominent rock several metres away. On reaching the pass at around 1,700 metres I thought I would have enough time to get down the other side to some accommodation at Kato Asites and phoned to make a reservation. I was finding that the steep, rocky and thorny slopes of Crete made it difficult to find a good camping spot, making a more conventional bed desirable. However, having reserved a room I felt under some pressure to get there at the agreed time. The distance was not great but the path was very, very slow and involved descending some 1,200 metres in a short distance. Underfoot, all was rough, loose or wobbly and I had to take it slowly and carefully, my feet complaining bitterly about all the hard work they had been made to do in the last two days. I was glad I had stiff boots as, even with these, I felt the sharp, angular rocks trying to push through into the soles of my feet. Towards the bottom I was getting frustrated with the interminable descent. The first milestone was a refuge, but the gentler slope it occupied did not last long, soon being followed by a steeply dropping gorge, fortunately with some helpful waymarks and a slightly clearer path. While the descent was tiring, this is not to say that the scenery, the limestone outcrops and flowers were not attractive, even beautiful. I was nevertheless relieved to walk into the village of Kato Asites. A shower, a beer and dinner had a miraculous effect on my wellbeing.

The next two days took me across an agricultural area, a patchwork of orchards, vineyards and fields of grass, set around some rocky mountains. A sign informed the traveller that the area produced most of Crete's labelled wines (as opposed, I presume, to the wine they pour from plastic bottles originally used for mineral water). At a nunnery I noticed silver coloured tokens hung from a tree. Parts of the body featured prominently on the tokens and I assumed accompanied prayers to the Virgin Mary, Jesus or some saint for help with some illness or affliction. There was one gorge to navigate. It was hidden by the folds of the landscape and much overgrown with tall and prickly vegetation. After what seemed a lengthy period of struggle, the path climbed up the side of the gorge in a gap between cliffs, rising to a viewpoint and then on through olive groves to a road. This took me to Archanes, a small town with an old area of little lanes to get lost in, from before the age of cars. Eventually, I found the door to the traditional rooms where I was staying. It opened into a courtyard off which there were a couple of rooms and stairs up to a larger courtyard with more rooms. I had a three-room affair all to myself with old taps and photographs to match the old buildings. Later, I ate my evening meal in the village square observing people riding up and down on motorbikes, scooters and ATVs (all-terrain vehicles)— nobody wearing helmets of course, men and women alike. Children were doing wheelies on their bicycles; tourists wandered around wondering which taverna to frequent and a lady opposite was trying (in vain) to encourage some amorous response from a man I took to be her husband. The fumes from passing cars detracted somewhat from the ambience, but the food was good and the ice-cold raki, given me with my dessert, courtesy of my hosts, gave me a warm and satisfied feeling.

I climbed up to the famous Lasithi plateau following an ancient mule track that zigzags up the mountainside, a gentle way to gain height, at the expense of taking a long time to get anywhere. Almost imperceptibly I moved from olive groves to holm oak to no trees at all, just rocks, thistles, sage and thorny vegetation. At the top there was a monument commemorating the death of some Turkish criminal and, shortly after, a view across the Lasithi plateau, an agrarian vista in which pasture, hay, potatoes and apples predominated. A few cherry trees had ripe fruit on them. Lasithi was once famous for its windmills with cloth sails that pumped water to the surface. Now the only complete examples seem to be for the tourists. As I crossed the plateau some of the tourists passed me on ATVs as well as the more typical coaches and rental cars. The locals passed in pick-ups, not all in a good state of repair, some loaded with bales of hay. In the villages I was seeing an increasing number of older women dressed all in black, usually bent over with a stick. One such lady was tending the grill at a small taverna, and, although I was not intending to stop, the enticing smell from the cooking souvlaki led me straight to a table for lunch.

The following day, I climbed into the mountains which ring the Lasithi plateau. After crossing the higher, smaller, Limnakaro plateau, dotted with trees, a number of farm buildings and the inevitable church, the path led me up a valley overshadowed by the bare, grey, limestone mountains rising high above. However, as I climbed higher, I benefited from some beautiful views. The day had started misty with clouds enveloping me, but I had climbed so high that I could now look down on the clouds, just as you can in an aeroplane but without the distortion of the windows. In the distance the Psiloritis Mountains poked through, fading in and out of sight as the clouds drifted across while I ate some biscuits. Crossing the pass, I had my first view of the mountains to come in the next few days (a little disappointing, as I was hoping for some gentler walking). Sheep were grazing on the high ground but it seemed to me there was very little for them to eat apart from a few thorny bushes. Much of the island seemed overgrazed to me, but then I know nothing of these things. The first part of the route down was painful, picking my way through the rocks, trying to avoid slipping on loose stone while also looking out for waymarks and E4 signs. My ankles were complaining. It was therefore a relief to find a dirt track, and a more moderate path in a small pine forest, a change from the prickly oaks that are more common. That evening my apartment in a small village had a four-poster bed, candles and smooth white pebbles in the bathroom. Very romantic but my wife was sadly far away...

For the next three days I crossed less visited areas, over mountains more modest than those I had recently crossed, through pine forests, and across valleys crowded with olive trees. My ankles enjoyed the flatter vehicle tracks and small roads the E4 followed, and the paths were mostly good. A particularly scenic path climbed into the mountains by the "Gorge of Ha". At the village of Thripti at the top I was delighted to find a taverna open for lunch despite the small size of the settlement. While I enjoyed a good lunch the staff and customers were all shouting at each other. I have noticed this before in Crete and the Peloponnese. Are people really cross with each other, or is it just the local Greek culture in which bellowing across the room is the norm? After Thripti the path disappeared and was replaced by thorny bushes. At the start there were some steel posts with E4 signs to aim for. Unfortunately, these stopped and I was following the route on my GPS, which then took me across a scree slope balancing on goat tracks. Finally reaching a track I made my way to Chrisopigi. On asking where I could get some water, an old lady in black pointed to the tap used to water the geraniums beside her in the village square. She and (I assume) her husband were just sitting there watching the world go by (which consisted mainly of me going by). That night I hid my tent in an olive grove, there being no other suitable place to camp.

After crossing a yellow gorse-spotted plateau for several kilometres, I reached the abandoned settlement of Skala, where the Turks massacred a group of Greeks. With sore feet after walking almost forty kilometres that day, the subsequent, and seemingly interminable, descent to Zakros was not pleasant, especially with gusts of wind trying to throw me off balance. It was with much relief that I picked up the key for my apartment. While I waited, the owner's mother smiled and gave me a banana. A shower was definitely needed to wash off the congealed sweat. Some wine and food at a nearby café also helped improve things, and the Metaxa brandy certainly helped to put me to sleep!

My last day walking on Crete was just 7.5 kilometres, through the evocatively named 'Canyon of the Dead', to the beach at Kato Zakros and the end of the E4 in Crete. Not as deep, nor as long, as some in Crete, this meandering gorge was popular with tourists, and made for a satisfying finale as I ambled among the low trees and pink-flowered shrubs that populated the base of the valley, dry jagged cliffs rising above. At the end of the gorge there were ancient Minoan ruins to visit, a culture that flourished at the same time as the Egyptian pharaohs. Reaching the beach where the E4 ended, I suppose I should have done something symbolic or romantic, like deposit a pebble a child had given me or run into the sea throwing off my clothes, shouting with joy. Instead, I had lunch.

Chapter 14: Cyprus —the final countdown

Before the Troodos Mountains

My final trip on the E4 was on a winding route across the island of Cyprus, the most recent country in which a route for the E4 has been devised. Evidently designed for the international traveller, it starts at Pafos (or Paphos) airport and ends at Larnaca (or Larnaka) airport. Cyprus is divided into a Greek south and a Turkish north. The E4 is entirely within the Greek area. It falls into three sections: the bit before the Troodos Mountains, the Troodos Mountains and the bit after the Troodos Mountains. The best section was the green, forested Troodos Mountains with its ancient churches and monasteries. Outside the mountains the trail visited some picturesque seashores, valleys and hills but at the time of year I visited, September, the grass was parched, dry, and a drab straw colour, burnt crisp by the summer sun. I suspect in spring, green with flowers blooming, I would have formed a quite different view.

Leaving for a trip is a stressful experience. Firstly, because it means leaving my wife for a few weeks. We say our goodbyes; I promise to be safe, look out for traffic on roads and not fall off any cliffs. I tell the dog to look after her; the dog looks at me with big brown eyes but I don't think she takes it in.

Secondly, I worry if all the travel arrangements will work out. Will the coach to the airport get stuck on the M25 due to some traffic accident? Will the airline lose my rucksack or will it be destroyed, mangled between conveyor belts? Sometimes I am told to send the rucksack through the normal system, at other times I am told to take it to the oversized luggage portal; which is correct? Will my sister think I am destroying the planet with the carbon dioxide released by my flying?

Then there are all the people crowding around me, filling the coach and plane, or waiting for flights in the departure area within a mall of shops selling very expensive watches and sunglasses no one seems to buy; presumably they rely on an enormous mark-up on those rare items they do sell. Having followed orders at security, I walk along the narrow, winding path between towers of duty-free perfumes, politely shuffling behind slowly browsing couples, trying to avoid people offering samples of perfume (which I don't use) while in search of a coffee at somewhere without a long queue.

Finally, there is the worry that I have forgotten something, or left it behind on some seat, so regular checks on my passport persist for a few days into my trip until I neglect to obsess about it.

In reality it all happened more or less as planned. The coach arrived a tolerable ten minutes late at Gatwick, and thankfully my rucksack arrived on the baggage reclaim belt in Pafos undamaged, although among the last bags to come through so that I was starting to fret about where I put the baggage receipt, no doubt needed if my baggage was lost.

As I flew into Pafos airport, the land looked dry and dusty. Steep sided valleys and ravines had cut into the soft, poorly vegetated soils. On flatter ground there were squares of stubble and orchards of some kind. Lines of villas followed, each with an unnaturally, bright blue swimming pool filling its backyard.

Walking out of the airport, then along the empty seashore, the airport fence on my right, I made my way to the busier, tourist beaches of Pafos, passing a line of hotels, resorts, souvenir shops, small supermarkets, agents for tourist trips, cafés and restaurants to reach my hotel. Before setting off on the E4 next morning, I visited mosaics from the Roman period in the Archaeological Park. These were among the best I have ever seen, graphically displaying competitions among the gods, geometric designs and animals. Helpfully, the mosaics also included the names of the gods depicted in Greek script. Some were of great quality, the colours and shading giving a three-dimensional impression that reminded me of the artist Cezanne. Pafos was also home to ancient churches and the pillar where St Paul was whipped thirty-nine times before he went on to the convert the island's governor to Christianity.

Over the next three days, I walked up valleys and around hills. Much of the land was straw-coloured grass with low trees and bushes a contrasting dark green. Bare white soil or dusty rock was visible on steeper slopes. Vineyards and olive groves were planted on terraces; the dazzling soil prominent between the plantings giving them a sparse appearance. Bougainvillea, draped over occasional walls, shouted out in brilliant pink against drab surroundings. I passed villages in various states of abandonment, although the two Bed & Breakfast establishments I stayed at showed how houses, with their rooms grouped around a courtyard, could be beautifully restored and put to good use. Old village houses and drab grassland contrasted with a very modern settlement of expensive houses, white concrete cubes with large windows grouped around a very green golf course, with tasteful Italian cypress trees.

I walked on dusty farm tracks and quiet roads, apart from one section through a stream bed. Fly-tipped rubbish was noticeable in a few places. As I approached the Akamas peninsula, convoys of ATVs drove by me, raising clouds of white dust in their wake. To avoid breathing it in I pulled up my bright yellow buff, which I had been wearing to protect my neck from sunburn, so that it covered my mouth and nose. In conjunction with my sun hat and dark glasses I must have looked like a demented, latter-day cowboy. I reached the coastal plain after a walk through pines, their new season's needle growth a vivid green, in sharp contrast with the dusty, grey green of most of the trees I had passed. After some banana plantations I started up the Akamas peninsula, supposedly a remote and undeveloped area of scrubby vegetation and sculptured limestone rocks surrounded by the sea. While it was indeed undeveloped as I started my walk up the gravel road, the frequent passage of cars and motorised buggies made it feel far from remote, although I guess it was just people like myself enjoying a holiday, although without wanting to walk. Most cars seemed to have red number plates, which I took to mean they were hire cars. I camped that night on the beach beside a café, a place where turtles nested.

By 6:30 a.m., I was awake and watching the colours on the cliffs opposite and in the clouds. It had rained during the night and the black rain clouds, tinged orange by the distant sun, were still a forbidding presence. Having spent much of the night tossing in the sweaty heat, all but naked on top of my sleeping bag, I had welcomed the rain which cooled the air and allowed me to drift into a peaceful slumber. As I munched on a biscuit for breakfast, sand-flies were trying to bite my legs, so, pretty as the beach was, I was keen to be on my way. After my experience yesterday, I was expecting to be troubled by passing vehicles, but only a police car, two white pick-ups and two cyclists passed me until I reached the north coast in the afternoon. During this time the E4 stubbornly followed the dirt road, initially two lanes wide and later single track, for some thirty kilometres. In consequence, the impression received was not of being among remote nature, even though there were no buildings in sight between Lara Bay and the Bath of Aphrodite.

Signs drew attention to the coastal juniper bushes which clothe the peninsula. As they are rare their habitat is protected by an EU directive and I had already seen several examples where my walk across Europe had touched the sea. The junipers beside the road were coated with dust raised by passing vehicles, unattractive to look at and not so pleasant for the junipers either. There were also pine trees, goats (including pretty brown ones and others with long beards) and lizards on the peninsula, and birds resembling small grouse that flapped into flight at my approach.

The fine, white dust on the road derived from the limestone, which, inland, outcrops as cliffs and hills or forms the shoreline, where it can be take on fantastical shapes, with sharp edges, as rain water, acidified by dissolved carbon dioxide, corrodes out hollows where it collects. In places, older, darker serpentine rock showed through. Channelling my inner geologist, I wet a few samples, and was rewarded by lovely green colours and veining.

The E4 climbs over the hills at the tip of the peninsula and then drops down to the northern coast at Fontana Amoroza, a bay boasting exceedingly blue water, and various tourist excursions by boat and four-wheel drive. My day's walk ended by the 'Bath of Aphrodite'. Legend has it that the goddess of love rose out of the sea in Cyprus and apparently bathed here in a small pool, partly hidden by rock and trees. Tourists are not allowed to bathe in it! Perhaps just as well as the people in front of me thought they saw a snake in the water.

For the first five days, the E4 had headed in a broadly north westerly direction, away from the walk's final destination in Larnaca. It now turned in a more easterly direction, first climbing the hills along the centre of the Akamas Peninsula. Sparse pine trees populated the higher ground, although not preventing long views across the coast I had walked along the previous day. Pines changed to rocky scrub, then terraces of stubble—the hay or wheat long since harvested, and finally, bright green vineyards and some rounded rock summits.

That night I enjoyed stiffado, a Greek dish I loved, with shallots and meat so tender it fell apart in a cinnamon flavoured sauce. In the morning my hotel, at 650 metres well into the hills, was surrounded by cloud. This soon burnt off as I walked down tracks and small roads across a broad valley and up the other side, passing fields of stubble, olive trees, and rough ground. The E4 seemed to bypass the centre of most villages in Cyprus, a mistake as they were one of the attractions of the route. I would divert into them for a coffee, fascinated by the expressive hands of the older villagers in conversation on adjacent tables.

The Troodos Mountains

After overnighting in the village of Lysos, I began my climb into the Troodos Mountains. First, I visited Melandra, a village abandoned by Turkish Cypriots following conflicts with Greek Cypriots and the 1974 invasion of the north of Cyprus by Turkish forces. A small number of buildings in various states of ruin — possibly as a result of shelling — collected around a small church and what I took to be a mosque; evidently, the two communities once lived side by side. The buildings were not completely obsolete, still doing duty as storage for bales of hay, and domiciles for chickens and the like. There were also various indications of the Greek Cypriot fight against the British in the 1950s, when Cyprus was part of the remnants of the British Empire. Signs pointed to EOKA hideouts, this being the organisation which battled against the British, and there was a memorial of some kind. The inscription was in Greek, but the date corresponded to the independence struggle.

Beyond Melandra, I followed gravel roads into the pine-covered Troodos Mountains, which I was to travel through for several days. My route contoured the mountains, making extravagant loops as it went in and out of each valley and ravine in order to maintain height. In a few valleys modern wells had been drilled to extract water. The other feature of interest was the geology. Rather than the white limestone of the coast, there were darker igneous rocks, formed by cooling magma. Occasionally there was evidence of lava flows: pillows of rock formed by underwater volcanic eruptions, or vesicles, little bubbles in the once molten rock now full of crystals. Elsewhere the rock would have been formed by magma intruding into older rock as sheets and solidifying underground. From some distant lecture I recalled the Troodos range was once part of the ocean floor that was pushed up to create mountains by the collision of Africa into Europe and Asia, the continents slowly moving towards each other over millions of years.

After some scrambling up a stream between brambles, I reached the Stavros tis Psokas forestry office and its campground, Conversation with one of the forestry officers was brief and largely non-verbal, owing to a mutual lack of the other's language, but I successfully pitched my tent on one of the earthen terraces among the trees. After refreshment at the café, I looked around the mouflon enclosure. Mouflon are wild sheep which inhabit the Troodos Mountains and other high places across Europe, but are shy and rarely seen. I had briefly seen some silhouetted in the twilight in France, now I wanted a clearer view of what they looked like. They were not woolly like sheep, the coat being more like a deer's. The rams had big curly horns, a dark-brown underbelly and neck stripe.

It was a popular area. Teenagers were using the road for skateboarding, and there were people having picnics. As they were packing up to leave, one of them gave me pizza they had not needed, still in its box. That was my supper for the night! After the visitors had left, I was alone at the campsite. The only sounds as I prepared for sleep were some nuts dropping from trees and the trickle of a nearby stream.

In the morning, after a strong Cypriot coffee (elsewhere known as Greek, Turkish or Arabic coffee) I climbed up a footpath among the trees. Beneath the sizeable pine trees, there were smaller trees in the 'under canopy'. A helpful sign described these as "Golden Oaks (*Quercus alnifolia*)" the national tree of Cyprus. Unlike the oaks I was familiar with, their leaves were oval and sported distinctive 'golden' undersides. Looking closely, I could see there were indeed a few thin acorns. At bush level, there were various aromatic herbs. The café was selling wild oregano, no doubt from among these trees. Later, in the valley beyond a fire-watch tower on the summit of Tripylos, I would start to see large numbers of Cyprus Cedars. Not as elegant as the Cedars of Lebanon, they are nevertheless a protected species, present at only a few places on Cyprus. The forestry officer on duty let me climb up the stubby fire watchtower to see the 360-degree view and pointed to various sights including places I had been and ones I was to visit in the next few days. These included the Kykkos Monastery and Mount Olympus.

That night I wild camped in the mountains; not so easy as the slopes were steep and a clear flat piece of ground difficult to find. I eventually settled on an abandoned forest track. Breakfast the next day was at one of the cafés by the Kykkos Monastery, arriving with the first tourists from the beach resorts. The monastery museum contained some old icons, beautifully presented using lighting to good effect and with appropriate background music. There were also ancient books, old liturgical vestments, church-related items and, somewhat incongruously, Bronze Age pottery. The monastery's church soon filled with people, some believers, crossing themselves and kissing icons before the iconostasis, others tourists wandering past them, waved on by a church official. Many of the tourists looked like Buddhist monks in long, purple robes. These were provided by the monastery to cover up the naked legs of any man wearing shorts, or for ladies showing too much flesh. This was one occasion for which I was prepared, in my long trousers. A couple near me took a selfie that would probably also show the 'no photographs' sign in the background. Of the several monasteries I visited on my route across the Troodos Mountains, this was by far the most popular with tourists, a popularity which reduced the religious atmosphere and the sense of communing with God.

Later I turned off the E4 to view two old, arched, stone bridges. Although not as good as some I had seen in the Pindus Mountains of Greece, the signs on the associated nature trail were useful. I now know that I have seen many oriental plane trees in the valleys of the Troodos, their leaves more serrated than those of the London plane tree I was more familiar with.

The following day I reached the Kalidonia waterfalls. On a worldwide scale they are not that spectacular, but after walking through dry landscapes in Cyprus, the waterfall looked really refreshing. Despite the two-kilometre walk from the road, it was a major tourist attraction, with lots of people climbing on rocks for pictures or taking selfies. The footpath from the falls was a pleasant amble beside the stream. At the top a sign advised that Troodos village was two kilometres up the road. However, the E4, never direct when a detour was on offer, took me on a seven-kilometre circuit. It did include some good views as the ground dropped away some 1,000 metres below the track, and it did lead to a nature trail back to Troodos but still...

Troodos village had my hotel, a Forestry Visitor Centre (closed due to a power cut when I visited), a working cash machine, and various cafés. Nearby was a military cemetery, which contained the graves of British soldiers from the 19th century. A couple of faded poppies were attached to the cemetery gate; I was glad someone remembered them. A little later there was an abandoned asbestos mine. I continued among the trees on roads, tracks and a footpath on slippery gravel across a scree slope. On this trip I had decided to wear hiking shoes rather than boots for two reasons: firstly, they are recommended by some long-distance walkers as they are lighter, and any less weight is a good thing; secondly, I thought it a possibility that the high ankle 'cuffs' on my boots were aggravating my Achilles tendon by constantly contacting it, causing me pain. However, I soon found that, especially on gravel paths, my hiking shoes had an annoying tendency to fill with small stones, burrs and sharp bits of grass, requiring regular stops to remove them. They did not prevent what was later diagnosed as Achilles tendinopathy.

I stayed two nights in some rooms at Spilia. The owner showed me around his winemaking and distilling hut. He made wine in the traditional way in large clay vessels *('pithari')* that were over a hundred years old. The local spirit, *'zivana'* he distilled from grape residues, and I can attest that it tasted pretty good. I asked about the Greek flags I had seen flying in many places in Cyprus, curious as to whether they meant that the Greek part of Cyprus wished to become part of Greece. He said this may have once been the case, but after the military junta in Greece in the early 1970s undermined the popular, elected president of Cyprus, Archbishop Makarios, supporting a coup against him, the desire for union with Greece evaporated. The Greek flags were a statement of identity, cultural rather than political, along with the yellow-and-black, double-headed-eagle flags of the Greek Orthodox Church. In the evening I was fed more than I could eat down in a coffee shop in the village, opposite a monument to those who fought the British for independence. As I ate, villagers wandered in and out, one over ninety years old; it seemed to be a mail collection point and general hub for assistance and information exchange.

I continued for three more days through the Troodos Mountains, wild camping at night. There were several monasteries on the route. On the first day I visited the 12th century monastery of Panagia tou Araka (the Panagia being the Virgin Mary). The priest waved me towards the church. Inside the colours of the frescoes were vivid blues and ochres despite their considerable age. Above them all in the dome at the centre of the church was Jesus looking down at me; below Him was the Virgin Mother, saints, apostles, and angels, whose wings looked rather inadequately attached. The building was a simple nave and the roof was extended to protect frescoes painted on the outside walls. I walked through several old, mountain villages with their stone buildings, and maybe terraced vineyards, often finding a café offering a coffee or Coke. At tiny Fikardou there were lines of cars stretched along the roadside, many people and the sound of things happening. I had fortuitously arrived for the village festival. There was traditional music by men and women in traditional costume and each house seemed to have produced something traditional. People clutched clay pots, just made, and sampled various foods and wine. I tried what seemed like salty rice pudding, bought some bread for my supper and sat down to eat a large number of round, fried, sweet dough things I bought. The village itself seemed to have no modern houses, just old stone ones separated by narrow alleyways, that day crowded with people. As I climbed a footpath out of the village, the reedy sounds of a violin followed me, gradually fading as I gained height.

From the higher points I could see back towards Mount Olympus, the name of the highest mountain in both Cyprus and Greece (although the Greek version is way more spectacular) and across to the city of Nicosia and the Kyrenia mountain range marking the north coast of Cyprus, with white clouds perpetually floating above them. One evening was particularly beautiful as I walked along a ridge from which Nicosia could be seen in one direction and the south coast of Cyprus in the other.

As I walked the sun was falling below the horizon, accentuating elements of the landscape with a warm, low light, the edges marked by shade. The beauty of it took my mind off my sore feet and blisters. As the sun finally set, I reached the Profit Ilias picnic site where I pitched my tent for the night. An old monastery that seemed no longer in use sat beside the picnic tables. On one of the tables someone had left their map case with a copy of a hike for the International Duke of Edinburgh's award. Also, a piece of cake three days out of date.

As I headed east the pine trees thinned, in favour of scrub and low bushes. Wide valleys sheltered cultivated areas with olive trees. Stavrovouni Monastery stood at the very top of a high mountain that seems to be the last gasp of the Troodos range across which I had been walking for the last ten days. Each monastery had a different character. Whereas the Kykkos Monastery was surrounded by stalls and a restaurant, encouraging visitors, Stavrovouni had no such thing. Ladies were denied entry to the main compound, and prohibitions on mobiles, etc. were enforced. While I waited for the monastery to open early one morning, I ate some biscuits for breakfast and admired the view. I could clearly see Larnaca and the salt lake beside it, that I was to walk around at the end of my trip. At 8.30 a.m., I followed a man into the monastery compound and on to the church. The man prayed fervently in front of a silver cross, which I assume held the sliver of the very cross on which Jesus Christ was crucified and for which the monastery is famous. After contemplating my good fortune in getting so far, praying for my wife's health, joy and safety, and admiring the walls covered with paintings of Jesus, Mother Mary and the saints and apostles, I left the man to his prayers.

After the Troodos Mountains — farms, military and tourism

After Stavrovouni, I walked through low hills of white marl and flatter, dry fields. On the map 'forests' were marked. These were usually on hills, which had been terraced and planted with pine and sometimes cypress and other trees. 'Forest' was perhaps too generous a term as the trees could be pretty sparse as they contoured the hills in parallel lines.

One day maybe they will be much larger and more like a forest, although the soil was so stony and dry, I wondered where they would get their water from. At one point a sign warned of a firing range and the risk of death. There was indeed firing in the far distance but domestic cars were using the road and there were no barriers or red flags. A tractor ploughed in the middle distance. An earlier backpacker had spoken in his video blog of this section, and as I knew he had managed to walk this route safely I continued on my way on a road between fields of ploughed stubble, and reached the next village unharmed. I was entering an area where the military was prominent. The previous day I had walked past armoured vehicles doing some kind of exercise, and in the next few days I approached the 'border' with the Turkish north. A sign warning of minefields dissuaded me from leaving the track. My map showed the E4 entering the United Nations (UN) Buffer Zone, and I was not sure what to expect. As I entered it a sign attached to two oil drums said 'No photographs, UN authorised persons only'. Was I a UN authorised person? I could find no details in guide books or on the internet other than I should not hunt, so I assumed I was acceptable and continued past a military post on the hillside to the village of Troulloi. This was a wonderful place for a hot day as the village shop was open and offered cold drinks and ice cream, simple pleasures. Diverting off the E4 to the village of Oroklini, I booked into a hotel. Listening over diner to the sound of British tourists and Queen on the sound system reminded me what a popular place Cyprus was for British tourists and expatriates, and also that I was now close to the sea.

I followed a dusty white track up a hill among lines of young pine trees. Contouring around the slope, I could see Larnaca spread out below and cargo ships on the sea beyond. Aircraft regularly crossed the skies on route to the airport, seeming to defy gravity by floating in the air. Pyla was a village notable for having both a mosque and a church, both Greek and Turkish communities still living together. I sat in a pub for a cup of Cypriot coffee, looking at a UN police station on the first floor of the building opposite. I had seen little evidence of UN personnel, other than a memorial to UN soldiers killed trying to bring peace, although a pick-up with a UN number plate was parked outside. The pub was an older building with a wide, graceful arch in the middle of the open sided room in which I was sitting. I had seen these arches before in the middle of rooms, they appeared to serve the function of a modern concrete or steel beam, allowing a wider room while using rafters of limited length. The lady serving me seemed to want me to stay, maybe as I was her only customer.

A kilometre or so after Pyla, by a landing strip, there was a fenced-in area, with old coaches and the remains of some classic cars: I recognized Morris Minors, Austin Cambridges and Triumphs. At the next village of Xylotympou a sign pointed to a park of Peace and Folk Poets. On a white wall there were details of a several poets, surprisingly all from this one village. In another area of the park there was a memorial commemorating the 2,200 Jewish babies born in Cyprus as a result of Britain trying to stop emigration to what is now Israel. Jews in transit were detained in camps on Cyprus in the late 1940s. The next part of my journey was across farmland, much of it recently ploughed; the soil a rich earthy red, some with irrigated potatoes or market garden produce. A bearded farmer in a pick-up stopped to check I was OK. Although I was still on the E4, walkers were thin on the ground in this flat, agricultural area (an exaggeration, there were none). In time the E4 reached the Sotira 'forest', an area of marginally higher ground where the limestone rock is close to the surface. There were not many big trees; bushes dominating the vegetation, sometimes spread out with rocks and dry, yellow grass between. Close to the highest point in the area, I came upon a picnic area and two churches. Leaving this modest summit, I walked through eucalyptus to Ayia Napa, the party capital of Cyprus.

From Ayia Napa, I made a day trip around Cape Greco. Walking on dusty tracks over a landscape of bushes, rocks and various aerials, I arrived at Konnos and the coast, where the scenery changed dramatically. There were hotels, bars, a beach full of blue umbrellas and crowds of people, usually in swimming costumes, some looking fit, others with a lot of flesh wobbling as they walked. Tattoos seemed popular for men and women. As I sat down for a lemonade and ice cream, my attention was drawn to the lady at the next table who had a tattoo down her spine telling me "you don't need a plan...", but the rest of the tattoo, lower down her back, was hidden by the back of the white plastic chair, so I am not sure what I did not need a plan for. Nor was she speaking English, which precluded my putting any enquiries to her. A path led from Konnos around the coast, close to the sea. I followed it to a small church and below it the cave of Ayioi Anargyroi. People were jumping off the cliff into the sea; not something I could recommend due to the risk of hitting a rock. However, with the cool blue sea on such a hot day, I could see the attraction. A little further on there was the first of a few natural arches on the coast that I would pass. I continued heading east until a fence prevented further progress. Beyond it there was what I took to be a military establishment with multiple aerials. So having reached the most easterly point on my trip on the E4 in Europe, I sighed and headed west along the coast.

Returning to Ayia Napa, the E4 followed a footpath over rough limestone, the sea to my left, with boats full of tourists; to my right, cliffs rising above me. I had to be careful to follow the trail, where the passage of feet had smoothed the sharp edges of the limestone, elsewhere it was unpleasant to walk on, slow dissolution by the rain having created a spiky surface that cut into the soles of my shoes. In time I reached the point at which the path was crudely paved, making progress easier. By now the cliffs had gone, superseded by resorts, with their sun loungers, umbrellas, bars and areas of unnaturally green grass, maintained by frequent watering. In the evening, Ayia Napa staged a medieval festival. People lined the street waiting for the parade. The wait was eventually rewarded. People dressed in costumes pillaged from history slowly moved up the street, beating drums with tremendous stamina, blowing trumpets, throwing flags into the air and swinging fire around their heads. Some were dressed for a masquerade, others on stilts wore fantastical costumes. Young school children waved, dressed in period costume. Later there was a crooner singing on a stage in the square but I had an early start in the morning so I climbed back up the hill to my rooms.

As I walked west beside the sea the next day, hotels and resorts continued for several kilometres, some well-established, others currently being built, with one or two small churches, once on lonely headlands, now surrounded by tourist developments. Sometimes I was on a paved path by a rocky shore, other times on a sandy beach, with the ubiquitous sun loungers and blue umbrellas. All kinds of people were stretched out on them: thin and fat, young and old, some brown, some pale, some red.

Whether Russian or English, they were enjoying a sun that I was finding a little hot. Later, I walked several kilometres following a gravel track along a quieter stretch of rocky coastline with a few pebbly beaches, on which the occasional family was enjoying their Sunday. There was a sign for a 'Fisherman's café' beside a small harbour with assorted boats. Looking for something cold I entered. There was coffee, cold water, questions about where I was going and comments on climate change, melting ice at the North Pole, the current heatwave in Cyprus and a friend's café in my home town of Cardiff (which was there forty-five years ago, the Anastasia; did I know it? he asked). A little further on was the British Military base surrounded by fencing but signage was discreet concerning nationality. A lone Union flag was flying at one location; the road I was walking along was called Waterloo Road. There was a British Legion, a café run by a forces' charity (where I quickly sank a large Coke before it closed) and 'No Photographs' signs but nothing explicitly declaring that this was British Sovereign Territory.

The last two days involved walking around the northern side of Larnaca. Sometimes through the outlying suburbs: concrete villas, many half-built, modern apartments, older dusty villages, a few churches and some light industry. Sometimes across farmland: dry stubble or pale, ploughed fields mixed with huge, open-sided sheds, full of cows with an arresting smell. Sometimes among trees: pines, fir and cypress sparsely planted in the dry, stony soil.

On my last day, there were three more impressive sights. Firstly, twenty arches of yellow stone carrying the Kamares aqueduct across a broad valley, built in the 18th century but looking Roman. Secondly, a large salt lake, white at the edges, red further in. I walked around it across rough grassland looking at the apartment blocks of Larnaca rising above it in one direction, and planes landing at the airport in another. Hidden at first from my view, the final sight was the Hala Sultan Tekke Mosque which shyly revealed itself, as I rounded a corner of the gravel track I was following. An important pilgrimage site, it is said to contain the tomb of Umm Haram, holy helper and aunt of Mohammed, who died here during an Arab army attack on Cyprus. Inside the mosque is quite plain but looking back as I crossed a causeway towards the airport, its location beside the salt lake makes it a striking monument, with its pointed minaret and domed roof set among palm and other trees.

And so I walked into Larnaca airport, the end of my trek across both Cyprus and Europe on the E4. The long wait for my flight home, and the last few days walking, was a bit anticlimactic, and my mind was already filled with thoughts of my next trip. As I had rambled across Europe from west to east, hiking across Israel on its National Trail seemed a good idea to continue my eastward drift.

Chapter 15: The reckoning

Some statistics: on my walk across Europe on the E4 European Long-Distance Trail I walked 10,660 kilometres or 6,662 miles over 440 days, an average of 24 kilometres (15 miles) a day including rest days. I covered this distance in 12 separate trips between August 2014 and October 2019, each typically five weeks in length but ranging from 3 ½ weeks to 8 ½ weeks. Crossing 11 countries, I failed to speak in eight different languages. I stayed in hotel, bed & breakfast or guesthouse accommodation for 273 nights; hostel, mountain hut or some other dormitory type accommodation for 35 nights; official campsites with facilities for 36 nights and I wild camped for 97 nights. I wore out six pairs of boots, one pair of hiking shoes, and two lightweight tents.

My equipment has evolved somewhat since the beginning of my trips, and I have developed warmer and cooler weather equipment lists. Having disposed of my original rucksack as the stitching began to come undone, I now have a light one for summer and two heavier ones for greater weights such as winter equipment (two as I am unable to decide which I prefer). The capacity of each rucksack is 65 or 70 litres. My original tent collected water above my legs and its four pegs were inadequate in windy weather, so I now use a better designed tent with ten pegs. I have a choice of sleeping bags: a lighter, more compact summer one in a brilliant yellow colour, and a heavier winter bag, both synthetic so they can withstand getting wet. I have never regretted not using a sleeping mat, being happy to curl around irregularities in the ground, after having cleared it of moveable stones, pine cones, tree saplings and thistles. However, in cold conditions, I use a three-quarter-length inflatable air mattress to lift me off icy ground. Surprisingly, I generally sleep better in my sleeping bag on hard ground, than I do in soft hotel beds. Instead of aluminium water bottles, having been saddened by the sight of paint peeling off them, I now use a plastic one-litre bottle and a two-litre plastic bladder for a reserve supply where required. For eating my durable, titanium 'spork' replaces a knife, fork and spoon, as the plastic 'sporks' I bought just kept breaking. In summer conditions I missed the opportunity for a swim on a number of trips, so now carry some extremely brief Speedo-type swimming trunks. These 'budgie smugglers' are worth the embarrassment for their very light weight (there being very little material), and the opportunity for a splash on a hot day or some spa-type experience. My final packing lists are given in Appendix 1.

While I have been congratulated for walking over 10,000 kilometres across Europe, the achievement is maybe not so great. It seems to me just a matter of putting one foot in front of another, again and again, more a matter of motivation rather than great skill or "ironman" endurance, especially as I took a rest day or short day whenever I felt like it. Walking across Europe was simply something I wanted to do and for which I was fortunate enough to have the time and money required.

People ask why I did it, what drove me on? A question I posed in my introduction. I find it difficult to articulate one reason. For many, a long walk is a time to think and reflect, a chance to reconcile oneself to death or divorce, or to come closer to God, your son or a sense of peace. However, I am not one of those people, although it is true that the solitude of solo long-distance walk does allow plenty of time for reflection (or daydreaming). My reflections have concluded that I enjoy long-distance walks for six reasons.

First, a varied trek such as the E4 adds bright colours to my life and memories that linger long after the walk has finished. Every day feels special, different, unique, the very opposite of a comfortable but repetitive routine. Colours are made more vivid by a bit of stress, living a little at the edge, struggling with language, finding somewhere to sleep, a long, steep climb or a big drop beside the path. Memories are also made when things go wrong, or in times of stress; however, recollections of pleasurable times are just as vivid.

Secondly, there are sights of great beauty and wonder. Panoramic scenes like the Iron Gates of the Danube below you in the morning light, or an ocean of clouds with mountain peaks poking through. Smaller-scale ensembles could be just as wonderful, multicoloured flowers in a summer meadow, an orchard of almond blossom in spring or the colour of leaves turning yellow at the start of autumn.

Thirdly, I enjoy learning a little (a very little I must admit) of the cultures of other countries; their food and history, their religion and attitudes to a passing stranger. Looking back at what I have written, food and drink seemed to have a significant place in my exploration of culture. However, learning of the battles fought, and blood shed across Europe was also revealing. Suleiman the Magnificent did not feature in my history lessons in school. I also captured a little of the current state of change, from a referendum in Catalonia, to refugees entering Hungary to the depopulation of villages in Serbia and Greece as people moved to work in towns and other countries, leaving whiskered old men to bemoan their loss in little coffee shops.

Fourthly, there are the unexpected, unusual or rare events you stumble across: a village festival, the wagging tail of a wild boar rooting about among pine needles, or dinner at a friendly taverna where none was expected. Of course, the unexpected can also cause distress, such as a café closed which you had thought would be open, and where you had planned for a coffee and cake.

Fifthly, some of the most intense pleasures have come from deprivation caused by my trek. For example after a hot, sweaty day walking, the water I carry unpleasantly hot, the first gulp of a cold beer on arriving at a destination is just sooo good (a second glass is invariably disappointing). Equally, a strong, black coffee in the morning is heavenly after a day or two without, suffering from caffeine withdrawal, especially with some breakfast. Equally wonderful is washing off the dirty, sticky sweat in a hotel shower after a few days of wild camping, tasting its salt as it washes past my mouth.

Finally there is a sense of achievement when you reach the summit of a mountain, cross a country or indeed, complete the E4. Maybe this is the most transient pleasure though for I am already dreaming of the next peak, the next country and the next path. As I write this during the Covid-19 Coronavirus pandemic, prevented by law from travelling outside my own city, I strain against the regulations that tie me to enjoy the trail again, to escape, to cross valleys and mountains, forests and plains; to enjoy freedom again.

So maybe if you are a healthy retiree, or planning a gap year before university or a job, or just wanting a long break from humdrum routine, the E4 may be something for you to dream about too.

John Pucknell, Cardiff, 2020

Appendix 1: Final Gear List

WINTER

	No.	WEIGHTS (KG)	
		Unit	Total
Rucksack	1	2.20	2.20
Terra Nova tent	1	1.08	1.08
Synthetic sleeping bag, 0C comfort level	1	1.35	1.35
1 litre plastic water bottle, full	1	1.17	1.17
2 litre plastic bag, full	1	2.05	2.05
Inflatable sleeping mat	1	0.26	0.26

CLOTHES

Scarpa walking boots, pair	1	1.56	1.56
Lightweight shoes, pair	1	0.38	0.38
Underpants, lightweight	2	0.10	0.20
Long johns, lightweight	1	0.15	0.15
Liner socks, pair	2	0.05	0.10
Walking socks, pair	2	0.15	0.30
Hankies	3	0.02	0.06
Waterproof jacket, lightweight	1	0.35	0.35
Waterproof trousers	1	0.14	0.14
Merino tee-shirt	1	0.13	0.13
Long sleeve base layer	1	0.24	0.24
Belt	1	0.03	0.03
Trousers	2	0.32	0.64
Fleece	1	0.20	0.20
Synthetic insulated jacket	1	0.60	0.60
Gaiters, pair	1	0.20	0.20
Liner Gloves, pair	1	0.04	0.04
Gloves, pair	1	0.11	0.11
Hat which covers ears	1	0.08	0.08
Buff neck scarf	1	0.05	0.05

TOILETRIES AND MEDICINES

Toilet bag	1	0.02	0.02
Toothbrush	1	0.02	0.02
Toothpaste	1	0.15	0.15
Dental floss	2	0.02	0.04
Comb	1	0.00	0.00
Disposable razor	1	0.00	0.00
Nail clippers	1	0.04	0.04
Nail file	1	0.00	0.00
Tablets for headaches etc	1	0.05	0.05
Travel towel	1	0.10	0.10
Sunscreen	1	0.10	0.10
Plasters and scissors	1	0.06	0.06
Savlon	1	0.02	0.02
Lip balm	1	0.02	0.02
Anti-chafing cream	1	0.02	0.02
Toilet paper and bags	1	0.17	0.17
Bar of soap and soap dish	1	0.20	0.20
Wet wipes	2	0.04	0.08
Sewing kit	1	0.00	0.00
Water purification tablets	1	0.04	0.04

		WEIGHTS (KG)	
	No.	Unit	Total
NAVIGATION			
GPS	1	0.30	0.30
Batteries for GPS	8	0.03	0.24
Maps if applicable	1	0.03	0.03
Guidebook if applicable	1	0.38	0.38
DOCUMENTS			
Itinerary and spare paper	1	0.00	0.00
Biro	1	0.01	0.01
Wallet	1	0.20	0.20
Credit card	1	0.00	0.00
Debit card	1	0.00	0.00
Passport	1	0.00	0.00
Boarding pass/tickets	1	0.00	0.00
Insurance details	1	0.00	0.00
Euros	1	0.00	0.00
ELECTRICS			
Cell phone	1	0.15	0.15
Charger	1	0.05	0.05
Camera and case	1	0.18	0.18
Camera batteries	2	0.01	0.02
Kindle	1	0.40	0.40
USB cable	1	0.05	0.05
Credit card sized back up power	1	0.11	0.11
OTHER			
Big dry bag	1	0.07	0.07
Sleeping bag dry bag	1	0.05	0.05
Little dry bag	2	0.03	0.06
Disposable luggage tag (remove on arrival)	1	0.00	0.00
Tent repair tape	1	0.05	0.05
Glasses	1	0.03	0.03
Head torch	1	0.10	0.10
Batteries for head torch	1	0.02	0.02
Spork	1	0.02	0.02
Sunglasses plus case	1	0.20	0.20
Walking stick	1	0.21	0.21
Phrase book	1	0.14	0.14
FOOD (typical emergency rations)			
Fruit and nuts	2	0.28	0.56
Flapjacks	4	0.12	0.48
Tins of tuna	2	0.17	0.34
Peanut butter in plastic jar	1	0.42	0.42
Oatcakes	1	0.33	0.33
Breakfast biscuits	1	0.33	0.33
Total			20.32
Total minus items being worn			17.02

SUMMER

	No.	WEIGHTS (KG)	
		Unit	Total
Lighter weight rucksack	1	1.60	1.60
Terra Nova tent	1	1.08	1.08
Synthetic sleeping bag, 5C comfort level	1	1.00	1.00
1 litre plastic water bottle, full	1	1.17	1.17
2 litre plastic bag, full	1	2.05	2.05
CLOTHES			
Scarpa walking boots, pair	1	1.56	1.56
Sandals, pair	1	0.48	0.48
Underpants, lightweight	3	0.10	0.30
Liner socks, pair	2	0.05	0.10
Walking socks, pair	2	0.15	0.30
Hankies	3	0.02	0.06
Waterproof jacket, lightweight	1	0.35	0.35
Waterproof trousers	1	0.14	0.14
Tee-shirts, light weight	3	0.13	0.39
Long sleeve base layer	1	0.22	0.22
Belt	1	0.03	0.03
Trousers	1	0.32	0.32
Trousers that convert to shorts	1	0.32	0.32
Fleece	1	0.32	0.32
Sun hat	1	0.20	0.20
Swimming trunks, very brief	1	0.07	0.07
Buff neck scarf	1	0.05	0.05
TOILETRIES AND MEDICINES			
Toilet bag	1	0.02	0.02
Toothbrush	1	0.02	0.02
Toothpaste	1	0.15	0.15
Dental floss	2	0.02	0.04
Comb	1	0.00	0.00
Disposable razor	1	0.00	0.00
Nail clippers	1	0.04	0.04
Nail file	1	0.00	0.00
Tablets for headaches etc	1	0.05	0.05
Travel towel	1	0.10	0.10
Sunscreen	1	0.10	0.10
Plasters and scissors	1	0.06	0.06
Savlon	1	0.02	0.02
Lip balm	1	0.02	0.02
Anti-chafing cream	1	0.02	0.02
Toilet paper and bags	1	0.17	0.17
Bar of soap and soap dish	1	0.20	0.20
Wet wipes	2	0.04	0.08
Sewing kit	1	0.00	0.00
Water purification tablets	1	0.04	0.04

	No.	WEIGHTS (KG)	
		Unit	Total
NAVIGATION			
GPS	1	0.30	0.30
Batteries for GPS	8	0.03	0.24
Maps if applicable	1	0.03	0.03
Guidebook if applicable	1	0.38	0.38
DOCUMENTS			
Itinerary and spare paper	1	0.00	0.00
Biro	1	0.01	0.01
Wallet	1	0.20	0.20
Credit card	1	0.00	0.00
Debit card	1	0.00	0.00
Passport	1	0.00	0.00
Boarding pass/tickets	1	0.00	0.00
Insurance details	1	0.00	0.00
Euros	1	0.00	0.00
ELECTRICS			
Cell phone	1	0.15	0.15
Charger	1	0.05	0.05
Camera and case	1	0.18	0.18
Camera batteries	2	0.01	0.02
Kindle	1	0.40	0.40
USB cable	1	0.05	0.05
Credit card sized back up power	1	0.11	0.11
OTHER			
Big dry bag	1	0.07	0.07
Sleeping bag dry bag	1	0.05	0.05
Little dry bag	2	0.03	0.06
Disposable luggage tag (remove on arrival)	1	0.00	0.00
Tent repair tape	1	0.05	0.05
Glasses	1	0.03	0.03
Head torch	1	0.10	0.10
Batteries for head torch	1	0.02	0.02
Spork	1	0.02	0.02
Sunglasses plus case	1	0.20	0.20
Phrase book	1	0.14	0.14
FOOD (typical emergency rations)			
Fruit and nuts	2	0.28	0.56
Flapjacks	4	0.12	0.48
Tins of tuna	2	0.17	0.34
Peanut butter in plastic jar	1	0.42	0.42
Oatcakes	1	0.33	0.33
Breakfast biscuits	1	0.33	0.33
Total			18.55
Total minus items being worn			15.99

Although from the above table I calculate I will be carrying over 17 kilogrammes in winter, when I weigh my fully loaded rucksack on the scales it comes to around 15 kilogrammes, I am not sure where I go wrong! Note that other backpackers quote base weight, i.e. without food, water, or the stuff you are wearing. On this measure I carry around 12.6 kilogrammes, way above the 6 kilogrammes some boast about. I have spent many an hour thinking what I could miss out, but whenever I drop something, I add something else!

As can be seen, the weight I carry in summer is a couple of kilogrammes lighter.

Appendix 2: Cape St Vincent to Tarifa

Via Algarviana, a possible E4 extension through the hills behind the Algarve coast

The E4 European Long-Distance Path officially starts in Tarifa, but while searching for a long-distance walk I could complete in the winter months, I came across the Via Algarviana. Starting from Cabo de São Vicente (Cape Saint Vincent) in the very southwest corner of Portugal, it extends to the border of Spain. According to the official website, it is intended to link up with the E4, presumably at Tarifa. It seemed a good idea in the winter of 2016 to see if I could make this link.

My trip would fall into four stages Firstly there was the Via Algarviana, also known as the GR13, which would take me east from Cabo de São Vicente to Alcoutim on the border with Spain. Secondly, I would walk from there to Seville. Visiting this great city was necessary as it was difficult to cross the Gaudalquivir River much further downstream. In the absence of recognised long-distance paths for this section, I had to work out my own route, with variable success. Thirdly, there was a pilgrim route, a Camino de Santiago, from Seville to Cadiz (although you are actually meant to follow it in the opposite direction). Finally, I found on the internet a route from Cadiz to Tarifa, along the coast of the Costa de la Luz ('Coast of Light'). At 755 kilometres (472 miles) long, the complete trek would take me 32 days.

After a flight to Faro, then a bus, train and another bus I arrived at the town of Sagres on 1st February. Calling in at the tourist office I asked about the Via Algarviana and was given a cardboard box, about the size and weight of a brick. Inside the box was the book-sized guide in Portuguese and English and a collection of maps. Since I had to carry everything on my back I discreetly threw away the superfluous maps for cyclists and linking trails, as well as extracts from the guide which I had already printed from the internet, using up a whole colour cartridge. After erecting my tent at a nearby campsite, I dined on some expensive fish (the waiter's recommendation for no doubt gullible tourists) at a restaurant overlooking the sea.

As I prepared to decamp, the sunrise was deep red through the pine trees of the campsite, heralding a sunny day, blue skies and a north wind keeping things cool. First, I walked to Cabo de São Vicente where the Via Algarviana and a few other long-distance paths start. This promontory is the southwest corner of Europe and lacked the commercial enterprises selling soft drinks and souvenirs so often associated with such strategic outposts. There was a lighthouse and some buildings, access forbidden, cliffs (with a few fishermen precariously practising their sport off some ledges on them) and a lot of open ocean. As in other places along the coast there were a number of motorhomes no doubt escaping, like me, the inclement weather in Northern Europe. From the cape, the path followed small roads and tracks through a flat landscape of grass and bushes, often left to grow wild and used for sheep grazing or hunting. Coming from the British winter I was struck by the number of flowers: daisies in densely packed patches; various yellow flowers, and others I could not identify.

The following day's walk was through more hilly terrain and after some farmland went through wooded areas with pines, eucalyptus, occasional cork trees and many wind turbines. I stayed the night at Barao de Sao Joao. The landlady of the rooms I was staying at was very chatty, but, unfortunately, as it was all in Portuguese, I understood very little and just smiled and nodded in a friendly manner. There was a great deal of art in the town with several tall, thin statues, paintings on walls and a sculpture of what looked like two rats or cats copulating(?) on a roof by a friendly restaurant and bar. In Spain as well as Portugal I noticed communal washing facilities, made up of concrete sinks and a water supply. In this village there was a line of washing hanging up, suggesting the facilities were still in use.

Most mornings I would stop at a bar for a breakfast of some strong coffee and a pastry or whatever else was available. These establishments were very much mens' bars, with half the customers drinking brandy or some clear spirit, all before eight a.m. In some, a calendar would be displayed, showing bare-breasted ladies of improbable bust sizes, a fixture of a kind no longer seen in the UK. The days were spent walking

260

through plantations of eucalyptus trees and orange groves, by ancient olive and cork trees and through forests of pine. Sheep grazed on rough pasture and there were areas with many cistus bushes in bloom; each flower had five white petals with dabs of dark red and a yellow centre, the type of plant you might buy for your garden in Britain. Many other flowers caught my eye such as iris, wild lavender, purple crocuses and numerous blooms of yellow and white I did not recognise.

In places the land was terraced, although the terraces were not always cultivated. I saw the remains of several old farms and rural buildings, now in ruins, often only yellow, mud bricks remained, probably once covered in plaster. Pumps to lift water out of wells spotted the route. There was an older type consisting of a chain of rusty buckets, with an arm to which some large animal must have been attached, such that as it walked around the well, it lifted the buckets, which deposited water into a trough. I also saw windmills devoid of sails. My impression was that the land had once supported many more people in the past, with some of the farmland having been abandoned. Plantations of eucalyptus and pine seemed to be the new way that land was being utilised, together with wind turbines.

Most of the Via Algarviana was on vehicle tracks or small tarmac roads, although there were some stretches of path between walls made of piles of rough stones. In general, it was easy going as the route rose and fell over hills and some mountains of which Fóia was the highest at 902 metres. When I was there, it was encased in cloud and I could see little (although thankfully the snack bar was open for a coffee and a slice of apple cake). Climbing across the bare rock up to the summit of Picota was more scenic; the path up was easy but tiring due to the amount of height gained that day. On coming down from Picota I admired the sprays of yellow blossoms on the mimosa trees in the valley beyond. There were several river or stream crossings, but only one proved problematic as the usual stepping stones were missing (or maybe I missed the correct crossing point) although I managed to avoid getting water in my boots. As red-and-white waymarks and signposts marked the route, I only occasionally had to consult my GPS, whilst the guidebook was more useful for background and context. Dogs in the villages and isolated farmhouses made it clear I was not welcome, chasing me out of town with their furious barking. Fortunately, the most vicious ones were behind fences or chained so I was never actually attacked, others I am sure were just bored and excited to see someone.

The Via Algarviana went through many villages and small towns. Houses with white walls and tiled roofs lined narrow cobbled streets. In the more attractive villages, the doors and windows were highlighted with lines of paint: blue; pink, or a yellow ochre. In Sao Bartolomeu de Messines, I stumbled on the town's carnival. Not a large event, a handful of floats and groups of people elaborately dressed in some theme or other, went up and down the main street. Stall holders sold beer and a fried dough affair, a bit like a doughnut.

On the western part of the route, up to the town of Alte, there was a reasonable amount of accommodation: guesthouses; small hotels, or rooms that could be booked on-line, some of them with excellent breakfasts. East of Alte, the countryside was wilder and the villages were small with empty or ruined houses left by people moving away, some with hopeful 'Vende Se' signs (meaning 'for sale'). The remaining inhabitants seemed to be old men with flat caps and old women with hats of a greater variety. Accommodation was limited to a 'Casa' (like a Bed & Breakfast) in the village at the end of each stage. No doubt the Via Algarviana was routed through this area to bring the local economy some much needed money. I wild camped in a quiet, narrow valley one night, and could have wild camped more but I felt it would deprive people of much-needed income and purpose. However, I had not discovered how to book the Casas in the easterly villages. My ignorance was circumvented by a lady at a café where I stopped for lunch in the village of Vaqueiros asking, entirely by miming (she was remarkably good at it), whether I wanted a room for a night. She not only provided one, she also booked my next night's stay in the following village. At that village the lady was less advanced in the art of mime and arranged for me to speak to an English-speaking lady on the phone, who not only told me the time I would get dinner and breakfast, but also arranged another night's accommodation.

While I met a few others walking the route, all in the opposite direction, it is not that popular. When I stopped for a coffee at a petrol station café, the people there gave me the silent stare treatment. Hiking is not a great pastime in Portugal, unlike cycling. Weekends brought out plenty of men in tightly stretched lycra.

The road to Seville

The Via Algarviana ends at Alcoutim on the Guardiana River, which forms the border between Portugal and Spain. There I spent my final night in Portugal in an almost empty youth hostel. In the morning, I boarded the passenger ferry, a small boat which took me across the river leaving Portugal and arriving in Spain in the town of Sanlucar de Guardiana a few minutes later. With its white-walled houses with their tiled roofs, Sanlucar de Guardiana looked very much like Alcoutim, although the fortress at the top of the hill above Sanlucar de Guardiana looked more dramatic than the fortress facing it in Alcoutim.

As no long-distance walking route had been defined between the area I was in and Seville, I created my own. Three options presented themselves. The first would involve walking down to the coast and following the seashore before heading back inland to Seville, a route that offered good prospects of accommodation, but more miles. The second option was broadly to follow the roads through agricultural areas, the A-490 then the A-472, the most direct route. Finally, I could head into forested mountains to the north, although there was little accommodation or information on this longer route. I chose the more direct route as my map reading suggested I could follow farm tracks instead of the roads for much of the way. Over the seven days I walked, there was more road walking than I initially expected.

A promising start took me along a dirt track for eleven kilometres, through grassland and areas of bushes and scattered trees, meeting only a shepherd who offered me a boiled sweet. At one point, I followed a modern concrete aqueduct on a small road. Then I hit the main road, with frequent cars. I had intended to follow vehicle tracks visible on my map that ran north of this road, but unfortunately there were padlocked gates and high fences with barbed wire discouraging access, so I was forced to walk several kilometres beside the main road to the town of Villaneuva de Los Castillejos and a *hostal* for the night. My walk to Bartolome de La Torre the next day ran into similar problems. I found a track off the main road through sunlit pine trees, but after a while it headed off in the wrong direction and I was obliged to climb over a padlocked gate to return to the road. As I walked along it, I was hooted at a few times by passing cars. These hoots were initially puzzling, as I was walking off the tarmac not causing a problem, although it later occurred to me that they were friendly greetings as sometimes a wave followed. Walking past grassland with scattered trees, used for grazing and in rougher parts maybe for hunting, the hike was not that exciting until I spotted four stork nests alongside the road on top of electricity pylons, complete with storks. In later days I realised they were actually quite common in the province of Huelva, nesting in church towers and even on cranes, but the first sight of these creatures caused me some excitement. Eager to record this natural phenomenon, I took photographs, but my basic digital camera was such that my subjects appeared as just a few dots against an empty sky, or in some cases there was just empty blue sky when I was not fast enough!

Finding a quiet route proved just as difficult the next morning. I followed an abandoned railway line, where marks in the dirt showed it was used by other walkers and cyclists, until I reached a large fence blocking further progress, which some farmer had meanly erected. Fortunately, I was able to divert onto a small road, much to the anger of a barking dog. The orange and olive groves each side of the road were protected with high fences, from what I do not know. In the afternoon I had better luck on a small, winding road, not entirely tarmacked, although even then a man called me over, apparently concerned that I was planning to camp in the area. I was not camping that night; instead, I was welcomed to the Hotel Cuidad Trigueros with a glass of orange wine. From Trigueros, signs helped me down quiet roads through open arable and pastoral farmland to the 'Dolmen of Soto'. The dolmen was a burial mound excavated and presented to show the large chamber within. Floor lighting brought out some of the crude drawings carved in the rocks used to construct the chamber. It was only spoilt by the lack of any information in English and the man at reception was not much help (although he must have been bored as there were no other visitors and there seemed little likelihood of any in February when I visited).

From the Dolmen, I made my way to Niebla on muddy tracks, happily with no gate blocking my way. Niebla was a surprise, the old area of town being surrounded by substantial walls and fortifications, started in Roman times and built in ever increasing size by Arabs and Christians. I visited the interpretation centre in the old hospital but again all was in Spanish including models of historical figures speaking using electronic projections in a very life-like way. I was sure they were looking at me! Most of the towns and villages I walked through appeared to have some history with an ancient wall or churches dating from the 13th to the 16th century with white walls and ornate decorative features around the doors, roofs and towers. Some of the older buildings were damaged by the Lisbon earthquake of 1755, surprising as Lisbon is hundreds of kilometres away. This part of Europe is not known for massive earthquakes, but history shows that they do occur.

For the next two days I had better luck following small country lanes, with names like the 'Camino de la Pastora'. These led me through largely unfenced arable land, with fields of ploughed brown earth or the green growth of some young grain crop. A distant field of yellow rape, occasional groves of ancient looking olive trees or some almond trees in glorious blossom added variety. Like most of my trip since I left Portugal, the land only had slight undulations and made for easy walking. One highlight was the seeing a solar power station, of a type that uses mirrors to focus the sunlight on the top of a tower. I recalled my childhood, using a magnifying glass to burn a hole in some paper, except instead of burning a hole, the focused beam of hot sunlight heats up water (or some similar liquid) turning it into steam which drives a power-generating turbine. An array of many mirrors is used and they must tilt and turn as the sun moves across the sky to keep its rays focused on the top of the tower. It was a technique that I had heard of but not seen in use before.

My final day of walking to Seville was along cycle tracks and on pavements beside roads though the urbanisations that surround the city. It was a Sunday and people were out on bikes or queuing up like me for some *churros* (a fried dough) and chocolate sauce from a roadside stall. The last section was along the banks of the Canal de Alfonso XIII where I saw couples hand in hand and people taking their small dogs or children for a walk. Seville is an amazing old city that I have visited twice before but I joined a 'free' guided tour (i.e. one where you feel obliged to give a substantial tip at the end). I learnt a few more things about the water supply and the need for people to buy up and restore the old houses.

Seville to near Cadiz — challenged by security patrols

Leaving Seville, I walked for the next five days towards Cadiz on the 'Way of St James', better known in Britain as the 'Camino de Santiago', part of a network of ancient pilgrimage routes to the cathedral in Santiago de Compostela in Northern Spain where the remains of St James are reputed to lie. From Cadiz to Seville, the section is also called the 'Via Augusta'. Pilgrims walk from Cadiz northwards, but I was heading south, which meant that the yellow painted arrows that occasionally mark the Camino were pointing in the wrong direction for me. I had downloaded the route onto my GPS, although, as it turned out, the particular 'track' I chose was a bit inaccurate and also missed out the twenty kilometres through the suburbs of Seville. At the tourist information office I had received blank looks when I asked about the route. So I headed off down the main road to the town of 'Dos Hermanos' through an urban landscape, making some deviations around the twin obstacles of a motorway interchange and a wide drainage canal. After Dos Hermanos things improved. As I followed the route on my GPS, it led me on a straight track beside a railway line with huge ploughed fields each side with the green sprouts of some crop poking through, or else fields of rape. The periodic train on the electrified line added some interest. Like the rest of the route to Cadiz, the land was flat or slightly undulating. Leaving the railway, the trail followed a 'green road', the Vereda de Dos Hermana—a corridor of pines and other vegetation which ran between large olive and orange groves. As I sat down to rest a hare hopped by. By the time I reached my pension in the town of Utrera, I was feeling pretty tired.

The next day I was stopped twice by security patrols. Things started well as I walked by large, open, ploughed fields. As the sun cleared away the morning mist, the route turned onto a track beside a concrete lined irrigation canal. A sign stating *'Prohibido el Paso por las Banquetas del*

Canal' did make me wonder if the route pilgrims were being directed along was permitted for pedestrians. At the end of the canal I followed the directions indicated by my GPS onto dirt roads beside fields. I was then stopped by a uniformed security guard in a pick-up, the latter marked with an emblem of crossed rifles. Although he spoke no English, it was clear he realised I was walking along the Camino de Santiago path. He said I could not continue and sent me back to the road, pointing to a route closer to the railway line. As I was following a track beside the railway line I was stopped by a second security patrol. This time one of them spoke English and understood I was following the Camino de Santiago route but with a resigned air said the road was private and I was not allowed on it. Evidently they had stopped other hikers. I had downloaded a guide to this part of the Camino de Santiago from the internet. It was in Spanish and I had used Google's automatic translation facility to convert it into English. Unfortunately the translation was not so good, but as I peered at it and the associated map in detail, it seems I should have been on the other side of the railway line at this point. The GPS 'track' I had downloaded was wrong or out of date. I was surprised at the high level of security I was seeing in Spain in this area: padlocked gates, high barbed wire fences and 'no pedestrians' signs before Seville and now multiple security patrols. It was not an attitude I had come across elsewhere in the country, or indeed anywhere else in my walk across Europe. The second time I had been stopped was on a dirt road, between a fenced railway line and a very large ploughed field. Access to the field was prevented by a deep ditch or high gates and fencing topped with barbed wire. It certainly seemed excessive. The land was very flat and seemingly fertile; from the remains of the previous year's crops, it looked like they were growing cotton and some maize. It was difficult to see what risk required so much security; did they fear someone would steal their yet to be planted crops; were they fearful of illegal immigrants squatting on their land, or was it an emotional issue, an assertion of the owner's rights to his property? After a telling-off, I was allowed to continue, but, at the next farm, where a sign said *'Prohibito el Paso'* I decided to take the longer, tarmac road route to the town of Las Cabrezas de San Juan which was centred on a rare hill.

For the next two days I walked on dirt tracks, passing irrigation canals, huge ploughed fields and motorways, and on roads to reach the city of Jerez, without being further castigated. Although the land was flat, with only the gentlest of hills, I was covering long distances day after day and getting tired, so decided on a rest day at Jerez, home of sherry, at a time when there was a minor flamenco festival. To reach the centre of Jerez there were many kilometres of modern outskirts, with hard, concrete pavements to pound. However, the old city at its heart made it worth it, with an impressive fortress or Alcazar with gardens, a mosque and baths, a cathedral and narrow streets of ancient houses, many sadly crumbling and in need of repair. In the evening I listened to mournful flamenco singers in packed bars while sampling the sherry. Nothing like the 'cream sherry' sitting at the back of my mother's drinks cupboard, left over from some distant Christmas; here, the sherry had a robust, vibrant taste and there were several types I had never heard of before. The barman wrote down what I had ordered in chalk beside me at the bar while the singer wailed accompanied by a few guitar cords.

After the town of El Puerto de Santa Maria, the path went through a very different type of landscape, a nature conservation area consisting of salt marsh with areas of water, various birds and pine trees and bushes. A little way after Puerto Real, where I spent the night, I left the salt marshes and the Camino de Santiago as it headed for Cadiz and instead returned to the sea at Chiclana de la Frontera.

Costa de la Luz — Sun and Sand

For the next four days I followed the coast to Tarifa, walking along wide, long, sandy beaches, climbing through coastal juniper in nature reserves overlooking the clear, turquoise sea or hiking through pine trees and rocks. A popular, but not (at this time of year) overcrowded, area with many visitors despite the windy days at the end of February. The white-walled buildings of the villages and towns I passed through had cafés, bars, shops and campsites where I stayed the night. There was also history, Roman remains and 16th century watchtowers. At Point Trafalgar, I saw no signs informing visitors on the sea battle that took place near here in 1805, at which Nelson defeated a combined French and Spanish fleet—a victory overshadowed by his death during the battle.

In one secluded bay among the dunes, I found several small, abandoned boats with Arabic lettering on their bows, slowly being engulfed by sand. Were they once occupied by refugees coming from Africa — visible in the distance — to find a better life in Europe? I wondered if this was why I had seen so many Civil Guards patrolling the coast. Not long after I arrived at Camping Torre de la Pena, where I camped 18 months earlier when I started my walk on the E4 across Spain. I camped at the same spot beneath the old tower, looking out over the sea to Africa. One more day's walk along the beach to Tarifa, then home!

Appendix 3: Northern route around the Sierra Nevada among the olive trees

Five years after I walked the southern route for the GR7 (and so the E4) around the Sierra Nevada in Spain, I walked the alternative route that goes to the north of the Sierra Nevada range. I returned to Antequera and then walked for several days largely through olive trees. At times they covered the low hills as far as the eye could see, the soil yellow, dusty and stony beneath them; at others, mountains reared up above a patchwork of olive groves, often with pine trees below a bare and rocky summit. As it was February, the olives were still being harvested. I often exchanged a *'Buenos Dias'* with small (family?) groups of men and women of all ages harvesting the olives near the track. This harvesting process involves shaking the tree's branches and collecting the olives in a net laid out below. Methods employed to do the shaking ranged from the simple expedient of beating with a stick, through to the use of hand-held, petrol-powered branch shakers, to the most sophisticated of all, the tractor-mounted shaker. The latter definitely offered the most oomph. Olives would then be packed into trailers, which were pulled by tractors to the local processing plants where they formed long queues. There seemed to be a lot of leaves among the olives being sent for processing. Smoke rose in places where the trees had been pruned and the branches were being burnt. Almond trees with their pink blossom dotted the road side.

The path periodically went through towns of whitewashed houses with red tiled roofs, where there might be a café, church, shop and accommodation. Priego de Cordoba was perhaps the most impressive town, with its castle, view across the valley from the town walls and narrow streets. Alcala de Real also had a large castle on the hill above the town. Added interest on my walk was provided by a ruined convent, a medieval bridge, a watchtower from Arabic times, an ancient waterwheel, remains of a stone-built farm (or *'cortijo'*) or a section of track that had slipped into the river. Where the GR7 briefly shared the same farm track as the 'Camino de Santiago', I met another long-distance walker, following this pilgrim's route. There are actually many Caminos de Santiago starting at various places across Europe and ending at the cathedral at Santiago de Compostela in northwest Spain. I was crossing a less popular route coming from Malaga.

To the south, I had occasional views of the Sierra Nevada Mountains, a mantle of snow covering their 3,000 metre peaks. My route was way below the snow line, but in the second half of the trip I crossed a number of mountain ranges. Here the olive groves were replaced by pines and oak, often with views back to the olive groves below. Above the trees there was grass and stone, outcrops of rock forming the summits. I had been walking on farm tracks through the olive trees, and in the mountains I was often on gravel roads, but footpaths formed some of the most enjoyable sections. Such paths were clear and well-marked, often old mule tracks, with some new bridges crossing streams. Occasionally they were overgrown and difficult to follow. In places, lines of wind turbines sprouted from ridges, symbols of the changes in the modern energy industry. On flatter patches of grass, there was sometimes rubble and a few walls remaining of abandoned farms, illustrating other changes, in which people had left the mountains for more prosperous livings elsewhere. Most of the time I was alone on these mountain paths, but on a sunny weekend near the town of Cazorla the pine-covered hills seemed to attract many day trippers.

Some interesting towns nestled in the hills, such as Quesada with its ancient town gates, and Cazorla with its castle (and plaza with its ice-cream parlours, bars and cafés). Outside the towns, I passed a few fortifications in various states of ruin. For example a little before the town of Bedmar, there was an Arab watchtower on the hill above the road. Below was a church, the *'Santuario de Nuestra Señora Cuadros'*, one of many religious buildings, hermitages and shrines I passed on my travels through Spain. Many were locked but I was fortunate on this occasion. As I walked into the flower-filled courtyard, a group was just leaving the church and I was allowed a look at the gold-leaf and pictures inside. The following day, crossing a broad valley, a railway line caught my attention. The rails seemed too far apart, maybe an example of the broader Iberian gauge railway? Such sights, often unexpected, added interest to each day of my walk on the E4. Some sights saddened me. In the town of Alcal la Real, on leaving the hostal early to find some breakfast, I noticed a group of Africans come out of an enclosure containing a cash machine. It looked like they had spent the night cramped inside there to keep out of the rain. I had noticed some of them the night before using a café's WiFi over a lengthy cup of coffee. I surmised they were migrants looking for a better life, struggling with little money in a foreign land.

I stayed at a variety of hotels and hostals, often rooms attached to a bar or restaurant. The rooms were always clean, although in some of the bars there seemed to be a habit of dropping the shells from nuts on the floor, so you made a crunching sound as you walked up to the bar, crushing shells beneath your feet. I spent a few nights camping in the mountains where other accommodation was unavailable and once at a campsite. Being well out of season I think I only found someone there as they were doing some work near the entrance.

In general, the weather was good, but as I approached the town of Pontonnes, I was caught in a cold and windy snowfall giving the stony landscape a bleak appearance. The town itself seemed jammed between cliffs of bare, grey rock. From there, it was a two-day walk to Pueblo de Don Fadrique, wild camping in the forest on the way, avoiding the long road section by resorting to forest tracks where I could. From Pueblo de Don Fadrique, having checked where the bus to Alicante went from, I had lunch and waited at the bus stop. The bus stopped on the other side of the road, necessitating a quick dash over the main road, but soon I was safely on my way back home.